BRICK

A WORLD HISTORY

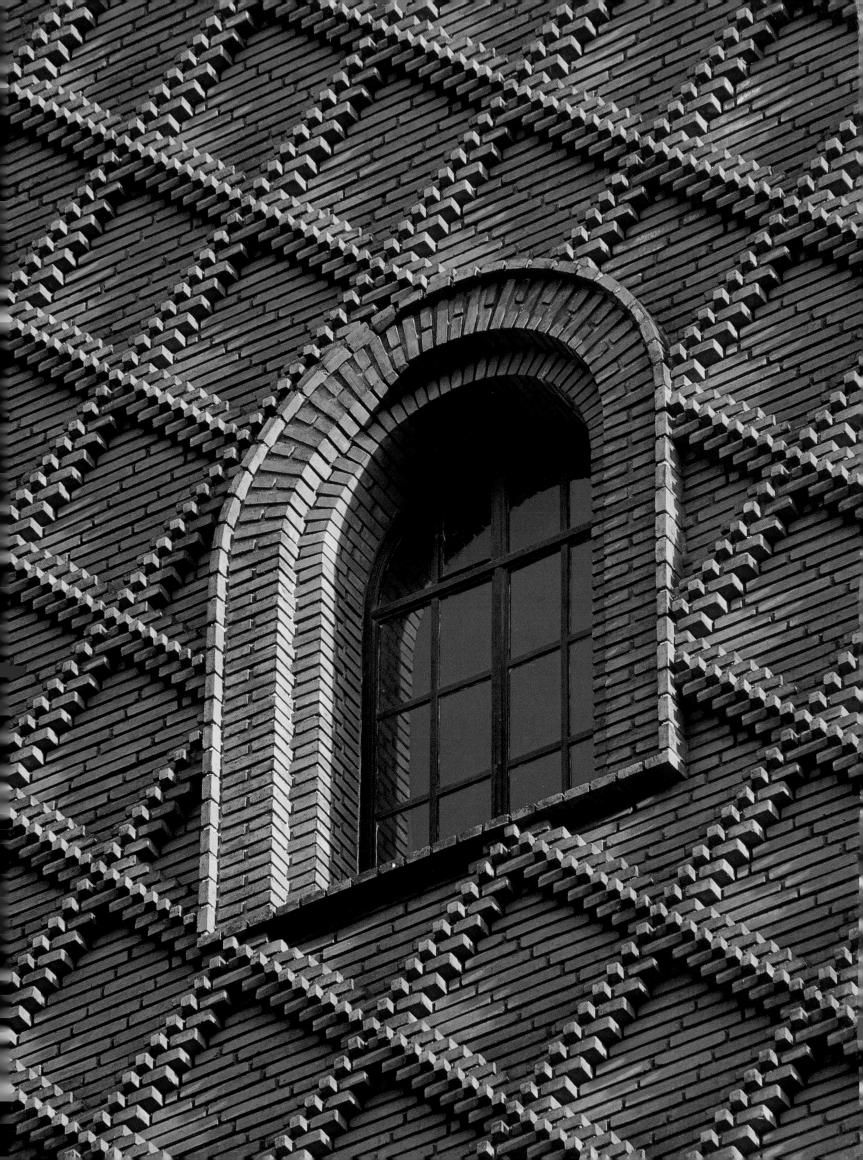

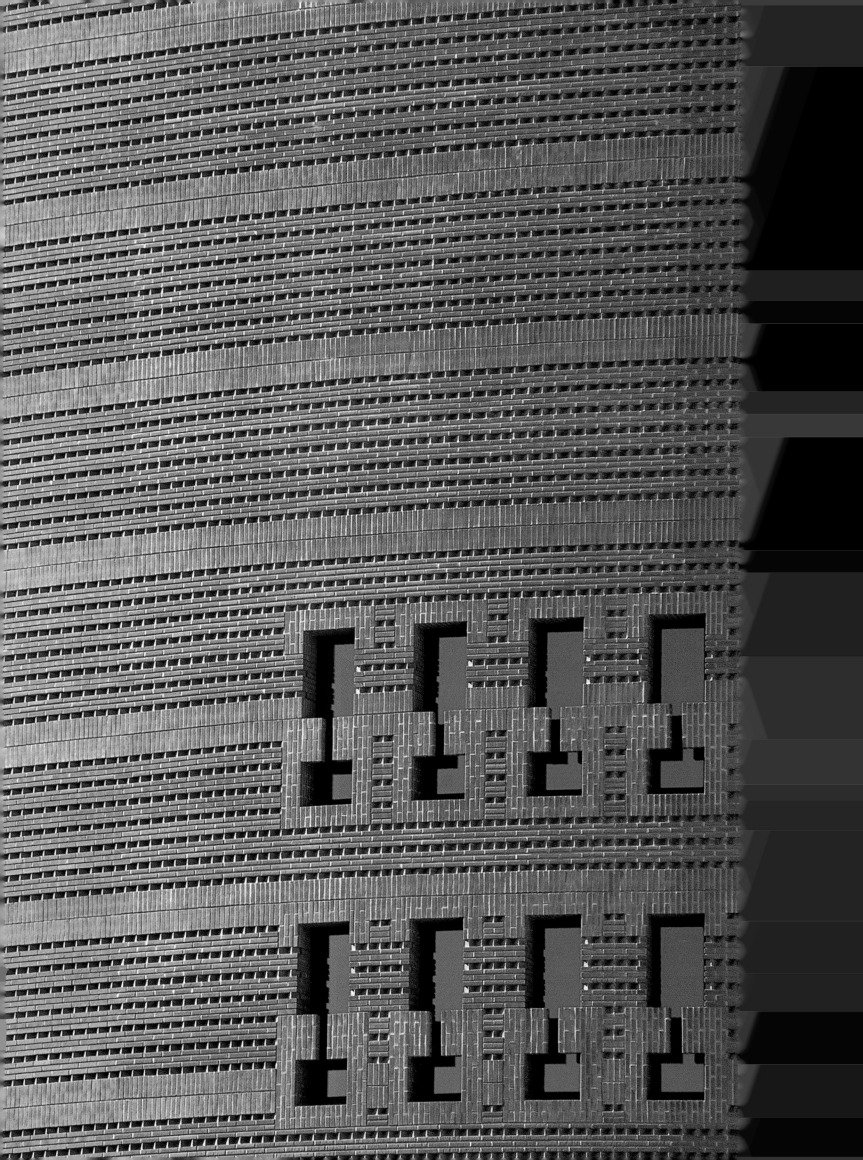

JAMES W. P. CAMPBELL

PHOTOGRAPHS BY WILL PRYCE

BRICK

A WORLD HISTORY

WITH OVER 600 ILLUSTRATIONS, 570 IN COLOUR

Thames & Hudson

For IMN. and CC.

On the preceding pages

Half title Inscribed brick from
Choga Zanbil, Iran.

Page 2   Grundtvigkirke
(1913–1930), Copenhagen,
Denmark, by Peder Jensen-Klint.

Page 3   Detail of Institut d'Art
et d'Archéologie, (1925–30).
3, rue Michelet, Paris,
by Paul Bigot.

Page 4   Detail of the
brickwork on the main façade
of Evry Cathedral (1988–92),
France, by Mario Botta.

Page 5   Small Mausoleum,
Sultaniya, Iran.

Title page spread
The Ark (destroyed 1220,
subsequently rebuilt), Bukhara,
Uzbekistan.

First published in the United Kingdom in 2003 by
Thames & Hudson Ltd, 181A High Holborn, London WC1V 7QX

www.thamesandhudson.com

© 2003 Thames & Hudson Ltd, London
Reprinted 2004

British Library Cataloguing-in-Publication Data
A catalogue record for this book is available from the British Library

ISBN 0-500-34195-8

Printed and bound in Singapore by C.S. Graphics

CONTENTS

ACKNOWLEDGMENTS 10   PREFACE 11   INTRODUCTION 12

CHAPTER ONE   22

ANCIENT CIVILIZATIONS
10,000 – 500 BC

CHAPTER TWO   38

THE CLASSICAL WORLD
500 BC – AD 1000

CHAPTER THREE   78

THE MEDIEVAL WORLD
1000 – 1450

CHAPTER FOUR   122

THE BIRTH OF THE MODERN WORLD
1450 – 1650

CHAPTER FIVE   160

ENLIGHTENMENT IDEALS
1650 – 1800

CHAPTER SIX   202

MECHANIZATION AND INDUSTRIALIZATION
1800 – 1900

CHAPTER SEVEN   244

INTO THE 20TH CENTURY
1900 – 2000

CONCLUSION   300

WHAT FUTURE FOR BRICK?

GLOSSARY 304   BIBLIOGRAPHICAL ESSAY 312   INDEX 318

ACKNOWLEDGMENTS

We would like to mention the following for their support: Richard L. Austin, Tony Baggs, Polly Barker, Marcus Bleasdale, Maddie Brown, Mike Chapman, Sophie Descat, Graham Finch, Ron Firmin, Andrew Forman, Jonathan Foyle, Ron Gough, Mike Hammett, Martin Hammond, Katie Jones, Con Lenan, Gerard Lynch, Robert McWilliam, Kitty Marsh, Peter Minter, Susan Olle, José Platis, Nicholas Postgate, Iraj Riahi, Andrew Saint, Trevor and Melodie Simons of Adventure Overland Travel, Terence Smith, Robin Spence, Henning Stummel, Daphne Thissen, Mike Trinder, Steve Voller, Lisa Warner of Trailfinders, and Christopher Wright.

Ruth and Paul Partridge, Alex Lush and Laurence Genée, Martin Harris and Linda MacLachlan, Adrian Richardson and Teresa Waldin, Simon Evenett, Deanna Griffin, Michelle Manz and Jonathan Sachs very generously provided accommodation and hospitality during our various travels. We would also like to thank the owners and custodians of the numerous properties included in the book who were kind enough to give us permission to photograph their buildings and extended their hospitality.

All the photographs were taken by Will Pryce with the exception of the plates from books on pages 44-45 which were taken by Michael Clifford and photograph of the mural in the tomb of Rehk-me-Re in Thebes on pages 28-29 kindly lent by Dr Alberto Siliotti. The isometric drawings on pages 64, 118 and 126 are reproduced by permission of Dr Rowland J. Mainstone and the drawing on page 218 by permission of the Soane Museum. The illustrations of patent floors on page 218 are reproduced courtesy of Laurence Hurst. We are most grateful for the rights to reproduce various plates from books in the library of the Faculty of Architecture in Cambridge and to all the staff at Thames & Hudson for their endless patience throughout the writing of this book.

Lastly, we are especially grateful to the Brick Development Association who have enthusiastically supported the project from the outset. They provided a generous grant towards the costs of photography and travel, introducing us to many in the industry who spent time showing us round their manufacturing plants and patiently answered endless questions. Without the help of all these people this book would not have been possible.

PREFACE

This book aims to provide the first complete guide to the development of brick across the globe, both in the sense of the object itself - the different sizes and shapes of bricks, and the techniques of their manufacture - and the way they have been used - the architectural achievements of brick.

One of the more pleasurable aspects of writing this book has been the travelling. The importance of visiting brickyards and factories for research is obvious and I would urge anyone who wishes to really understand the processes involved to go and witness them at first hand. However, it's equally important to experience the buildings. Photographs can describe what a building is like and can provide unique insights into how it is put together, but you can only really appreciate a building by walking up to it, through it and around it. Therefore it was agreed from the outset that Will Pryce and I, as photographer and author, should visit every building we were going to include in the book together.

As a result, the photography for this book has taken almost three years to complete and in that time Will and I have travelled the equivalent of twice round the world in ten separate expeditions visiting over twenty countries. He has taken photographs in the heat of the desert in Iran and as the snow fell in Chicago. Such trips were not entirely without incident, not least because on our longest expedition we set out on September 11, 2001 to visit fourteen countries, three of which border Afghanistan.

Any attempt to encompass thousands of years of history in a single volume naturally involves leaving out a great deal. Others would no doubt have chosen different buildings to highlight, devoted more space to certain topics or omitted some of the things I have decided to include. Everyone will have his or her own favourite brick structure or personal interest as I have mine. I have simply endeavoured to select those buildings and topics which I thought were most characteristic of a particular period and region and that had something important to say about the development of brick as whole. It is, I accept, a personal selection and I leave it up to the reader to judge how successful I have been.

Ultimately history is a cumulative task. It is written by building on and revising the works of others. I have spent a great deal of time studying the history of building construction and talking to those in the industry, but I have also relied heavily on the research of those listed in the bibliographical essay at the end of this book. I hope the result will not only provide an entertaining introduction for all those interested in how things were made, but also prove to be a useful basis for future research in years to come.

JAMES W.P. CAMPBELL
2003

Notes. This book contains names and terms from many different languages and cultures that do not use the Roman alphabet. Sometimes there are agreed systems of transliteration, but in the case of proper nouns I have tried to use those names by which the monuments or places are most commonly known or easily recognised rather than sticking rigidly to any particular system. Likewise I have used the Christian calendar for no other reason than it is widely understood.

Introduction

The Hanging Gardens of Babylon, one of the Seven Wonders of the World; the Great Wall of China, the largest man-made object on the planet; the Hagia Sophia, one of the most beautiful churches ever built; the great medieval castle of Malbork, Poland, which is the size of a small town; the 2000 temples in Pagan in Burma that have survived intact for 900 years; the engineering achievement of Brunelleschi's Dome in Florence; the structure of the Taj Mahal in India; the 1200 miles of sewers which the Victorians built under London; the unforgettable profile of the Chrysler Building in New York City – all these have one thing in common: they were built out of brick. Brick is at once the simplest and the most versatile of materials, the most ubiquitous and the least regarded, all too familiar yet strangely neglected.

Above and opposite
Details of the Institut d' Art et d' Archéologie, Paris, by Paul Bigot 1925–30, an example of virtuoso brickwork at a time when modernism was favouring concrete and glass.

This book looks at the development of a simple object – the brick – examining the techniques of its manufacture and use from the distant past to the present day. It is not strictly a book on architectural history, although it contains many pictures of buildings and has much to say about architecture. It is essentially a book on the history of technology and ideas that concern brick, and aims to dispel many popular myths. Take a simple example: colour. Most people think of bricks as being red. In fact they have been produced in every colour under the sun, including the pale yellows of the desert, the bright green glazes of the Middle East, the purples and blacks of so-called Staffordshire Blues. It is also commonly assumed that brick is always a second choice after stone, but, as this book intends to demonstrate, brick has its own logic and advantages. Skilled architects, engineers and craftsmen have long known how and when to exploit them. To some extent the bias of architectural historians for stone rather than brick has been responsible for the lack of appreciation of its richness and diversity. It has also led to general underestimation of the significance of brick in the history of architecture and building construction. It is this imbalance that the current work seeks to address.

Brick is one of the oldest building materials and its story starts at the very beginning of the history of civilization. The mud brick was invented between 10,000 and 8000 BC; the moulded brick was developed later, in Mesopotamia about 5000 BC; but the most significant landmark was the invention of the fired brick in about 3500 BC. It was this that enabled the construction of permanent structures in areas where it had not been previously possible. Firing the brick gave it the resilience of stone but with the added advantages that it could be more easily shaped and provide potentially endless exact repetitions of decorative patterns. With the subsequent development of glazes it became possible not only to make rich

ornament in brick, but also to produce it in vivid colours.

The ancient Romans built many of their greatest buildings using brick. Their combination of brick with concrete for the structure in the Pantheon and the great baths of Caracalla is well appreciated, but their use of brick in engineering and the way it was used for ornamental purposes in the 2nd century AD is easily overlooked. Arguably, the changes in Roman use of brick had more to do with changes in manufacture of brick and techniques in laying than an interest in architectural style. In Byzantium, Roman brickmaking was refined and its use resulted in the great church of Hagia Sophia, which remained unsurpassed for centuries. In the East, China developed ways of making bricks that made them harder and stronger, processes that eventually led to the construction of slender pagodas and the Great Wall.

By 1200 AD, bricks were found across Europe and Asia from the Atlantic to the Pacific. While Islam spread brickmaking and bricklaying techniques across North Africa and Central Asia, Christian monasticism introduced it across Europe and Buddhism passed it from India to Burma and Thailand.

From the time of the Renaissance to the 17th century, advances in technology in Europe changed the way brick could be used. Most importantly it became cheaper and its use became more widespread across the social spectrum. Thus, while it is true that the period saw a flowering in academic knowledge and trade, leading to such masterpieces as the Duomo in Florence, the terracotta of northern Italy, Mughal architecture in India, and the mosques and bridges of Isfahan, it also saw more widespread use of brick in housing in cities and in fortification and the use of brick in the new settlements of colonial America.

The 18th century saw the beginning of the Industrial Revolution in England. Books were published in Europe on methods of making bricks and techniques

were developed that allowed them to be manufactured in enormous numbers and transported across long distances. By the 19th century and the introduction of mechanization, brick had become the standard material for industrial and commercial applications, as well as for the highly inventive forms of the Gothic Revival and early skyscrapers. This trend continued into the 20th century. Architectural historians tend to suggest that bricks lost their pre-eminence to more 'modern' materials such as concrete steel and glass, but this was far from being the case. Brickmaking increased steadily and large numbers of new products and techniques were introduced which allowed brick to be used in innovative and more imaginative ways. At the same time, in the developing world bricks proved their suitability in terms both of cost and sympathy with local traditions.

At present new techniques in the manufacture and structural use of brick promise an exciting future, offering a world of diversity and aesthetic possibilities. After 10,000 years the outlook for the humble brick looks bright.

In view of this rich history and the importance of building technology to the history and development of civilization, it is extraordinary that the study of brick (and indeed construction history in general) has been neglected for so long. That situation seems to be about to change. Journals are beginning to appear on construction history and more academics are working in the field, partly driven by growing interest in conservation.

The aim of this book is to provide a complete guide and introduction to the world of brick not only for the specialist, but also for the general reader.

employed that will determine the style, structure and appearance of the final work.

One of the aims of this book is to provide a historical overview of the development of these two trades, brickmaking and bricklaying, but it is also a history of the results, a study of bricks and the structures (buildings, walls, bridges, etc) made out of them. However, before we begin, some definitions are required. Where possible technical jargon has been avoided in the text, but it is important to explain here certain basic concepts, as an understanding of these is essential for a full appreciation of brickmaking and brickwork.

Basic concepts in brickmaking

There are two basic types of brick: those that are fired and those that are simply baked in the sun. This book is concerned mainly with the former. Building with bricks that are dried in the sun (or adobe as it is generally known) is one the oldest and cheapest methods of building construction. It requires very little in the way of technology and the raw materials are generally available on site. In many of the poorer parts of the world the method is still used today. The main problem with mud bricks is that they wash away and even the usual practice of plastering the outside of adobe buildings will not protect them against serious downpours.

The firing of bricks overcomes the basic problem of waterproofing. Nevertheless, it is not as simple a process as it might at first seem. Simply placing a brick in an ordinary fire will not work. In order for the brick to vitrify, it must be heated to a temperature between about 900 and 1150°C and this heat has to be maintained for at least 8–15 hours. The exact temperature is dependent on the type of clay used. The bricks must then be allowed to cool gradually to avoid cracking. Under-fired bricks will be too soft and tend to crumble. If they get too hot the clay distorts and fuses into a glass-like substance. Thus the skill of brickmakers lies in part in their ability to build and operate kilns which can generate these temperatures with a degree of accuracy and control.

All bricks are made from clay. The geology of clays is complicated and the term covers a large number of different substances that share similar properties. However, it is not necessary to have an in-depth knowledge of geology or material science to understand that certain clays are more useful for brickmaking than others and that clay alone is not sufficient for making bricks. The material used must also contain sand or other matter. The percentage of clay used will determine the properties.

Understanding brick

The first step in appreciating any object, whether it is an everyday object, a work of art or a building, is to understand how it was made. Many elements of the eventual appearance of a building are determined by the initial choice made by the architect or builder to use a certain material. One can only begin to understand the more profound reasons behind a work if one knows what part the building process itself has had in determining its shape and why the builder chose the material he did.

With brick the situation is more complicated still because there are two objects involved. The first is the brick itself and the second is the object produced from it. These are the products of two distinct manufacturing processes: making and laying. Although both may be done at the same place, they are rarely done by the same person.

The way a brick is made affects its colour, shape, texture, strength, resistance to fire and weather and longevity. If the brick is not well made, the walls will crumble and the structure will fall. It is thus essential that those who are responsible for designing and constructing buildings understand enough about brickmaking to know what to ask for and to appreciate the limitations of the processes involved, while the architectural historian needs to know how these choices have affected the end result. For everyone concerned an understanding of the methods involved in bricklaying is essential, for it is the way that a brick is placed in relation to the others, the colours that are selected, the forms that are built up, the surface textures that are created and the decorative motifs

Top The Colosseum, Rome, begun by Vespasian (70–76 AD) and completed by Titus in 80 AD.

Above Tomb of Anna Regilla (mid 2nd century), mistakenly called the Temple of Rediculus, off the Appian Way, near Rome.

Opposite The Tomb of the Saminids, Bukhara, c. 900 AD.

Unbaked bricks are made with mud, often mixed with straw, and will generally have a relatively low clay content (perhaps less than 30% by weight), while at the other extreme terracottas will be about 75% clay. In modern brickyards, clays dug from deep pits are carefully mixed with sand to produce the correct mixture, but in the past surface deposits were often specifically chosen because they already contained the right amount of clay and other materials. In the eighteenth century the usual test applied by a brickmaker looking for a new site was to put a small piece of soil in the mouth and taste it. The ready-to-use material was called brickearth and its availability was an important factor in determining the geographical spread of brickmaking.

The right type of clay having been selected, it is then dug up (English-speaking brickmakers talk about 'winning' the clay) and mixed to ensure that the consistency is even. Stones left in the clay make cutting the bricks more difficult and, depending on their nature, may also explode on heating. To avoid this they must be removed or crushed. The clay is then mixed with water, ready to be shaped.

Strictly speaking, all bricks are cuboid in shape, but as the plan dimensions are the most important (closely followed by thickness) they are usually described as being either square or rectangular. Where dimensions are given in the text they are described as length, breadth and thickness and given in millimetres. However, all such dimensions are approximate. Even among bricks fired in the same batch there may be great differences (perhaps as large as 10%) in their dimensions due to inconsistencies in moulding, drying and firing. Measurements are supplied only to give a rough idea of the shape of the brick in question. They were taken with a simple pocket tape measure applied to a handful of bricks and should be treated as approximate.

The uniformity of the brick is one of its most important properties and is traditionally achieved by making them in moulds. The most common type, the open mould, is simply a box without top or bottom. The brickearth is pressed into the top and then the mould is lifted off to leave the brick behind. Another alternative, the box mould, is similar, but has a bottom. It is commonly used for making tiles but rarely for bricks as the suction created in the bottom of the mould makes it difficult to turn them out. Today of course most bricks are moulded by machine.

Most methods of moulding brick require the use of quite wet clay, so after moulding the brick must be dried sufficiently to prevent it cracking on firing. In the past bricks were typically set out in hacks for several weeks and covered from the rain. Today they are often

dried in heated sheds. During the drying process the bricks shrink.

Most bricks are fired in permanent kilns, which have to be constructed from incombustible materials (typically previously fired bricks) and are designed to be easily loaded and unloaded and to last for many hundreds of firings. However, it is possible to stack up the unfired clay bricks in such a way that when fires are lit underneath them the gases will pass through the bricks and fire them. Such a structure is called a clamp. The advantages of clamp firing are that it is cheap and quick and that no fired bricks are required.

In the past it was chiefly used by itinerant brickmakers who either rented land for brickmaking or were using the clay from the site to make bricks for one particular project. Clamps are still used in many parts of the world today for similar reasons. Their drawback is that they are highly inefficient. The bricks on the outside of the clamp, in contact with the air, do not reach sufficiently high temperatures to fire properly and need to be fired again, while those in the middle are often over-burnt and unusable. To make them slightly more efficient and seal in more of the heat, clay was often plastered over the outside of the clamp,

Above The minaret of
Kalan Mosque, Bukhara,
Uzbekistan. *c.* 1120 AD (p.114).

Top right Chiang Mai,
Thailand, 12th–14th century
(p.89).

Above right The Twin
Pagodas, Suzhou, 982 AD.
The two towers are 33m high.

a process which is called scoving and resulted in the
so-called Scove kiln.

The way the bricks are stacked within a kiln or
clamp (a process called setting) is crucial in ensuring
that they are evenly fired. It also affects the colour of
the products, as parts of bricks will become more
oxidized than others. In general colour is determined
by the minerals in the brickearth or clay used. Those
with an iron content, for instance, will fire red or pink

as the iron oxidizes. Those that are rich in lime, but
lack iron, will tend to turn yellow or cream. However,
the exact colour will be determined by the position of
the brick in the kiln and how much oxygen is let into it
during the firing process. Even within a single batch of
bricks there can be wide colour variations.

Once the brick has cooled and been removed from
the kiln, it is ready for use. It passes out of the hands
of the brickmaker and into those of the bricklayer.

Basic concepts in bricklaying

The bricklayer starts with the results of the brickmaker's art. He or she must turn a pile of identical bricks into a structure. Each layer of bricks, called a course must be laid horizontally on a *bed* of mortar. (The use of the term mortar here is important. The word cement should not be used as it implies a particular type of mortar: one that dries under water).

When laying bricks the thickness, colour and finish of the mortar joint is very important for the final appearance of the wall. Cut stone walls tend to be laid with the minimum thickness of joint and this is achievable because each stone is cut to fit. In some cultures bricks too have been sanded down so that they can be laid with the slightest of joints but in general they are used straight from the brickmaker. The more the bricks supplied vary in shape and size,

Top Temple of Htilominlo (1218), Pagan, Burma.

Above left The great plain of Pagan, Burma.

Above right Castle of Malbork, Poland, 14th century (pp. 106–07).

the thicker the mortar joints they must be laid in. The colour of the mortar is determined by its chemical composition. The most common ingredient, lime, is naturally white but mixing it with sand can turn it yellow. Other substances have differing effects: for instance, the Byzantines added brick dust to turn their mortar red while Victorian builders in London preferred to add soot to make it black. Finally the finish of the joint can be altered by putting stones in it (a technique called galletting) or by scraping it. The Romans finished their joints with a second layer of mortar applied after the wall was complete (a technique called pointing). Over the centuries bricklayers have experimented with a number of different types of pointing, creating recesses to accentuate shadows, scoring lines in the mortar to suggest regularity and even impressing objects into the joints to create decorative patterns.

Bricks are normally set out against a piece of string to ensure that they sit with their upper surfaces in line and the joint remains constant. Between each brick is an upright piece of mortar called the perpend. Usually the perpend is the same thickness as the depth of the mortar bed but varying it will likewise change the appearance of the finished wall.

Nowhere is the difference between stone and brick more obvious than in the art of bonding. Bricklayers traditionally talk of the thicknesses of walls in terms of multiples of the length of a brick. Thus a 'half-a-brick thick wall' is the breadth of a brick thick (about 100mm using most standard English bricks, 115mm for standard German ones) and a 'one-brick thick' wall is the length of a single brick thick (215mm in England, 240mm in Germany). Walls of half-a-brick thickness are not strong enough to support much more than their own weight so historically most walls have been several bricks thick. In such walls it is possible to place rectangular bricks either along the wall (in which case they are called stretchers) or at right angles to its face (in which case they are called headers). The ability of the brick to be laid in this way has traditionally determined its size. The length is twice the width plus a mortar joint to allow both sides of a single brick thick wall to be laid flush.

Bricklayers seek to lay bricks in such a way that they result in the strongest wall possible. Bonding describes the various patterns created by the alternation of headers and stretchers. The simplest example is a wall where one course is laid with all the bricks showing the short side on the face of the wall (a course of headers) and the next course laid with the long sides visible (a course of stretchers). This is called English bond. A list of the more common bonds can be found in the glossary at the end of the book. Bonding is peculiar to

bricklaying. The stonemason simply uses larger stones that bind the outer leaves of the wall together while still providing an even appearance on the wall face. Only with the use of bricks does bonding become necessary and that necessity becomes elevated into an art form in its own right. The use of consistent bonding patterns is a way to distinguish a brick wall built by a stonemason from one built by a bricklayer or to distinguish an experienced bricklayer from a novice.

The appearance of a flat brick wall is therefore determined by a number of factors, some of which are controlled by the brickmaker and others by the bricklayer. The situation is similar when it comes to decorative brickwork. Bricks can be shaped in four ways: moulding, sculpting, carving and rubbing.

Opposite above left Church of S. Antonio, Padua, Italy.

Opposite above centre The terracotta façade of Santo Spirito, Bologna, Italy, 14th century.

Opposite above right The entrance to the Lutfullah Mosque, Isfahan, Iran, early 17th century (p.152).

Opposite below Herstmonceaux Castle, England, 15th century (p.104).

Top and above right Palazzo Pubblico, Siena, 1259–1305 (p.101).

Above left Beneath the Khwazi Bridge at Isfahan, Iran.

Top left Groombridge Place, Kent, England, built in the mid-17th century (p. 177).

Above left Folly Farm (1906–12), Sulhampstead, England, by Sir Edwin Lutyens (1869–1944).

Top right University of Virginia (1817–1826), Charlottesville, USA, designed by Thomas Jefferson (1743–1826).

Above right The Arthur Heurtley Residence (1902), designed by Frank Lloyd Wright (1869–1959).

Below Battersea Power Station (1933), London, designed by Sir Giles Gilbert Scott (1880–1960).

Moulding involves pressing the clay into wooden box moulds which have been specially made to provide the profile in question. Quite complicated shapes can be made this way by designing the box so that the sides and other parts come off to release the completed brick. Making box moulds is expensive. Simple shapes can be made by putting different inserts into the same moulds but normally each special brick will require its own mould. Moulding is thus reserved for elements that will be used in large numbers. Sculpting is shaping the clay by hand or using simple tools. The clay is then fired in the kiln in the normal way. Every sculpted piece will be different. If the piece cracks in the firing process it will

be useless. Both moulding and sculpting are processes carried out by the brickmaker before the brick is fired. Carving and rubbing are done by the bricklayer. Bricks are carved or sawn using chisels (called brick axes) or metal saws. Complicated profiles can be accurately sawn by using a wooden form as a guide. Rubbing involves shaping the brick by rubbing it against a hard stone or file. All these various methods leave their own characteristic marks on the final product.

As glazes have to be applied before firing, any glazed work must have been shaped by the brickmaker. Much decorative brickwork, however, was created by the bricklayer cutting normal bricks on site, which needed less co-ordination between brickmaker and bricklayer and less forward planning. The chief difference between terracotta and moulded brick is in size. When the unit is no larger than a brick it is called a moulded brick. When it is bigger it is called terracotta. Both tend to be made with more refined earths than conventional bricks.

Differentiating cut decorative bricks from moulded ones is not difficult, but requires close observation. In moulding or sculpting, stones in the clay will be pushed below the surface and they will thus be concealed in the final product, which will have a relatively smooth surface. Cutting and rubbing will remove the surface, leaving cut stones or holes where they have been torn away. The presence of cut stones in the surface of decorative work thus implies that it was shaped by cutting or rubbing by the bricklayer. Tool marks are another indicator, although these are often eroded or removed.

The use of cutting or moulding provides clues to the interaction between brickmakers and bricklayers, but a history of brick and brickwork does not involve only those individuals. Buildings are constructed through interactions between many parts of a society. Knowledge of how the builders lived and where they stood in the hierarchy is essential to understanding how and why bricks or buildings were made the way they were. The history of the brick is as much about people as it is about objects and, as will be seen, not just bricklayers and brickmakers have been involved but architects, kilnsmen, legislators, engineers, inventors, town councillors, aristocrats and kings have also all had their parts to play. The way bricks have been made and used has altered according to economics and politics, fashion and architectural style. Much of this book is therefore concerned with these issues.

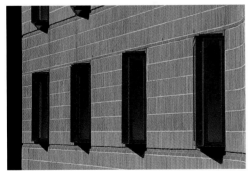

Organization of the book

For ease of use the book is organized strictly chronologically. Each chapter covers a specific period and is further subdivided into sections on particular topics. At the beginning of each chapter is a brief outline of its layout and a summary of its contents. The whole book is thus devised as a collection of short pieces which together seek to provide a complete history of brick from its invention to the present day.

Naturally in a book of this scope most topics can only be summarized, but a detailed bibliographical essay is included at the back directing the interested reader to sources where more information may be found and providing an overview of current scholarship on each subject. The aim is to provide the reader with a clear overview of the history of brick and why it has become one of the most successful building materials yet devised.

Top Langhaus, Woningbouw Housing, Java Island, Amsterdam (2001), by the Swiss architects Diener and Diener.

Above left Keble College, Oxford, extension (1991–95), designed by Rick Mather.

Above centre Hilversum Town Hall (1924–30), Netherlands, designed by W. M. Dudok (1884–1974).

Above right St Peter's Church (1963–66), Klippan, Sweden, by Sigurd Lewerentz (1885–1975).

CHAPTER ONE

ANCIENT CIVILIZATIONS 10,000 – 500BC

The 9,500 years covered by this first chapter saw the development of many of the most important features of brickwork today. The invention of the mould, the development of kilns for firing bricks, the introduction of glazes and ways of shaping bricks to form sculpture, the division of labour between brickmaker and bricklayer and the development of complicated patterns of bonding all belong to this period, making it one of the most important in the whole history of the subject. Nevertheless there are great difficulties in establishing an exact chronology for events that happened up to 12,000 years ago and much still remains to be discovered.

The period which the present chapter describes runs from roughly 10,000 BC to 500 BC and covers the rise of the first settlements and civilisations. The term 'roughly' is used deliberately and should be emphasized. Our knowledge of this period is primarily archaeological and the dates involved are highly speculative. Buildings and artefacts do survive from this period but written records are rare. The writings that remain are mostly inscriptions on buildings and monuments and although significant fragments on clay tablets have survived in some areas, most that have been recovered are simply tallies of goods. For many thousands of years there are no written records at all, a period which can only be described as 'pre-history'. Ascribing dates when there are no written chronologies to fix them to is extremely difficult. The traditional method used in archaeology involved meticulous recording of the depths at which objects were buried. Working on the principle that the highest layers were the newest and that the lowest were the oldest, it was thus possible to draw up an approximate chronology for a particular site, which was then further refined by comparing artefacts recovered in particular layers with those located elsewhere. There are obvious drawbacks to such a method when comparing sites in different areas. In any case stratification methods were often not applied particularly systematically. Artefacts were frequently recovered in a more haphazard manner and dating them in relation to new finds is correspondingly difficult. Moreover, the most significant step forward in dating archaeological remains was not made until 1949 when Willard F. Libby (1908–80), an American atomic scientist, invented carbon dating. This made it possible to date organic materials from early periods to a degree of accuracy previously unimaginable. Modern archaeological excavations using both

stratigraphic excavation techniques and carbon dating can thus estimate with greater certainty when a particular object was deposited. Unfortunately most ancient sites were excavated before carbon dating was available. As a result information about dates from these excavations is unreliable and must be given a large margin of error. Thus, even accounting for the fact that not all imaginable sites have yet been excavated, it is not possible to say exactly when early events happened. At best we can make educated guesses, which no doubt will be refined and revised in the future. It is the current state of knowledge that this chapter seeks to summarize.

The first section of this chapter looks at the very earliest bricks ever made. It is currently believed that the first human settlements date from between 10,000 and 8,000 BC in what is generally called the Neolithic period. Before this mankind had been nomadic. Settling down to grow crops and rear animals, these first farmers formed small walled settlements for mutual protection. The first settlements pre-date the invention of pottery and the discovery of metals and contain the earliest bricks. These were roughly made by hand and dried in the sun.

The next section looks at the development of bricks from simple kneaded lumps of mud into regular mass-produced rectangular units (called 'adobe'). Egypt is used as an example, even though the moulding of bricks pre-dates Egyptian civilization, because more records and artefacts survive there relating to these developments than elsewhere. The technology that was developed in this period for making mud bricks is still used in many parts of the world today.

The third section looks at Mesopotamia. It was here that both the first moulded and first fired bricks were made. Various written sources survive giving some

idea of the structure of building works and the hierarchy and number of individuals involved. These cultures also saw the veneration of the brick as a religious object, such was its importance to society. The various brick sizes and ways of laying bricks are described, along with the methods used for working bricks into decorative elements. With the invention of brick came the necessity for mortar, an agent to bind the bricks together. In simple adobe construction the obvious solution was to use mud, often mixed with straw or animal dung. Mud can also be used for fired bricks but it easily washes away and has comparatively little adhesive power. Three alternatives, gypsum, lime and bitumen, were available to the earliest civilizations. Bitumen was only used where it was readily available in tar pits. It had the advantage that it needed little preparation and dried to a waterproof layer, yet its comparative rarity meant that its use never spread much beyond the narrow confines of the oil fields of southern Mesopotamia. Lime in the form of limestone needed to be burnt at 1000°C to break it down into quicklime which when mixed with water created an adhesive paste ideal for plasters and mortars. Lime plasters are found from roughly the same period as the invention of the fired brick which required kilns operating at about the same temperature. Gypsum mortar was made by burning gypsum that occurred naturally normally in deposits close to limestone. It only needed to be burnt at about 125°C, temperatures obtainable in a normal bonfire. Some authors have suggested that its use pre-dated lime mortar but there seems to be little evidence to support this case. All three types of mortar seem to have been employed in early Mesopotamia.

Opposite Dramatic panel of glazed bricks from the Palace of Darius I (521–486 BC) at Susa, Iran, now in the Louvre in Paris.

Following pages The great ziggurat of Al-Untesh-Napirisha (c. 1260–1235 BC) now known locally as Choga Zanbil ('basket mound').

Beginnings: brickmaking in Neolithic Jericho

The world's oldest bricks were discovered in excavations in Jericho, on the banks of the River Jordan, by an international team of archaeologists led by Kathleen Kenyon in 1952. The remains of the ancient city amounted to no more than a large mound or tell when excavations began. Tells are hills formed from the ruins of thousands of years of settlement deposited on top of each other, each new town built on the remains of the old. The Jericho tell was particularly important because, as work progressed, it became clear that it contained the remains of one of the oldest human settlements ever discovered. It was so old that it belonged to the Neolithic or Stone Age, pre-dating the invention of pottery or the discovery of metals.

Prior to the excavations carried out by Kenyon's team, it had always been assumed that pottery was invented when man first settled down to make permanent communities. As digging progressed it became clear that people must have built towns before they used pottery, when they still had only simple flint tools. These very early towns were made of mud brick. There were two types of early bricks found at Jericho. The oldest dated from the period Kenyon termed Neolithic Pre-pottery A (c. 8300–7600 BC). They varied in size but measured approximately 260 x 100 x 100mm. These first bricks were shaped like loaves of bread and were made by scraping the mud from the ground using a stick, mixing it with water by hand before kneading it into a roughly rectangular shape. Each brick was then set out to dry in the baking hot Middle Eastern sun and when hard they were then laid in courses to make thick walls, using more mud as the mortar. The second sort of bricks found in Jericho are more distinctive. Termed 'bun bricks' and dating from the Neolithic Pre-pottery B period (7600–6600 BC), they were formed in a similar manner to the former but were longer, thinner and more consistent in size (400 x 150 x 100mm) with distinctive herringbone patterns of thumb marks in their upper surfaces.

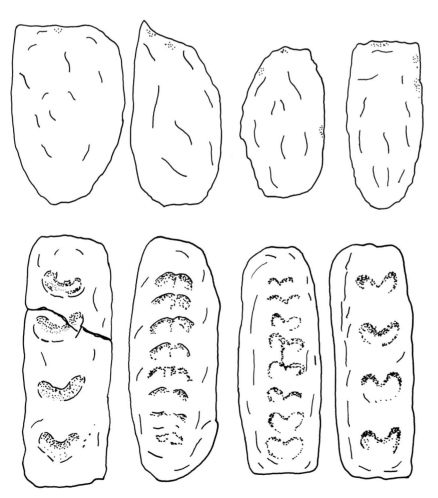

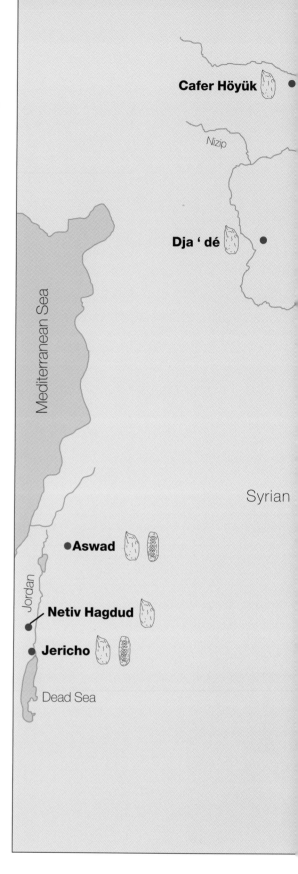

Above left Bricks of the Neolithic Pre-pottery A period found at Jericho dating from 8300–7600 BC.

Above Map showing the major archaeological finds of Neolithic Pre-pottery.

Left Bricks of the Neolithic Pre-pottery B period found at Jericho dating from 7600–6600 BC.

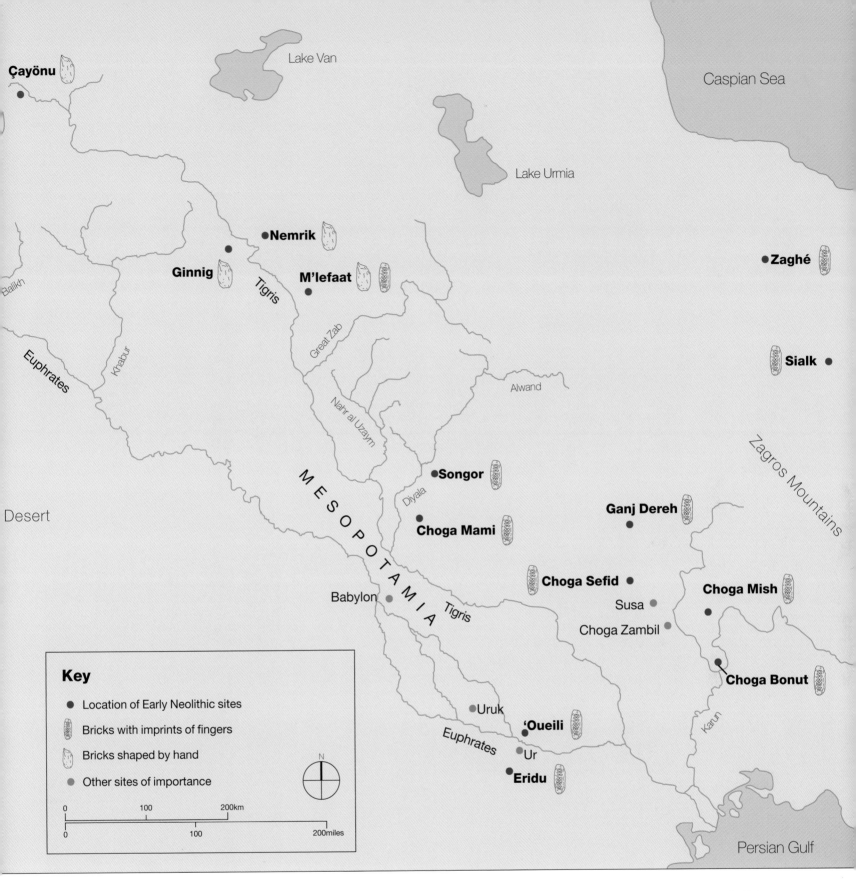

Çayönu

Lake Van

Caspian Sea

Lake Urmia

Nemrik

Balikh

Ginnig

Tigris

M'lefaat

Great Zab

Zaghé

Euphrates

Khabur

Nahr al Uzaym

Sialk

Alwand

Zagros Mountains

Songor

Diyala

Ganj Dereh

Desert

Choga Mami

Choga Sefid

Choga Mish

Babylon

Tigris

Susa

Choga Zambil

Choga Bonut

Karun

Uruk

'Oueili

Euphrates

Ur

N

Eridu

Persian Gulf

MESOPOTAMIA

Key

- Location of Early Neolithic sites
- Bricks with imprints of fingers
- Bricks shaped by hand
- Other sites of importance

```
0        100        200km
0            100        200miles
```

It is, of course, possible in such a climate to make solid mud walls without using bricks, but the sun-dried brick (or adobe, as it is more properly known) had a number of advantages. Firstly, bricks, unlike mud, were easily transportable, so that a wall could be built some distance from the source of the mud. Secondly, and probably more importantly, a brick wall was stronger because each brick was fully dry before it was put in place. Thirdly, the use of bricks removed the need for any form of support to the sides of the walls to keep

them upright while the mud dried (in effect the bricks acted as a form of permanent shuttering).

Although these are the earliest bricks of any kind so far discovered it is unlikely that they were isolated cases and by the seventh millennium the idea of making hand-made bricks seems to have become widespread.

The major disadvantage of these hand-moulded bricks was that they did not fit properly together because they were inconsistent in size and shape. Such

bricks relied on thick mortar joints of mud which were inevitably weaker than the bricks themselves. In hot countries where timber was scarce they provided a valuable alternative to wood, and mud is more plentiful and easier to carry and work than stone. Nevertheless the next step, which was the development of the moulded brick, marked a substantial improvement on these early attempts at brickmaking.

The development of brickmaking in ancient Egypt

The brick mould is a tool for making bricks. It represents the first great technical innovation in brick manufacturing. Its apparent simplicity can easily conceal the fundamental shift in the nature of brickmaking that it represented and, like any tool, it did not appear overnight. It went through a series of adaptations and refinements before arriving at the form with which we are familiar today.

The oldest surviving images of workmen using moulds to make bricks were found in the tomb of Rekh-mi-Re in Thebes. Rekh-mi-Re was the vizier of Egypt in 1450 BC. In these remarkable pictures we see workers getting water from pools and brickmakers then mixing it with mud and straw and pushing it into open-bottomed wooden moulds on the ground. The top of the mould was then scraped with a piece of wood to remove the excess clay and the mould lifted off and placed onto the next piece of open ground where the process was repeated. By this method it was possible for a single brickmaker to mould many hundreds of perfectly rectangular

identical bricks in a day. These would then be left to bake in the searing Egyptian sun. The murals show that the ancient Egyptians used single moulds with handles, some of which have been found, and mud bricks are still made using much the same process on the banks of the Nile today.

It should be emphasized that the Egyptians were not the first people to use wooden moulds to make bricks. The earliest kings of both Upper and Lower Egypt ruled from about 3000 BC and this method of brickmaking seems to have been adopted there from the beginning of that First Dynasty, but it is likely that the method was first introduced to Egypt from Mesopotamia. Moulded bricks seem to have become common there much earlier, from what archaeologists call the Ubaid 2 period (5900–5300 BC), well before the use of metals.

Although Neolithic man may have appreciated the advantages of wooden moulds, making them must have offered a considerable challenge. The sides of moulds have to be cut straight, which is easily done with a saw, but that would have been extremely

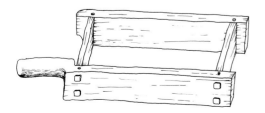

difficult with the flint tools that had to be used before the discovery of metals. Similarly Neolithic man lacked the tools to join the parts of the mould together. How he did so remains a mystery because the earliest surviving moulds date only from the Egyptian period, by which time metals had been discovered.

There was an intermediate stage between the development of hand-modelled bricks and bricks made in wooden moulds, in which bricks were shaped by hand and the sides flattened with boards. Such bricks are recognizable in having flat sides, but without the dimensional uniformity of bricks thrown into rectangular moulds. They have been discovered at 'Oueili in southern Mesopotamia, dating from c. 6300 BC.

The Egyptians may not have invented the rectangular moulded brick but once they had adopted it, they used it in some of the most imaginative ways. Most importantly they developed a sophisticated brick architecture of arches and vaults. This is in sharp contrast to their use of stone in which they never used the arch, preferring to restrict themselves to a simple beam and lintel system.

Egyptian mud bricks were rectangular and varied in size and it has been suggested that these differences can be used for dating archaeological remains. The bricks made for state buildings were generally larger than those used for private dwellings.

Those at Thebes in the Middle Kingdom period (c. 1800 BC) are typically 280–320 x 150–160 x 75–100mm; earlier examples at Giza were 360 x 180 x 115mm. The very largest weighed 40–50lb and must have required several people to lift it. Others were no larger than a modern brick, but most were designed to be lifted with two hands. They were typically laid in mud mortar in consistent bonding patterns (most commonly, what we call English bond).

While stone was used for grand buildings, mud bricks were typically employed for walls, houses, pylons, stores etc. of which a number survive in Thebes (now Luxor). Wood was in short supply so where possible the Egyptians tried to avoid its use. The Temple of Rameses II in Thebes had massive grain stores, some of which remain intact, which consisted of long vaulted chambers. To avoid using timber formwork to build the vaults, they were constructed with each course leaning backwards on the previous one. By this method it was possible to span 3.8m using 350 x 210 x 60-70mm bricks without any centering.

Although the Egyptians perfected the use of mud bricks, they showed little interest in fired ones. They did use them in isolated instances in buildings from the Middle Kingdom period onwards, but they are rare before the arrival of the Romans. With such a good supply of building stone Egyptians had little need to make them.

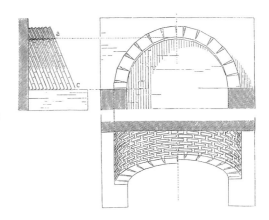

Top   Wall paintings from the tomb of Rekh-mi-Re, vizier in Egypt (1450 BC), Thebes (Luxor), showing bricks being moulded by hand in the traditional way.

Opposite, far right   A drawing of an Egyptian brick mould, the remains of which are in the University of London collection.

Above   Cutaway drawing showing the method of vault construction of the grain stores in the Temple of Rameses II at Thebes (Luxor).

The fired brick in Mesopotamia

Jericho may have boasted some of the earliest brickwork but it was crude. In ancient Mesopotamia, by contrast, great civilizations developed sophisticated methods of manufacturing and using bricks which would remain unmatched for centuries after they disappeared and still appear remarkable today.

Fired bricks

That clay formed a hard material when burnt was well-known in the ancient world. The earliest pottery in Europe and the Near East dates from c. 7000–6000 BC, not long after the manufacture of the earliest mud bricks. The idea that the same technique could be applied to building materials had no doubt occurred to our distant ancestors long before they chose to act upon it. The earliest fired bricks so far discovered were used in Mesopotamia, in the Ubaid 3–4 period (c. 5000–c. 4500 BC) in Maddhur, to make a drain. However this instance appears to have been exceptional, if not unique, and fired bricks remained very rare before the Uruk /Djemdet Nasr period (3100–2900 BC). It is this date that should perhaps be properly ascribed to the earliest use of fired brick. Thus the first fired bricks were not manufactured in any numbers until some 5,000 years after the first recorded use of the mud brick and 4,000 years after the first pottery, an enormous gap that is worthy of further explanation.

In hot climates mud brick is an adequate and economic building material. Even today it remains the most commonly used building material in the world for the construction of houses. Its advantages remain the same as they have always been:

the manufacturing process is cheap and it can be done adequately by anyone, without the need for skilled labour. With a little know-how, house owners can build their dwellings from the earth on which they stand.

The fired brick is an entirely different type of object. To fire clay effectively into a hard mass it must be heated to temperatures between 950 and 1150°C: too hot and the brick will melt, fusing into a misshapen glass-like mass; too cold and the brick will be so fragile as to crumble easily on the lightest blow. Moreover, while the test of whether mud is the right consistency to make adobe is straightforward (simply make a few bricks and see if they work), the choice of clay for fired bricks is much more important and the mistakes are only discovered when all the bricks have been moulded and valuable fuel has been wasted. Making fired bricks is also expensive, particularly in countries where suitable fuel for burning is in short supply. It thus requires a knowledge of the selection of clay and of the process of building and maintaining the kiln at steady firing temperatures. These are the skills of an experienced professional brickmaker. Mud bricks can be made at home: fired bricks have to be made in an industrial process

by someone sufficiently skilled to know what they are doing.

Yet there are many reasons for wanting fired bricks over mud ones. Mud bricks are washed away in the rain and disintegrate in floods. Fired bricks, meanwhile, are waterproof and resilient.

Because of its strength and apparent permanence the brick in antiquity became a symbol of eternity, of man's power over time itself. To our ancient ancestors then there was nothing mundane about the fired brick. Far from being everyday, it was seen as a luxury item: a building material so valuable it was suitable only for temples and palaces, the houses of gods and kings. Records surviving from the third Dynasty of Ur (2111–2003 BC) record that with a piece of silver you could buy 14,400 mud bricks while the same amount would purchase only 504 fired bricks. Fired bricks thus cost about 30 times as much as mud bricks. Even by the Babylonian period (612–539 BC), which had a very sophisticated brickmaking industry, fired bricks were still between two and five times more expensive than mud ones. Neolithic man may have had the technology to make burnt bricks, but it took a civilization of much greater sophistication to be sufficiently developed to be able to afford them.

Left Bricks from the temple of Insusinak at Susa, now in the Louvre in Paris. These are some of the very earliest examples of bricks moulded in relief and date from the 12th century BC.

Opposite The central staircase of the ziggurat which is commonly called Choga Zanbil, 40 km south-east of Susa in western Iran. It is actually the ziggurat of Ishushinak and Napirisha (c. 1250–1235 BC), built by King Untesh–Napirisha at the centre of his new capital Al-Untesh-Napirisha (also called Dur-Untesh-Napirisha). The site was supplied with water by a 50-km long canal to the River Dez.

Shapes and bonding

Four shapes of brick were commonly used in Mesopotamia: plano-convex, rectangular, square and those which archaeologists have called 'Riemchen' bricks (which are rectangular in plan, but square in section). Plano-convex bricks bulged upwards on their upper surfaces, which made them difficult to lay on top of each other. As a result they tended to be laid on their sides in herringbone patterns. The other bricks lent themselves to more orthodox bonding methods. Often the outer wall would be made in Stretcher bond, but would conceal more elaborate bonding systems beneath. Many of the bonds used (such as English bond), would be familiar to modern bricklayers, but they also employed many patterns involving bricks on edge which have not been widely used since. Square bricks tended to be laid flat, but to make walls they had to be mixed

with half bricks, which were rectangular, making it difficult to tell on casual inspection whether most of the bricks in any given wall are square or rectangular.

Fired bricks were often stamped and inscribed and bricks were also sculpted before firing. Such bricks were used to make round pillars and decorative reliefs. Some of the most remarkable examples dating from the 12th century BC were uncovered in excavations in Susa.

The brick in Mesopotamian society

Mesopotamia is the general term for the fertile area between the Tigris and the Euphrates rivers which developed into city-states between 4000 and 3000 BC. Certain cities (like Uruk or Ur) controlled large areas, while others only ruled the area around them and over the centuries some rose to dominance for

long periods before being subdued by others. Defensive structures played a key part in all Mesopotamian cities, which were from the beginning surrounded by stout walls. The other important structures were derived from the system of government. Despite their political rivalry the different states all held certain fundamental beliefs in common and at the heart of all of them was a king who saw himself as a direct link with a large pantheon of gods. The king needed a palace and a temple and the two were intimately connected. The largest structure that dominated the city and the palace was the ziggurat.

A ziggurat was a stepped pyramid similar to the pyramids of ancient Egypt and perhaps inspired by them, but while the Egyptian pyramids were vast mausolea, built to house the bodies of the pharaohs, Mesopotamian ziggurats were grandiose bases for temples. In this respect they were closer in use to the stepped pyramids of Mesoamerica. The ziggurat was the setting for an elaborate ritual of renewal enacted every New Year by the king and a high priestess, which aimed to ensure the future prosperity of the state.

Rituals generally played an important role in pre-modern cultures and continue to do so in one way or another in many modern ones. Ancient Mesopotamian rituals were not restricted to religious matters, but entered into every part of daily life. This even extended to building works. There were strict rules as to what could and could not be done on certain days, and astrologers and geomancers had to be consulted on when and where a building should be built before works commenced. The brick was central to this ceremonial. The word brick (*sig* in Sumerian) was also used to mean both 'a building' and 'a city' and, more importantly, it was also the name of the god of building. We know from inscriptions that, before the laying of foundations of any building, offerings of food and drink had to be made to the brick god, represented in the ritual by the first brick. The situation for public works was even more involved. The King himself enacted the most important ceremony, the preparation of the first brick. A description of the ceremony survives:

> [the King] put the blessed water in the frame
> of the brick mould. For the ruler drums and
> kettledrum[?] accompanied the adab song.
> He set up the appropriate brick stamp so that
> [the inscribed side] was upwards; he brushed
> on honey, butter and cream; he mixed
> ambergris and essences from all kinds of
> trees into a paste. He raised the impeccable
> carrying-basket and set it before the mould,
> he acted precisely as prescribed, and behold
> he succeeded in making a most beautiful brick
> for the house. Meanwhile, all the bystanders
> sprinkled oil, sprinkled cedar essence, while he
> let his city...rejoice. He struck the brick mould:
> the brick emerged into the daylight. He looked
> with complete satisfaction at the stamp on
> the clay...he spread on it cyprus essence and
> ambergris. The sun god rejoiced over [his]
> brick, which he had put in the mould which
> rose up like a swelling river...

The first brick so dedicated was called the *asada*, meaning 'the invincible one'. To make it so it needed one final act which is not described: firing.

Building industry

Such rituals lay at the heart of a complex system of building construction. Important Mesopotamian buildings were set out to detailed drawings. One such plan survives, inscribed on a clay tablet. It is so detailed that it marks the position of individual bricks and contains detailed measurements in brick dimensions, to enable the builders to set out the structure. The brick thus seems to have been the standard unit of measure in all building works.

Mud bricks were laid to these drawings in mud mortar, often with layers of matting at regular intervals to bind the courses together. No trowels were used, the mortar being spread with bare hands. Bonding timbers were also used within the walls to hold larger structures together.

The core of the ziggurat was always mud brick, but mud brick is easily washed away by floods and rain, so the outside was often made of fired brick. This was laid in bitumen mortar. Bitumen lay about in pools in parts of the region and was easily collected. Herodotus tells us that it was used for its waterproof properties and this seems likely: the rivers regularly flooded and mud bricks were easily washed away so it made sense for precious structures to be protected with a layer of waterproof fired brick firmly bonded by the most waterproof mortar readily available.

Building a ziggurat was an enormous undertaking. It has been estimated that the ziggurat at Babylon contained some 36 million bricks and that, of these, about a tenth were fired and the rest were mud-baked, requiring some 7,200 working days to mould the fired bricks and 21,600 working days for the mud ones. By the same calculation it was estimated that the ziggurat would have employed some 1,500 workers (87 moulders, 1,090 masons and 404 porters) just to make and lay the bricks. From various documentary sources we know the names of some of the trades involved: digger of mud, mixer of mud, mud specialist, porter of mud, maker of baskets for transporting mud/bricks/mortar, brickmaker, maker of fired bricks or kiln-man, glaze preparer, bricklayer, architect/chief builder. Texts have also survived describing the hierarchy of the various individuals involved in running a brickyard but the yards themselves and the kilns have not been properly excavated and recorded because firstly they mostly stood apart from the cities to avoid fire and secondly they have so far been considered less important than the central ruins.

The great civilizations of Mesopotamia conducted trade far and wide and the techniques they employed

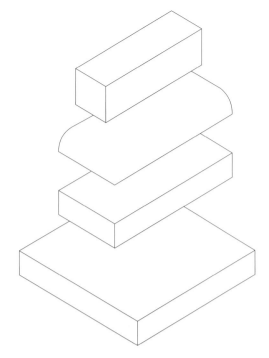

could be easily copied. Fired bricks appear in the Indus valley in the third millennium, where they were used extensively in the great cities of Harrappa and Mohenjo Daro which similarly suffered from flooding. It is possible they were developed there independently, but it is likely that they were at least inspired by advances already made in Mesopotamia. Nowhere were there structures to rival the ziggurats or the palaces that surrounded them, which remained the largest brick structures for some time to come.

Babylon and the glazed brick

Babylon is remembered for its legendary Hanging Gardens, one of the Seven Wonders of the World. The Gardens were said by Quintus Curtius Rufus to have included trees 50 feet high and 12 feet across and to have been built by Nebuchadnezzar to remind his concubine Amytis of her mountainous homelands in Media (north-western Persia), which she greatly missed. If they existed, the Gardens would have been built of brick, probably consisting of terraces of burnt bricks with vaulted halls beneath. Sadly, no contemporary accounts survive and little trace of a suitable structure has been found. It seems likely that they were always nothing more than a myth. Nevertheless, excavations at Babylon have yielded some startling finds.

The ancient city of Babylon was founded as a provincial capital in the third dynasty of Ur (2111–2003 BC). It later became the temporal and spiritual capital of Mesopotamia under the Amorite ruler Hammurabi (1792–1750 BC) but fell from importance after it was sacked by the Hittites in 1595 BC. Frequently fought over and destroyed, the city reached its architectural height under King Nebuchadnezzar II who ruled from 604 to 562 BC.

The city of Babylon, home of the Hanging Gardens and long presumed to be the site of the original Tower of Babel mentioned in the Bible, fascinated early travellers and explorers. Leonhart Rauwolff, a physician from Augsburg travelling through Syria, Palestine and Mesopotamia in 1573–76, was convinced he had rediscovered the ancient city when he came across the colossal remains of the ruined ziggurat at Dur Kurigalzu, which soars 55m into the air. The actual site of Babylon, when it was subsequently located, was less impressive, consisting of little more than a mound in the desert. In the 19th century it was carefully investigated by the British antiquarian Claudius James Rich who published his discoveries in his *Memoirs on the Ruins of Babylon* (1815), but it was not properly recorded until the end of the 19th century, when the Royal Prussian Museum

sponsored two excavations of the site by Robert Koldeway, an architect who pioneered systematic excavation in the Near East.

The city that Koldeway revealed to the world was more remarkable than anyone expected. He uncovered a great wall with towers at regular intervals that enclosed 850 hectares and was broad enough to justify Herodotus's claim that a four-horse chariot could turn on top of it. Inside this defensive ring there were a number of great building complexes including a walled inner city (the summer palace), which was the sacred and political centre of the whole of Babylon. The palace contained hundreds of rooms around a few large courtyards. The scale of the complex was staggering and through painstaking excavation Koldewey was able to reveal that a succession of buildings had occupied the site, including a subterranean complex of rooms and wells with traces of hydraulic lifting gear which he optimistically took to be the foundations of the Hanging Gardens.

Most of the palace was made of moulded mud-brick. This presented problems in excavation as it was similar to the earth being removed, but was unremarkable in itself. The great discoveries, however, were the Ishtar gate and the interiors of the royal apartments, which were carefully dismantled and transported to Berlin, where they remain the centrepieces of the Pergamon Museum today.

These revealed that the Babylonians had perfected the art of first moulding and then glazing fired bricks, new technologies that they took to a high level of sophistication. Bricks in relief were made by hand, sculpted in the wet clay. They would have been pre-assembled to check that they fitted together, perhaps with a plank or palm leaf between each block to simulate the mortar and stop the bricks sticking to each other. The shape was then carved in the wet clay. The blocks would then be left to dry before firing. Bricks of roughly the same size were used to reduce the problems associated with shrinkage. Colour glazes would then be applied to them, probably in the form of a liquid slurry which would turn to glass on firing. What is remarkable is the control which Babylonians were able to exert over the colours in their glazes, which can only have been discovered by a long process of experimentation. Sadly, they left no records of their methods behind them.

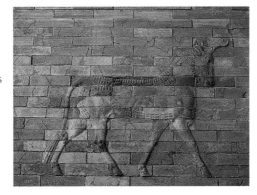

Opposite, top and bottom Processional Way (604–562 BC), Babylon.

Left, bottom Wall from the throne room of the palace (604–562 BC), Babylon.

Right, top An early example of moulded brick from the temple of Karaindash at Uruk (14th century BC).

Right, bottom Ishtar Gate (604–562 BC), Babylon.

The magnificence of Susa and the decline of Mesopotamia

The ancient city of Susa contained some of the most remarkable examples of glazed brickwork ever produced. The settlement dates back to 4000 BC and was the capital of Elam, an area of what is now in south-western Iran, to the east of the Mesopotamian basin. Elam was at various periods under the control of Agade and Ur, but it reached particular importance under Darius I (521–486 BC), the Persian king, who made it his administrative capital and rebuilt the city using the most skilled artisans he could find from across the empire he had conquered, which stretched from the Indus to the Aegean.

The site of ancient Susa was first studied by the British geologist and explorer William Loftus in the 1850s, but it was a series of French archaeologists who made the great discoveries there. The first was a civil engineer, Marcel Dieulafoy (1844–1920), who in an excavation from 1884–86 uncovered the Apadana, the pillared hall of Darius's palace, which included the 'Frieze of the Archers', now in the Louvre in Paris. Thereafter the French were given a monopoly on Persian archaeology in Iran, of which they took full advantage. They explored widely in western Iran but concentrated most of their excavations in Susa, building a fort there to protect the archaeologists. They continued to work there until the Iranian revolution in 1979.

The excavations at Susa proved valuable because Darius and his successors brought trophies to the city from their conquests throughout Mesopotamia and the Middle East. It was here, for instance, that the law code of Hammurabi, (king of Babylonia in the 8th century BC) was found. Darius imported not only precious objects, but also skilled workmen. Inscriptions in the foundations of the palace revealed that he bought stone workers from Lydia (now eastern Turkey), goldworkers from Egypt and Media, cedar from Lebanon, ivory from Nubia and lapis lazuli from Sogdia. His brickmakers and bricklayers were imported from Babylon. The result was a city that in its heyday must have been spectacular.

As no doubt he had demanded, the brickwork of Darius's palace equalled and perhaps even exceeded that at Babylon. The range of colours employed was certainly far greater, including greens, as well as the blues, whites and yellows of the Babylonian examples. Like their Babylonian equivalents, each glazed brick used in Susa was tapered in section so that its front face could be laid with the thinnest joint possible. Investigations of the Babylonian examples also revealed that each brick was marked, indicating its place in the wall. No doubt a similar system was followed at Susa. The bricks had to be stacked in the kiln and came out like a giant jigsaw puzzle.

Some type of key was essential to fit them back together in their correct locations.

Of all the capitals so far discussed, only Susa remained a town into medieval times, but the empire it had administered had long since disappeared. The importance of the region as a centre of civilization was finally brought to an end by the invasions of Alexander the Great (356–323 BC), who created a Greek empire that stretched from India to North Africa. After Alexander's death, the great centres of political power were in the Mediterranean, leaving the cities of Mesopotamia to fall into decline. The spoils of war no longer flowed into the coffers of Babylon and Susa. The money and the justification for great and lavish building projects disappeared and the skills that they involved ceased to be required. The continuity of a tradition of brickmaking that had lasted 6,000 years was finally broken.

Opposite far left Glazed brick relief from the palace of Darius at Susa showing 1.46 m high archers who were probably the king's bodyguard.

Opposite above The lower part of the excavation site at Susa.

Opposite below The foundations of the palace of Darius at Susa, an early example of bricks laid in Flemish bond.

Above and below Glazed brick reliefs from the palace of Darius, Susa, which are now on display at the Louvre in Paris. The reliefs were made with wedge-shaped bricks so that the visible joints were as narrow as possible. Inscriptions suggest that they were made for Darius by Babylonian brickmakers brought to the site for the purpose.

CHAPTER TWO

THE CLASSICAL WORLD 500BC – 1000AD

This chapter begins with the fall of Susa and the rise of ancient Greece and ends with the construction of the exquisite Tomb of the Saminids in Bukhara. It covers the rise and fall of the great classical civilizations in the Mediterranean and the first emperors in China. It also encompasses the appearance of two great religions: Islam and Christianity. In terms of brickwork it was a period of innovation and re-invention. New techniques were devised for making and laying bricks and for mixing and using mortar. Brickmaking became an established and profitable line of business and tools like the trowel first appeared in bricklaying. The new technology allowed more daring buildings, many of which still remain some of the finest examples of brick architecture anywhere in the world today.

As is clear from the previous chapter, the Romans did not invent brick or brickwork, but as a building material brick is nevertheless frequently associated with Roman construction. What is noteworthy is the apparent lack of influence of ancient brickwork on subsequent developments in the Mediterranean. This chapter begins with an examination of the origins of Greek and Roman bricks and tiles, dispelling various myths along the way.

Roman brickwork is undoubtedly highly important and after the first section the following six are devoted to exploring various aspects of the manufacturing and use of brickwork in the Roman Empire. The first of these looks at the sources for information on Roman building techniques and particularly at the contents of the first major treatise on the subject by Vitruvius. The next section examines brickmaking, looking at the various sizes of bricks that the Romans commonly used, how they moulded them, the ways they marked them, and the various types of kilns they employed. It also discusses the way the trade was organized. There was a clear distinction between bricklayers and brickmakers in this period. Bricklayers seem to have been masons in Roman times and their business was less lucrative than that of the brickmakers. The next section is devoted to their craft, the techniques they used, the tools they employed and how they organized their work. It is often assumed that Roman brickwork was originally intended to be faced in marble or render. While this may often have been the case, by the end of the 2nd century the Romans had mastered various bricklaying techniques that allowed them to produce highly intricate decorative effects in brick alone.

The following three sections deal with specialist areas of brickwork in which the Romans made further innovations. The first looks at baths and aqueducts, which required special types of bricks and new structural forms. The second looks at arches and vaults, which played an important part in many Roman buildings such as the Colosseum, while the third looks at domes, which the Romans built in a number of ways.

The Roman Empire declined in the 4th century and divided in two. The Eastern half was based in the city variously called Byzantium, then Constantinople, and finally Istanbul. The Western Empire, which was the weaker, had its capital in Rome and then Ravenna, before it was conquered by invaders from the north and broken up in 476. Ravenna subsequently became the capital of the Ostrogothic kingdom under Theodoric. The Eastern or Byzantine Empire, however, continued in a depleted form until Constantinople finally fell to the Ottomans in 1453. This period marks the transition between Roman brickwork and later traditions. Byzantine brick is dealt with in two sections. The first looks at the general changes in brickmaking and bricklaying techniques. The other deals with the specific problems involved in constructing the Hagia Sophia, which features one of the largest brick domes ever constructed.

Brickwork in Ravenna is dealt with separately. Although it shared certain features with the Byzantine tradition (and indeed the Byzantine Empire captured the city in the mid-6th century and held it until 751), various features of Ravenna's brickwork also prefigure later developments in medieval European brickwork.

The history of brick in China has been complicated by somewhat partisan claims made under previous administrations in state sponsored works that the Chinese invented brick. Recent research has thankfully been more scholarly and it is now generally accepted that the first bricks did not appear in China before 1066 BC and that they were probably not widely used before the Warring States period (475–221 BC). However, whether the Chinese developed brickmaking technology independently or acquired it through contact with the Middle East and India has yet to be established. What is clear is that once the Chinese had developed brick they proceeded to use it in new and exciting ways which were not paralleled elsewhere. The section on China looks at the various types of bricks produced in this period and the various ways they developed for firing and laying them that set them apart from the Western tradition.

The two final sections in this chapter examine Islamic brickwork in the period. The Islamic calendar is traditionally numbered from 15 June 622, the *Hegira*, when Mohammed (c. 570-632) fled to Medina. The religion he founded spread rapidly across the Middle East and North Africa, reaching from Spain to the Indus by 711. The Islamic invaders absorbed the building techniques of the peoples they conquered and transferred them across continents. The materials used depended on local availability, and in those areas where brick had predominated it continued to be used by the new rulers. The first section traces the spread of Islamic brickwork and its general characteristics. The last section looks at a particularly remarkable building, the Tomb of the Saminids in Bukhara. This delightful building was constructed under the enlightened rule of Ishmail the Saminid (862-907), who gathered round him a great court of artists, academics and poets. He took a particular interest in garden design and the building he constructed as his tomb was set in a garden on the edge of the city. The building itself is a perfect essay in the possibilities of brick decoration. It survived Mongol invasions and was discovered buried under later buildings in the 1930s and carefully restored. It now stands in a public park on the edge of the town centre. Constructed in the 10th century, it marks the end of a remarkable millennium of architectural history and prefigures some of the developments yet to come.

Opposite The Basilica of Constantine/Maxentius (c. 310 AD) in the Roman Forum. When completed this building was 100m long and 65m wide. The arches of the nave were 35m high. On the left is one of the coffered barrel vaults opening off the central space which had a quadripartite groin vault.

Following pages Trajan's Markets (98–117 AD) viewed from the forum of Trajan. The markets are on both upper and lower storeys and continue up the hillside behind.

Greek and Roman architectural ceramics

Ancient Greek civilization can be divided into four periods: Bronze Age, Dark Age, Hellenic and Hellenistic. The roots of civilization in ancient Greece and Asia Minor have been traced back to 3000–2800 BC. In Crete this represents the Early Minoan period while on the mainland it is called the Early Helladic period. Architecture was recognized as an art chiefly in the form of palaces and tombs. Between 1000 BC and about 700 BC the whole area descended into poverty and little of any value remains from this period, normally called the Greek Dark Ages. It is in the subsequent Hellenic period, running from 700 to 300 BC that the great temples commonly associated with ancient Greece were constructed. This is the age of Plato and Aristotle. In the last period, after Alexander until the birth of Christ, the architecture merely reinterpreted what had gone before, as the power of the Greek world diminished and the Romans gained control.

Early Greek architecture was, as one might expect, extremely simple. Normal buildings were constructed out of mud bricks covered with a coat of more mud to protect them from the rain. They were roofed by a layer of timber beams covered by a thick layer of clay. This simple form of flat roofing laid to a slight fall was perfectly adequate for small spans in the moderate rainfalls of the region. Larger buildings were made using timber frames and had pitched roofs covered in thatch. Terracotta was used to make decorations for these buildings and it was only natural that it came to be seen as an alternative for roof coverings.

The precise date of the invention of the terracotta roofing tile is not known. Early tiles have now been found reportedly dating back to between 2600 and 2000 BC in Lerna near Argos in the Peloponnese. Certainly the technology was widespread before Greek culture reached its height. The Greeks used three main types of tiling systems, although each region made tiles in particular and identifiable way. The earliest general types are referred to as Lakonian and

Corinthian. The Lakonian type consisted of curved tiles laid alternately with the concave side upwards and downwards, the latter covering the joints in the former. The Corinthian consisted of two distinct shapes of tile. The first was flat, with edges turned up, and the second was a ridge tile placed to cover the gaps between the former. This type of tile was also later made in marble. A third system was employed in Sicily and Aeolis where the flat tiles of the Corinthian system were covered by the semi-circular tiles of the Lakonian. These roofs often had semi-circular tiled gutters with a spout at each end. Where this was not the case, the roof projected to throw the water well clear of the walls and decorative antefixes were placed in the ends of the tiles. These could be quite elaborate, in the form of heads or animals, but were most often a simple palmette or scroll. Ridge tiles were decorated with similar motifs. Terracotta was also used for sculpture in early pediments and for decorative acroteria (statues that were placed at the four corners of roofs).

However, despite the presence of a complex trade in architectural ceramics, fired bricks for building walls were not commonly employed in the Greek world. They were not completely unknown, however. Excavations of an unidentified circular building at Tiryns (also near Argos) revealed what could be the first fired bricks in Europe, possibly dating from as early as 2000 BC. This seems to be an isolated instance, suggesting that the bricks were not necessarily fired on purpose. Mud bricks were more commonly employed. Where fired bricks occur at all it is more commonly in the plinths of mud-brick houses where the brick is used instead of stone to separate the adobe or timber work from the ground. A fired brick of this type has been found separating a wooden column from the earth in the remains of a house in Olynthos dating from c. 400 BC. In an empire as widespread as ancient Greece, which traded with and later conquered many Eastern lands, it would have been surprising indeed if brickmaking had not appeared at all, but it never seems to have been widespread.

Some writers have attributed the change from mud brick and timber frame to stone construction in larger buildings to the wider use of terracotta roof tiles. Tiled roofs were too heavy to be supported on mud-brick walls and stone, which was relatively plentiful in the mountainous regions of Greece, was an obvious alternative. It is generally accepted that the various features of a Doric temple started out as imitations of their timber-framed counterparts. Eventually even the tiles themselves were replaced in the grandest buildings with marble imitations. The use of stone for the walls from about the 7th century onwards saw the disappearance of the terracotta decorations that had previously adorned them. Thereafter terracotta was mainly restricted to roof decorations where stone was not generally employed.

(a)

(b)

(c)

The three systems of tiling used in ancient Greece:
(a) Lakonian
(b) Sicilian
(c) Corinthian

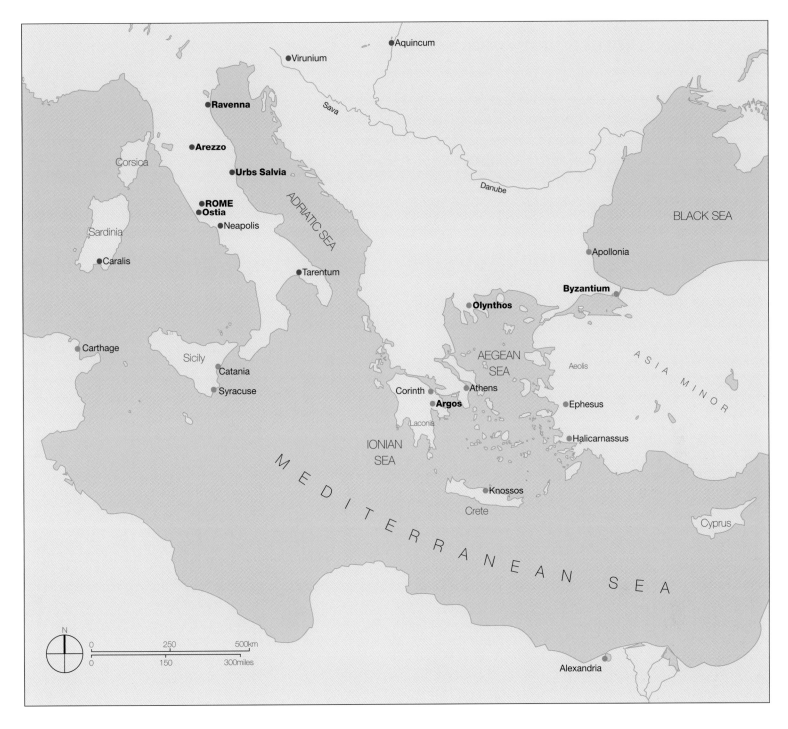

The arrival of the Romans

The Romans had conquered most of the Italian peninsula by 274 BC and in the following 250 years they gradually expanded their dominions to cover Greece, Asia Minor, Egypt, France (then Gaul) and the Iberian Peninsula. Further conquests were made under Augustus in Germany and the Balkans so that by the end of the 1st century AD they controlled a massive empire from the Atlantic Ocean to the Red Sea.

Well before the Romans had conquered Italy, the Etruscans who lived there had used terracotta roof tiles on buildings with mud-brick walls and had experimented with firing bricks. The Romans subsequently adopted the tiled roof for their buildings. Their tiling system with its two parts, the tegula (a flat tile with upstanding ribs at the edges) and the imbrex

(a semi-cylindrical covering tile), was similar to that used in Sicily in Hellenic times.

The Romans, like the Greeks before them, used mud bricks to build the walls of their houses. However, they did use fired bricks in the 1st century BC for town walls. Half-fired bricks were used in the walls at Arezzo measuring 440 x 290 x 140-mm. The earliest fully fired Roman bricks were used in Sicily and southern Italy. The city walls of Urbs Salvia were made in 470-450 x 320-300 x 50-65-mm bricks neatly laid in 10-15mm joints in the reign of Julius Caesar (49-44 BC) but no bricks have been found in Rome itself dating from before the reign of Augustus (27 BC – 14 AD). Even then the bricks used in the capital actually seem to have been roof tiles recycled from other sites and placed in

walls as a facing, with the moulding of bricks specifically for the purpose only coming later. By the end of the 1st century AD use of brick was widespread and the legions who set up brickyards wherever they went were responsible for carrying the technology across the Empire.

Thus, although it was probably the Greeks rather than the Romans who should be credited with the first use of fired brick and the introduction of architectural ceramics into Europe, it seems fair to say that it was the Romans who should take the credit for disseminating the technology, exploiting the full potential of brickwork and using it in new and daring ways to produce some of the most extraordinary buildings the world has ever seen.

Early writing on brick: Vitruvius and other writers

The earliest building manual to survive from ancient times was written by a Roman called Marcus Vitruvius Pollio. The Romans were not the first classical civilization to write on architecture: Vitruvius himself mentions a number of previous writers in the introduction to volume seven of his book, but all earlier works have been lost. Vitruvius's *Ten Books on Architecture* thus remains the most valuable written source for Roman architectural practice and any history of building construction. It also acted as an important source for other writers in the period.

The *Ten Books* deal with all aspects of Roman architecture from the education of the architect through the use of building materials, the types and arrangement of ornament, the setting out of towns, the making of military machinery, to drainage and sewerage and even astronomy, but bricks and tiles are only mentioned in five places:

1] Under building materials, where Vitruvius deals with sun-dried bricks (II.3.1-4).
2] In his discussion on types of wall which lists the methods of making wall out of sun-dried bricks (II.8.16-20).
3] On baths, the use of square tiles in vaults and in flooring for the construction of the under-floor heating systems are noted (V.10.1-5).
4] In the section on finishing, when dealing with floors, he lists the uses of brick laid in herringbone patterns and of large two-foot tiles in paving (VII.1.4-7).
5] When covering methods of plastering in damp conditions, Vitruvius advocates creating cavity walls

using two-foot tiles (*bipedales*) and suspended floors held on eight-inch tiles (*bessales*) (VII.4.1-2).

Apart from these (and a short note on the advisability of using terracotta pipes instead of lead ones for the carrying of drinking water), Vitruvius is strangely silent on the use of bricks and other fired-clay products.

Many scholars have attributed Vitruvius's reticence on the subject of bricks to the date at which he was writing, some even citing it as direct evidence that fired brick was unknown in Rome in Vitruvius's time. This argument is complicated by the fact that we are not exactly sure when Vitruvius wrote his books. It is currently believed that they date from sometime between 30 and 20 BC. Brick in this period was certainly still relatively new in the city of Rome, but it had been used for several centuries in southern Italy, an area with which we know Vitruvius to have been very familiar.

Monumental buildings in Rome in Vitruvius's time were faced with stone, while normal flats and houses were often timber-framed with adobe infill panels. Concrete was becoming increasingly common, usually faced with rectangular pieces of tufa (a soft volcanic stone) set in a diamond pattern (*opus reticulatum*). This was not an ideal facing because it tended to crack.

Brick was beginning to replace tufa as a facing and had been used in this way outside the capital for some time, but it was still relatively new in Rome. The most likely explanation for Vitruvius's reticence on the subject is that he mistrusted it and preferred to concentrate in his treatise on what he thought of as tried and tested technologies.

Whatever the reason, later Roman authors writing on building had no such excuse. It is thus indicative of how reliant they were on Vitruvius as a source, that they had little, if anything, to add to what he had already said on the subject. Pliny the Elder, for instance, does briefly discuss bricks in his

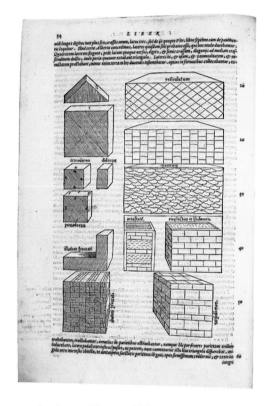

massive *Natural History*, which contained no fewer than 37 books and covered topics as diverse as astronomy, meteorology, geography, mineralogy, zoology and botany. He deals with bricks after pottery in book XXXV (chapter XLIX lines 170–174), but his description adds little to Vitruvius, whom he cites as a source. Of the other writers on building contruction, Sextus Julius Frontinus barely mentions bricks in his book on building aqueducts (*De Aquis*) written c. 100 AD, Cestius Faventinus only discusses them in the context of lining wells in his *De Diversis Fabricus Architectonicae*, written in the 4th century AD, while Rustilius Taurus Aemilianus (Palladius), whose *De Re Rustica* was based on Faventinus, omits brick altogether.

From this brief description it can be seen that although bricks and brickwork were to become a distinctive feature of Roman construction and the Romans wrote treatises on many technical matters, they produced frustratingly little on the

A. *Tavolozza triangolare martellinata delle mura d' Aureliano.* B. *Opera incerta d' ogni sorta di scaglie* C. *Tegoloni quali legano i corsi della tavolozza, ed opera incerta* D. *Merco del Mastro della fornace*

Piranesi Architetto . dis. inc.

subject of bricks. As a result, our knowledge of the development of Roman brickwork is based mostly on archaeological observation, supplemented by material gathered from inscriptions on monuments. The piecemeal nature of such sources makes interpretation extremely difficult. For instance, the name of a brickmaker is sometimes found on bricks or the name of the builder carved in a wall. Occasionally accounts are found detailing prices. In Ostia we even have a list of members of a *collegium* or guild. Gathering together material of this kind, archaeologists and historians have gradually pieced together a picture of what life might have been like for the Roman brickmaker and bricklayer in the Roman Empire but such conclusions are tentative and much of the information is still missing.

Opposite, left
The frontispiece from Daniele Barbaro's famous Renaissance edition of Vitruvius with plates by Andrea Palladio (1567).

Opposite, right
The original drawings for Vitruvius's treatise were lost. Subsequent editors have added new ones where the text demands it. This page shows brick and stone cutting and laying from Barbaro's edition.

Above An engraving by G. Piranesi showing how cut bricks were used as a facing for concrete. Only those used in bonding courses are left rectangular. The rest are cut into triangles.

Brickmaking in the Roman Empire

By the 2nd century AD brickmaking had become a sophisticated industry, one of the few in which the aristocracy actively invested and from which they derived considerable profit. Thorough and well-preserved records survive for Rome and its neighbouring port of Ostia, enabling historians to build up a reasonably clear picture of how the trade operated.

In both Ostia and Rome it seems to have been common for landowners to exploit the brickmaking potential of their estates to feed growing demand, and brickyards were seen as valuable investments. Brickmaking itself was overseen by *officinates* who ran the yards. The legal relationship between *officinates* and the landowner remains a mystery. They may have leased the land or been employed by them. While research has shown that the *officinates* were free or freedmen, their underlings were probably not. Like virtually all heavy work in Rome, the work of digging the clay, tempering it and the moulding of the bricks would almost certainly have been done by slaves. In outlying territories brickmaking was often carried out by the army. Early bricks in Rome itself were of poor quality because the clay tended to be used raw and suffer from excessive shrinkage. Later sand was added which reduced this problem.

In his discussion of mud bricks (II.3.2) Vitruvius writes, 'bricks should be made in springtime or autumn, so that they dry at a uniform rate'.

The direct action of the sun dried the clay too quickly. A similar method was no doubt followed for burnt bricks.

The Roman method of moulding bricks remains a subject of considerable controversy. Bricks were made in 'standard' sizes but they were rarely very uniform in shape. This has led to some scholars to suggest that they were made by what is called the 'pastry cutter method', where a flat sheet of clay is laid out on the ground and sliced with a knife roughly to produce bricks of the correct size. Most brickmakers think that this method is impractical and that it is more likely that Roman bricks were made by placing a conventional open wooden mould on a bed of straw on the ground and throwing the wet clay into it, using water as a releasing agent. This type of slop moulding produces a brick identical in appearance to the Roman one, which normally has one rough side. Differences in size could be put down to differences in moulds and in poor mixing of clay, leading to different rates of shrinkage during drying and firing.

Brick sizes

Roman bricks are normally distinguished by being square and flat. Vitruvius (II, 3) lists three types of brick: the *lydion*, which he says is one foot by one and a half; the *pentadoron*, which is five palms in each direction; and the *tetradoron*, which is four palms in each direction (*doron* being Greek for the palm of the hand). Pliny (XXXV.49.171) more or less repeats Vitruvius (whom he cites as a source), but provides measurements in Roman feet and inches and substitutes the word *didoron* for Vitruvius's *lydion*. Both state that only the term *lydion* was invented by the Romans, while the others were Greek in origin. As we mentioned above both authors were writing about unbaked bricks. When it comes to naming the various types of baked bricks that have been found, building historians have turned to more disparate and fragmentary references in inscriptions and accounts.

The smallest Roman brick is the *bessalis*, derived from the *bes* meaning two thirds of a unit, the unit being a Roman foot which is 12 Roman inches or 11.64 English inches. The *bessalis* is thus a brick measuring 8 inches square (about 200mm). Vitruvius states that bricks of this size were used to make the *pilae* that supported the floor above a hypocaust in Roman baths (see pages 54–55), but *bessales* were versatile and easy to handle and are commonly found cut into smaller pieces in wall surfaces. They were generally about 45mm thick.

The *pedalis* was a Roman brick measuring one foot square, conforming to the *tetradoron* mentioned in Vitruvius and Pliny. The word *pedalis* is taken from the section 'De Fictilibus' in Diocletian's Edict on Maximum Prices; it is unclear how commonly it was used in Roman times, but sizes of tiles and bricks seem to have been based on the foot so it would seem logical to have a one foot brick. Whole *pedales* were used at the top and bottom of *pilae* in hypocausts. Elsewhere they were generally used cut into smaller pieces. One Roman foot was 295mm long. Found examples tend to be slightly smaller. On average they are a couple of millimetres thicker than *bessales*.

Two larger types of square bricks are also listed in Vitrivius: the *sesquipedalis* and the *bipedalis*, measuring one and a half feet square and two feet square respectively. These are very large bricks, closer to flooring slabs, and Vitruvius cites them as being used for the floors of hypocausts. Because they were so large they also had to be correspondingly thicker. *Sesquipedales* should measure 443mm square and the found examples tend to be about 50mm thick. *Bipedales* should measure 590mm square, although examples up to 750mm square have been found. They are usually 60mm thick. *Bipedales* are not common but are found in arches, bonding courses and subdivided into triangles for use in walls. Weighing up to 65kg, they were hardly practical for day-to-day use.

Rectangular bricks (usually grouped under the term *lydion* by archaeologists) were commonly used in bonding courses. The average size is about 400 x 280 x 40mm. The name, which is found in Vitruvius, is derived from Lydia in Asia. The size on plan is similar to Minoan bricks (which were about twice as thick) and it has been speculated that the origin of this type of brick is Etruscan.

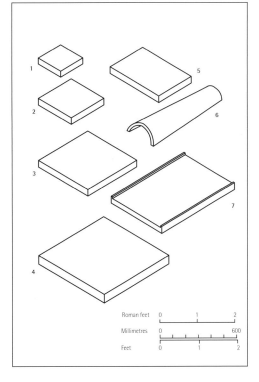

Roman feet 0   1   2
Millimetres 0   600
Feet 0   1   2

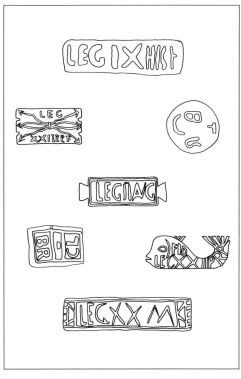

Opposite The Colosseum (left) and the so-called Temple of Rediculus (right).

Top Detail of a doorway to a warehouse in Ostia

Above. left Roman bricks: (1) Bessalis, (2) Pedalis, (3) Sesquipedalis, (4) Bipedalis, (5) Lydion, (6) Imbrese, (7) Tegula.

Above Examples of Roman brick stamps.

How useful are these terms? In truth, however convenient it might be to have neat categories, there is very little proof that the Romans used a term such as *lydion* widely or generally took as much care over sizing bricks as might be wished. We believe that each *collegium* or guild imposed its own rules, and as a rule of thumb bricks became thinner later in Roman history while the mortar joints became thicker, but size alone is not a definite indicator of origin or period.

Stamps

The last act of the shaping of the bricks prior to firing was the application of a stamp to the upper surface. These stamps do not seem to have been applied to all bricks. Perhaps only the last brick in a batch was stamped or one in so many to ease the counting process. Roman brick stamps have been noted since the beginning of archaeology in the 18th century, but it is only in the 19th century that study of them became systematic. Lists have been drawn up and published which allow bricks to be matched with others and dates to be put to a particular specimen. Brick stamps varied greatly in size and content. Up until the end of the 1st century they seem to have

been relatively simple, often providing nothing more than initials. In the second century under Trajan (98–117) they became much more elaborate including the name of the landowner, the head of the brickmaking operation and dates. The text is often bounded by a frame or enclosed within a circle or other device; some typical examples are shown on page 47.

Kilns

Once marked and dried the bricks were ready to be fired. It seems likely that most Roman bricks were burnt in kilns. Certainly no evidence for the use of clamps in this period has yet been found. A surprising number of Roman kilns have been excavated, providing a clear picture of production. Because of the similarity in shape and size between Roman bricks and tiles, the same sort of kilns seem to have been used for both and the two were probably fired together.

Roman brick and tile kilns consisted of two storeys. The lower storey housed the fire, which was fed through a stoking hole from the outside. This storey was roofed by a perforated floor which supported the objects being fired and through which the exhaust

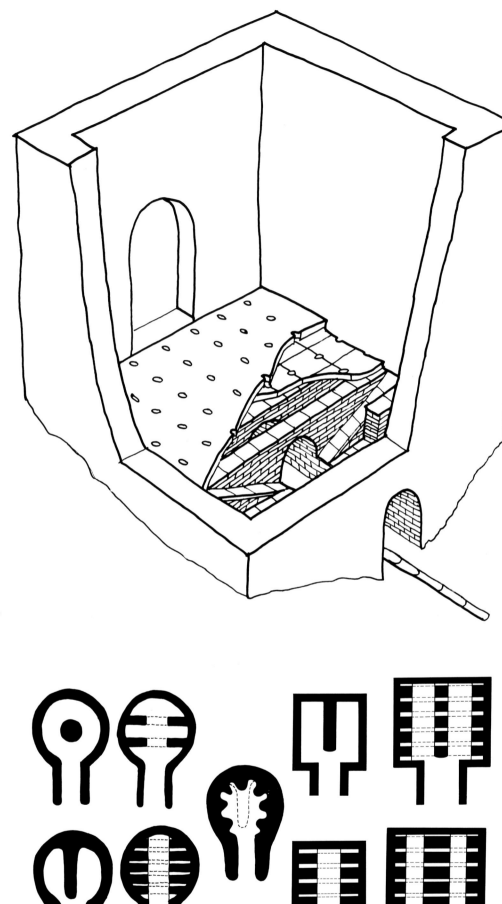

Right A cutaway isometric of a typical Roman brick and tile kiln. The fire was lit in the lower chamber, the gases escaping through holes in the floor. The upper chamber held the bricks or tiles.

Below right Plans of the various types of Roman brick and tile kiln excavated so far.

gases could escape. The upper storey had no permanent roof and was surrounded by high walls which kept the heat in. In general these do not survive. The green tiles and bricks would be stacked in the upper space for firing and then covered with broken tiles or shards to protect them from the rain and provide a final layer of insulation. Access to this upper storey could be through a door in the side walls, but kilns were often built into hillsides so that they could be filled from above.

In plan, Roman kilns could be round or rectangular. For many years it was presumed that brick kilns were rectangular because this shape was more suited to stacking bricks and tiles, while the round kilns were used for pottery, but excavations in southern Italy have shown that the Romans did use round kilns for both purposes. Roman kilns appear to have been mostly wood-fired, although coal-fired examples have been found.

Left Detail of the façade of
Trajan's Markets, showing
decorative brickwork.

Opposite The entrances to the
shops on the upper floor of
the arcade of Trajan's Markets.

The Classical World

Bricklaying in the Roman Empire

Many of the monumental brick buildings that survive from the Roman period were originally
clad in plaster or in marble, but this was by no means universally the case. Augustan Rome
did not boast much in the way of decorative brickwork. Like most innovative materials
it took time for exposed brick to become acceptable and for the skills to be acquired to
work it in new ways. By the 2nd century AD, however, the Romans were producing
highly sophisticated decorative brickwork.

The simplest type of brick wall is solid brick. This is
comparatively rare in Roman brickwork although it was
necessarily used for thin walls of a single brick
thickness (18 inches or under) and for door and
window surrounds. It is so unusual to find whole walls
built this way that the method does not warrant its
own descriptive term in Latin. *Opus testaceum,* which
means 'brick work', is reserved instead for concrete
walls that are only faced with brick, the most common
form of brick construction used throughout the Roman
Empire. From the outside the bricks appear to be
rectangular but actually the walls were faced with cut
bricks. Initially the bricks were cut in half and thus
roughly rectangular, but later the practice was to cut
larger bricks into triangles, laying them with the
longest side outwards. It is this cutting of bricks that
leads to the dimensions of the bricks which are visible
in Roman walls. A *bessalis,* for instance, would typically
be cut in half. When placed in a wall its exposed face
would thus be 282mm. A *sesquipedalis* would produce
four 443mm long bricks while a *bipedalis* would be cut
into eight bricks which would be 425mm long when

laid. To provide a clean edge, bricks were cut with saws.

Opus caementicium is a general term covering all
concrete work. Concrete is a mixture of mortar and
aggregate (a mixture of rocks varying in size from
stones just liftable by hand down to grains of sand).
The Romans used lime mortars. Lime was extracted
from limestone and burnt in a kiln. It was then mixed
with water and slaked on site. Both Pliny and Vitruvius
provide detailed descriptions of the preparing and
slaking of lime. The Romans were, of course, by no
means the first to use lime mortar, but they were the
first to realize that it could be used to bind rubble
together to form a viable building material in its own
right: concrete. Their other great innovation was the
addition of pozzolans.

Pozzolans in general are additives to lime mortar
that make it react hydraulically, a chemical process that
speeds up the drying time, leads to a much stronger
mortar and means that it even dries under water, a fact
that made it useful for building bridges and harbours.
The Romans discovered that a volcanic ash from the
region of Pozzuoli had this effect, (hence the term

pozzolan, which has since been applied to all additives
to lime mortar which have the same effect). Brick dust
can also be used in this way and the Romans often
added it to mortar.

Walls filled with concrete could be made quickly,
using any rubble lying around. Such walls could be
constructed in wooden shuttering that could be
removed when the mortar was dry, and such a system
was used in Roman construction, typically for vaults
and domes (see below), but more commonly the walls
were faced in a form of masonry which acted as a
permanent shuttering. One of the earliest and most
common forms used was a facing of tufa blocks laid in
a diamond pattern (called *opus reticulatum*). Tufa,
which is a form of lightweight volcanic stone, is easily
mistaken for brick, but although similarly shaped clay
blocks could easily been used, there are no recorded
examples of fired clay in *opus recticulatum* work.

The last type of walling which employed brick was
called *opus mixtum*, a general term which just meant a
wall made out of several materials, normally brick and
stone. The stone facing would be interrupted by regular
bands of brickwork which would be binding-courses
running through the whole depth of the wall.

In all these types of wall the important factor to
note is that the brick was normally cut. In other words
it was treated very much like stone. The brick from the
kiln supplied to site was seen merely as another form of
block that had to be cut to shape to fit on site before
being laid.

For fine brickwork the Romans used the thinnest joints possible, in some cases tapering the bricks as the Babylonians had done so that the outside of the joint was thinner than the inside. Elsewhere they often paid great attention to the finishing of the joint, applying a further finishing layer of mortar after the bricks had been laid, a technique which we would now term 'pointing'. The object was to make the wall as smooth as possible and flush pointing was typical but they also used cut-to-shape pointing and concave pointing.

Trajan's Markets

The most dramatic surviving example of decorative brickwork, Trajan's Markets, dates from the reign of Trajan (98–117 AD), nearly a century after Augustus and Vitruvius. They were the Roman equivalent of a shopping centre. Hundreds of individual shops were reached via arcades and corridors on four levels, built into the side of the Quirinal Hill. The lower part of the complex formed a huge semi-circle, mirroring another on the other side of the Forum. The façade of this consists of shops on the lower floor and an arcade on the upper storey giving access to shops on an upper level. It is decorated with entablatures and pediments of carved brickwork with marble capitals and door surrounds.

Ostia

The development of the coastal town of Ostia coincided with the height of Roman brickwork. Virtually every building was constructed of brick and many were ornamented with fine carved brickwork decoration, of which sadly only a fraction remains. The most striking examples of decorative brickwork are found in the few carved shop fronts which survive, particularly the *horrea Epagathiana et Epaphroditiana*. These were warehouses built by two eastern freedmen, Epagathus and Epaphroditius, whose names are recorded in a plaque above the entrance. The front façade is made of carefully cut brickwork assembled with thin mortar joints. It was once surmounted by two further storeys which may have been similarly ornate.

The builder of the *horrea Epagathiana* was a member of Ostia's *fabri tiguarii*, a *collegium* with some 350 members. *Collegia* are often compared to guilds. They consisted mostly of freedmen (slaves who had been released) and provided them with a certain amount of security (for instance, they paid for burials). More importantly the *collegium* provided the organization of building workers. Each had a rigid hierarchy based on military ranks and strict rules. Through the *collegia* the large bodies of workers necessary for substantial building works could be easily

controlled. It seems likely that they were the most common form of building organization.

Temple of Rediculus

The period around 150 AD seems to represent the high point of Roman decorative brickwork. The warehouses in Ostia date from this period. So too does the building which was called the Temple of Rediculus in the 17th century. More recently it was renamed the Tomb of Annia Regilla, the wife of Herodes Atticus, because it was constructed near his villa, just off the Appian Way.

That attribution too is now in doubt. The building, which is currently in a private garden down a back lane, is remarkable for its exceptional brickwork. Two colours of bricks are carefully mixed. The wall planes are constructed from pale yellow bricks, while the decorative details are picked out in fine red bricks. The Roman brickmaking industry was by this time providing moulded decorative elements which were used along with carved brickwork. By the end of the 2nd century, however, the quality of brickwork began to decline.

Opposite Close-up of the side of the so-called Temple of Rediculus near Rome; in fact probably the tomb of Annia Regilla, wife of Herodes Atticus, mid-2nd century AD, on the Appian Way.

Below left Ostia Antica, where two-storey buildings remain giving a clear idea of Roman urban life.

Above Entrance façade of the *horrea Epagathiana et Epaphroditiana*, Ostia.

Below right A typical street in Ostia, which flourished as the port for goods coming in and out of Rome.

Bricks and water

The Romans used bricks and concrete for civil engineering works including aqueducts, bridges and baths, and these contain some of the largest and most complicated brick structures.

There had been aqueducts serving Rome since 312 BC, but the aqueducts composed of great lines of high vaulted arches belong to a slightly later period. The earliest, like the Aqua Marcia (114 BC), tended to be constructed (or at least faced) with stone. By the 1st century brick was replacing stone as the material of choice, perhaps because the growth

in brickmaking was making it more readily available. The brick remains of the Aqua Claudia (built between 38 and 52 AD) are still visible behind the Porta Maggiore (itself part of an aqueduct) in Rome.

Aqueducts were built to supply Roman cities with water. Once in the city, the water was kept in cisterns

(which were themselves often built of brick) and distributed through lead or clay pipes. Vitruvius suggests that terracotta pipes were healthier than lead ones because of the dangers of lead poisoning. The clay pipes were made of fired terracotta. Tapering along their length, they fitted into each other and were sealed with lime mortar.

Storm drains were also constructed under the city, although few have survived. Terracotta rainwater pipes fed the water from roofs down into this system. Remains of these features of Roman life survive in Ephesus, Pompeii and Herculaneum and detailed descriptions of the construction and maintenance of water supplies are provided in Frontinus's *De Aquis*.

It was the Romans' fondness for baths that provided the largest consumption of water within Roman towns or cities. Roman baths were sophisticated buildings in terms of hydraulic engineering. Not only did they contain numerous

rooms with pools, all of which had to be filled with clean water, continually emptied and refilled, but they also had advanced heating systems. The chief method of heating both the pools and the rooms in which they were contained was by hypocaust.

The hypocaust system relied on heat generated by furnaces in the basement of the building, which were continually stoked by teams of slaves and served by corridors for the access of men and fuel. The hot smoke was channelled through the floor, which was raised up for the purpose. The pillars on which the floor rested had to be heatproof and incombustible. Brick was the obvious answer. The *bessalis* was a brick specifically made for the purpose. They were stacked up with thick mortar joints between and then covered by larger tiles. A thick layer of concrete would then be laid on these tiles. On top of this was the layer of mosaic tiles which formed the bottom of the pool.

The space under the floor was only part of the bath heating system. The hot flue gases were also drawn up the walls, which were made hollow by using special hollow bricks or tiles with spacers on the back. There were different types of tiles used for the purpose:

1) Box-shaped tiles. These are commonly found in Ostia.
2) Half-box-shaped tiles.
3) Square tiles with nibs on (*tegulae mammatae*). The nibs could be at the corners or offset. An example providing a 75–80mm cavity survives in the House of Julia Felix in Pompeii.
4) Plain tiles with ceramic bobbin spacers. (55–80mm in length) through which iron nails were passed to fix the tile to the wall.

A similar system was even applied to the ceilings, with vaults made of curved versions of the hollow bricks. Usually these are simply ceramic pipes, designed to be laid in the mortar, and plastered over, but rectangular versions have been found and there are even examples of hollow voussoirs designed for the purpose.

Left The Aqua Claudia, one of the first aqueducts in Rome, begun by Caligula in 38 AD and completed by Claudius in 47 AD. It was 74km long.

Below Box-shaped tiles in the walls from a set of baths in Ostia.

Above The ruins of one of the hot baths in the Baths of Neptune, Ostia, showing the stoking hole on the left and the space under the bath supported on square bricks.

The great Roman technical innovation was the use of the voussoired arch. The brick arch had been used since the beginning of building, the shape being made by varying the size of the joints. The voussoired arch, however, was a more recent innovation, possibly stemming from Etruscan or Greek precedents. Nevertheless, the voussoired arch was essentially a stone structure. Converting it to brick presented a number of challenges.

The voussoired arch uses wedge-shaped blocks to form a stronger structure. Stone Roman arches were constructed using voussoirs, but most Roman arches were brick not stone. Roman brick arches were normally built using large two-foot bricks (*bipedales*) set on edge, the arch shape being made following ancient precedent by tapering the joints. Sometimes one ring of bricks is used but often two or even more rings are employed for greater strength. The reason for using tapering joints in most brick arches is that it was simpler to construct. In stonework every stone has to be cut to shape, but the brick is most easily produced as a regular block. The large flat bricks that the Romans habitually used could not easily be cut to a taper. The alternative was to actually mould the bricks to shape. Wedge-shape bricks made for this purpose had to be made especially for the job in hand according to the width of arch required and this must have rendered them impractical for all but the largest projects, such as the Colosseum in Rome.

The Colosseum, or Flavian Amphitheatre as it was originally known, was started in 70 AD by the Emperor Vespasian (ruled 69–79) and completed in 80 AD by his son Titus (ruled 79–81). The term *Colosseum* first occurs in the works of the Venerable Bede (c. 673–735), quoting an ancient prophecy: 'While the Colosseum stands, Rome will stand; when the Colosseum falls, Rome shall fall; when Rome shall fall the World shall fall'.

Externally the Colosseum was clad in travertine marble, much of which was pillaged for re-use in buildings elsewhere in Rome in the Middle Ages and the Renaissance. Its main structure was made of concrete, which was covered internally in brick and tufa. Despite its massive appearance, every effort is made in the construction of the Colosseum to minimize weight and maximize space for circulation. The core of the building is honeycombed with arches and vaults which transfer the loads to the ground.

The amphitheatre is elliptical: 188m long, 156m high and 50m high. It was entered through 80 huge arches from which the spectators climbed to their seats via numerous stairs and corridors.

All arches have depth, but relatively deep arches are normally known as vaults. Roman vaults were typically constructed out of concrete, as is the case of all the main vaults in the Colosseum. The flexibility of concrete meant that it could be laid in tapering shapes and into cross-vaults without the complexity that would have been involved in cutting stones or bricks to make those shapes. In the Colosseum many of the vaults are conical: that is, the radius of the arches on the outside is larger than that on the inside. Concrete laid on timber formwork allowed such shapes to be simply constructed. Brickwork was typically employed in simple arches and to provide extra strength. The French historian Choisy, in his book on Roman building construction written in 1873, shows the use of bricks employed as ribs in groin vaulting on the Palatine Hill. This use of bricks prefigured the later use of ribs to reinforce Gothic arches.

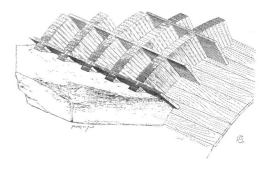

Below left External view of the Colosseum. The structure was used as a quarry for building stone in the Middle Ages and the marble burnt to make lime for mortar.

Above Plate from Choisy's *L'Art de bâtir chez les Romains*, showing the system of brick ribs used in the vaults on the Palatine Hill.

Opposite Two views of the Colosseum as it survives today.

Brick in the engineering of domes

As they had perfected the voussoired arch, it might naturally be presumed that the Romans would have used similar techniques to construct masonry domes. In fact, although they did construct brick domes, the earliest Roman examples were built of concrete and had nothing in common with masonry arches employed elsewhere in the same period. The most dramatic of all these domes was the Pantheon, which was built by the Emperor Hadrian between 118 and 128 AD.

Internally the Pantheon is one vast single space 50m high and 43m across, forming a room so large that it can fit a sphere 43m in diameter inside it. Its walls form a massive cylinder into which niches are cut at regular intervals, surmounted by a great coffered dome. There are no windows. Instead there is a great circular hole (*oculus*) in the centre of the dome. No dome of this size was built again for 1,500 years. It is larger in diameter than the domes of St Peter's or the Hagia Sophia or indeed any dome built before the use of iron and remains one of the most remarkable buildings ever constructed

The dome of the Pantheon is not brick: it is made of solid concrete, but brick does play a significant part in the construction of the drum that supports it. The bricks seen on the outside are with a few exceptions not rectangular as they appear, but formed using the familiar method of cutting square ones into triangles and laying them with only the longest sides being exposed. Nor are the walls of the building as solid as they look. They appear to be 6.05m (20 Roman feet) thick, but at the lower levels this thickness is diminished by the deep-cut niches and by tall inaccessible hollow spaces which run through the walls between to reduce weight on the foundations. The weight of the dome is transferred to the solid piers between these voids by massive relieving arches. These are solid brick, consisting of two rings of *bipedales* and one ring of *besales*. Because the crown of these arches and the feet remain at the same level on the inside and the outside of the dome, the vaults they create are much more complicated than they first appear (they are conical). Thus the arches that appear to be almost incidental on the outside of the building are not only key to the building's structural integrity, but also the only solid brick elements in the walls.

After the construction of the Pantheon, solid concrete domes seem to have diminished in popularity, starting a trend towards the solid brick and masonry domes of the Byzantine period. The first stage in this development was the introduction of brickwork ribs into the concrete in a similar way to the

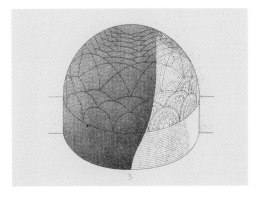

brick ribs found in Roman concrete arches. One of the best examples of this type of construction is the dome of the so-called Temple of Minerva, Medica built in the middle of the 3rd century. These ribs were probably introduced to strengthen the dome rather than reduce the amount of formwork required during construction, and their effectiveness can be seen in the fact that the dome survived even when large sections of the concrete infill panels between the ribs had been destroyed.

Later domes increasingly relied on the brickwork rather than the concrete, probably influenced by Eastern buildings of the period. Choisy, in his book *L'Art de bâtir chez Les Romains*, illustrates a number of examples of brick domes including those of the Mausoleum of Diocletian at Split and of Galerius at Salonika where the bricks were set in layer upon layer of superimposed arches to add strength. Elsewhere earthenware jars and hollow tubes were employed to lighten the domes, a method which was also a feature of the later Byzantine examples.

Opposite, below left The upper side of the Pantheon showing the arched vaults which penetrate through the depth of the wall and transfer the loads evenly to the piers.

Opposite, below right Piranesi's illustration of the interior of the Pantheon, showing the coffered dome.

Above The Pantheon now sits in a square. Originally it was approached through a lowered court up a flight of stairs so that only the portico would have been seen from the front.

Above top Piranesi's illustration of the Temple of Minerva Medica

Above right Choisy's illustration of the system of superimposed arches used in the dome of the Mausoleum of Galerius at Salonika.

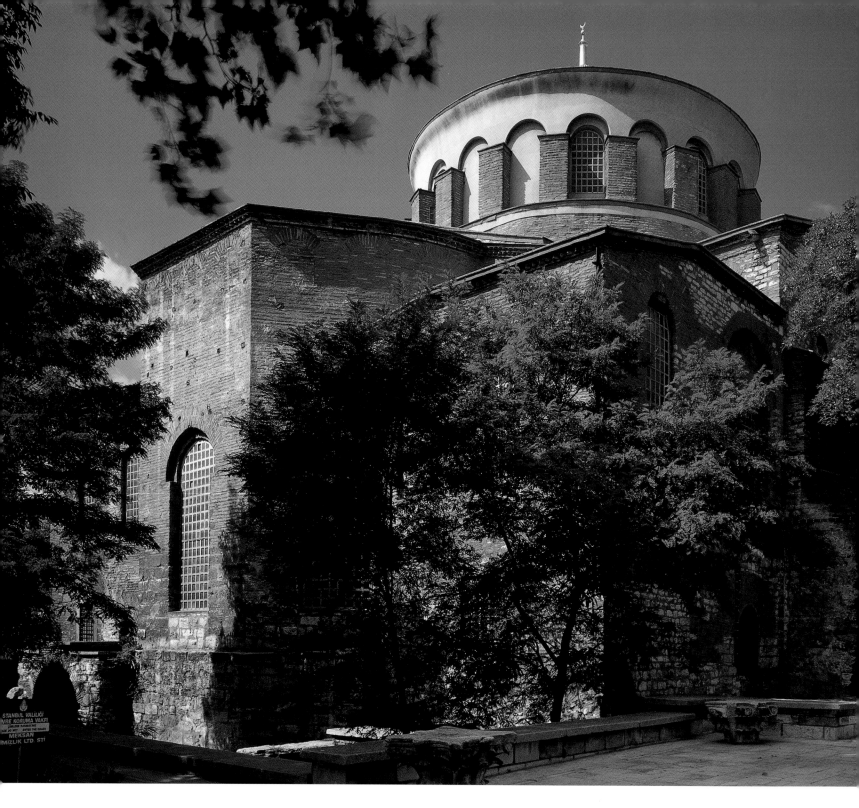

Byzantine brick

The Emperor Constantine moved his capital from Rome to Constantinople (now called Istanbul) in 330 AD, founding an Eastern Roman Empire that lasted until 1453, well beyond the collapse of Rome itself and the invasions of Italy by successive generations of tribes from the north.

Byzantine bricks were made in much the same way as their Roman counterparts. Brickmakers are identified in manuscripts as *ostakariori* (clayworkers) or *keramopoioi* (brickmakers). The wood - or charcoal - fired kilns were round or square and similar to Roman ones in form, with low stoking chambers under perforated floors and upper firing open chambers. A brick works at the Lavra Monastery on Mount Athos was sited by the seashore to allow easy transport of bricks. The numbers of bricks required meant that brickmakers were much in demand. The writer Theophanes recorded that the rebuilding of the aqueduct in Constantinople in 766–67 required 500 *ostakariori* from Greece and 200 *keramopoioi* from Thrace.

The early Byzantine brickmakers followed the Roman practice of stamping their bricks, although like the later Roman brick stamps, Byzantine ones tend to provide little information. Examples of stamps from outside Constantinople are rare and the practice of stamping bricks in the city seems to have died out entirely in the 11th century. Byzantine brickmakers followed Roman practice in making square bricks.

The standard brick seems to have been based on the Roman *pedales*, being about 320–360mm (slightly greater than one Byzantine foot) square and between 35mm and 50mm thick. There seems to have been little variation in the dimensions during the Byzantine period so brick sizes cannot be used for dating.

It is not clear whether bricklaying was a distinct craft in Byzantine times. It was certainly not specifically recorded as such. It seems more likely that bricks were laid by masons. A number of illustrations in early Bibles of the construction of the Tower of Babel show bricklayers using trowels and bricks being carried in bowl-shaped hods up the wooden scaffolding. They also show other labourers slaking lime in wooden troughs using long hoes and turning mortar out into

bowls for use. The *Book of Eparch*, which records details about trade guilds in 10th-century Constantinople, also shows that the trade was strictly regulated. Builders could only work on one project at a time and for brick buildings they remained accountable for faults for ten years after construction. Moreover, the book recognized that bricklayers required specialist skills, stating that 'those who build walls and domes or vaults of brick must possess great exactitude and experience lest the foundation prove unsound and the building crooked or uneven'.

On casual inspection Byzantine brickwork appears similar to its Roman counterpart but while the Romans used brick as a facing for concrete, Byzantine architecture often used walls of solid brick. Sometimes

Far left The Church of Hagia Eirene, Istanbul. The building was converted from a basilica to a cross-domed church in the 8th century.

Top The 12th-century brickwork of the dome of the church of the Kalenderhane Camii, Istanbul.

Above Close-up of the brickwork of Hagia Eirene.

Byzantine brickwork was in the form of *opus mixtum* with bands of stone alternating with those of brickwork, but more often the brick was used on its own. The reason for this switch from concrete construction to solid masonry is unclear. Perhaps the Roman settlers mistrusted the strength of their mortar when they could not use familiar sources of pozzolans or perhaps they began to be influenced

by earlier Eastern traditions. Whatever the reason, the switch had an important effect on the architecture.

Byzantine brickwork was characterized by thick horizontal mortar joints. Indeed the horizontal joints were as thick as the bricks and usually thicker, while the vertical joints were often only a few millimetres wide. The effect of thick horizontal joints in providing a richly textured wall was so popular that sometime in the 10th century a new method of bricklaying was invented which has been called variously the recessed-brick or concealed-course technique. In this method the bricks in every alternate course are recessed into the wall and completely covered by mortar so that from the outside it appears that the wall consists of half as many bricks as it does, each laid in an exceptionally large joint. It has been suggested that this may have helped the outside of the wall to bind to a rubble core behind, but the primary motivation was probably purely aesthetic.

Mortar was made from slaked lime. Brick dust was often added, which not only gave a pink colour which went well with that of the bricks, but also acted as a pozzolan, although it is not clear how well this was understood at the time. Sometimes finer mortar would be applied to the outer surface of the joints to bring it flush, an early example of what is now called pointing. The edges of the resulting joints were often scored with a sharp implement, sometimes using a straight edge. It was also not uncommon to impress lengths of cord into the mortar joint to leave a rope-like pattern imitating the cord that was probably used to level the joints. Both techniques made the brickwork appear more regular.

As well as employing new techniques, Byzantine builders were highly imaginative in devising elaborate decorative bonding brick patterns. The thick walls and wide mortar joints allowed considerable flexibility in approach. Round patterns are common, the simplest being made from radiating bricks, while the more complex ones employ curved roof tiles to provide a frame and spirals. Bricks are set vertically and horizontally to produce herringbone patterns, zig-zags or alternating squares. Square mortar joints are framed in brick networks in every conceivable orientation and bricks are laid in long raking diagonal patterns. In general, early Byzantine work is comparatively plain, with the number of patterns increasing into what we would call the Middle Ages and patterns varying from region to region and from builder to builder.

Left The church of Christ Pantepoptes, Istanbul, built in 1080, seen from the south-east. The wide-spaced bricks are laid using the recessed-brick technique.

The great dome of Hagia Sophia

Legend has it that when the Emperor Justinian first laid eyes on Hagia Sophia, the great church which he had commissioned, he was so taken aback that he exclaimed, 'Glory to God who has thought me worthy to finish this work. Solomon, I have outdone you.' There is no doubt that Justinian, with his architects Anthemius of Tralles and the elder Isadorus of Miletus, succeeded in producing an extraordinary building that is as admired today as it was nearly 1,500 years ago. It is less frequently realized that the Hagia Sophia was built out of brick.

Much of what we know today about the history of the Hagia Sophia is derived from an anonymous work, the *Narratio*, that appeared two or three centuries after its completion. It related the story of Justinian's remark quoted above and provided details of the building works. From it, we learn that the building was constructed by two teams, each consisting of 5,000 workmen, supervised by 50 master workmen, who worked in competition to build the sides of the church at the greatest speed. It also tells us of how the plan was given to Justinian by an angel and relates that the mortar from the foundations was made with a broth of barley and bark of elm. More importantly, from our point of view it tells how special bricks were made for the dome. They were imported, it says, from the island of Rhodes and were so light that 12 of them weighed the same as a single normal brick. The *Narratio* goes on to tell us how relics were placed between every 12 bricks laid in the dome, accompanied by prayers from the church below.

The bricks used throughout the building are approximately 375mm square and 40–50mm thick, although later bricks tend to be slightly smaller and thicker. The only major deviation from these dimensions are the bricks used in the arches which are roughly the same as Roman *bipedales* (700mm square) and may have been reused from Roman sites. All the bricks are used whole rather than cut in the Roman manner, except where they need to be cut to make openings. They are set in lime mortar in joints 50–60mm thick (that is, thicker than the bricks themselves). Thus the mortar plays a significant part in the strength of the wall. The walls are not filled with concrete like Roman walls, but are instead made of continuous coursed brickwork. The mortar is mixed with brick dust and small shards of brick. No doubt the brick dust acts as a pozzolanic agent while the small pieces of brick saved on the use of sand.

The construction of the original dome is something of a mystery. Justinian selected as his architects two men who were chiefly renowned as mathematicians (both published books on mathematics). No doubt it

was they who came up with the ingenious system of supporting domes and buttresses that transmit the forces from the base of the dome to the ground. The present dome is a later replacement. The first dome was probably about 1m thick, that is one and a half bricks, and the bricks were probably laid radially on timber centering. It is possible to lay a dome like this without formwork, but it would be extremely difficult to provide both a working platform and support for the course of brick being built: a continuous centre is thus the most likely solution. The second dome which was constructed after the earthquake was similar to the first but taller and the *Narratio* tells us that it was built on a system of light centering that remained in place for a year.

Above Hagia Sophia (begun 532) dominates the Istanbul skyline.

Opposite Both internally and externally the brickwork is mostly covered by finishes, only small areas being visible.

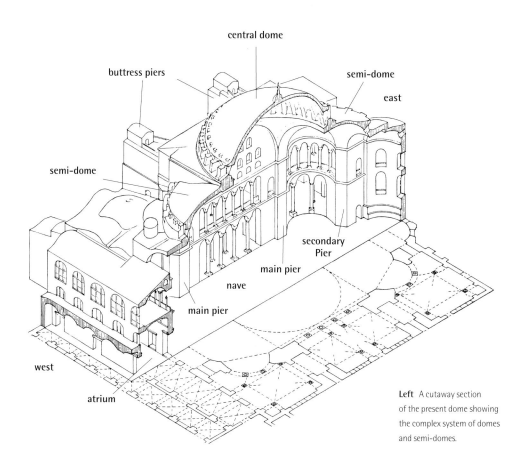

Left A cutaway section of the present dome showing the complex system of domes and semi-domes.

Ravenna and the brickwork of the late Western Roman Empire

Nowhere can we see the division between medieval and Roman brickwork more clearly than in the precinct of San Vitale in Ravenna. Here Roman and Byzantine techniques were mixed and new types of brick (which were much thicker than those used before) were developed that would become typical in the Middle Ages.

The church of San Vitale was built in 526–537 by Julianus Argentarius. Its brickwork at first glance looks Roman: the bricks are long and thin, with close-fitting vertical joints and wide (20–50mm) horizontal ones. On closer inspection it seems more Byzantine: the walls are solid brickwork and the bricks are rectangular (varying in size but commonly 340 x 510 x 35–45mm). The cornice is five courses high, two of which are set in a saw-tooth pattern. The building is octagonal on plan, surmounted by a semi-circular dome. The transition between the two is made by the introduction of concave squinch-arched niches. The dome itself is brick, and it weight is reduced by making the upper surface out of a spiral of amphorae (wine jars) which are bonded to the inside with lime mortar.

Only a few yards away, in the gardens of San Vitale, sits a building of completely different character: the so-called 'Mausoleum of Galla Placida'. This consists of a central block which is square on plan surrounded by four equally-sized bays forming a Greek cross. The bricks here, like the building, could hardly be more different. They are laid in the medieval manner with roughly equal vertical and horizontal joints and are much thicker than Roman bricks, averaging 300 x 150 x 80mm (with some measuring 430 x 250 x 100mm). The walls are laid without a distinguishable bonding pattern, with a simple set of brick cornices. Internally the building consists of intersecting barrel vaults and a central dome, with the arches made from

Opposite Arian baptistery, Ravenna, built by Theodoric (493–526) using 300 x 180 x 65-mm bricks with 30-mm joints.

Below The mausoleum of Galla Placida (5th century) built using 300 x 150 x 80-mm bricks with 20–30-mm joints. These bricks are of similar proportions to later medieval buildings.

thinner bricks and the vault constructed from concentric horizontal courses, inset with amphorae to reduce the weight.

The idea of using hollow elements to form domes is repeated in the baptistery of Neon. There the dome is formed of thin purpose-made curved and ribbed terracotta tubes laid in concentric horizontal rings and then plastered. Unfortunately, little of the original exterior brickwork remains. This is particularly true in the upper sections where the blind brick arcades just below the eaves are now thought to

be part of a major vertical extension of the building in the Middle Ages. Previous observations had placed them as the earliest example of this type of motif.

The Arian baptistery, built by Theodoric (493–526) next to the Arian Cathedral, was confiscated after the Byzantine reconquest together with all the other buildings dedicated to Arian worship, and was reconsecrated in the Orthodox cult (561). Architecturally it is very similar to the Baptistery of Neon and, like the others, it is also partially

buried and has to be entered down a flight of steps. Its brickwork is also basically medieval in appearance. Thick rectangular bricks are laid with headers at intervals and a saw-tooth cornice like that at San Vitale sits beneath the roof.

Early brickwork in China

Some authorities have claimed that the Chinese invented bricks. Although this is no longer generally accepted, it is clear that the Chinese did develop a highly sophisticated brickmaking industry that was radically different from that in the West in the period 500 BC–1000 AD.

It has been claimed that the earliest examples of ceramic tiles and facing bricks in China date from the Western Zhou period (1066–771 BC) but the earliest verified use of fired bricks in a building is in the shaft of a smelter in Xinzheng County, Henan dating from the Warring States period (475–221 BC). The next occurrence is in a section of wall in the pottery figurine pit of the tombs of the first emperor of the Qin Dynasty (255–206 BC). Chinese bricks thus belong to a period after the discovery of bricks in Mesopotamia but before their development in the Roman world.

Chinese brickmakers seem to have experimented much more imaginatively than any of their Western counterparts with different sizes and shapes for architectural ceramics. For instance, in the Warring States period (475–221 BC) large hollow terracotta slabs (1.3–1.5m in length) were used to make the floors, walls and ceilings of hollow-brick tombs which were barely larger than the coffins they enclosed. The building bricks from the Western Han period (206BC–24AD) were more conventional, occurring in two basic sizes (400 x 200 x 100mm and 250 x 120 x 60mm). This ratio of sides (4:2:1) is close to that of modern bricks. The Chinese also made large flat bricks with ratios of 6:3:1 and 8:4:1. The tongued and grooved bricks of the Eastern Han period (25–220 AD) are some of the most unusual bricks ever produced and were designed for use in vaulting to tie the courses together.

Later Chinese bricks were burnt in quite sophisticated downdraught kilns using reducing techniques which were employed in pottery manufacture in China many centuries before they appeared elsewhere. Early bricks were probably made using less complex methods. It seems likely that they were burnt by stacking bricks up, leaving gaps for fuel

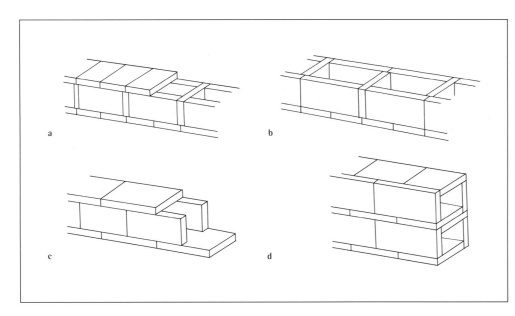

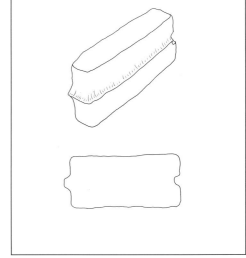

Above Some of the many bonding patterns used in the construction of hollow walls:
(a) lined-up box bonding
(b) alternating box bonding
(c) all-through channel bonding
(d) piled-up box bonding

Above right 'Tongued and grooved' or 'mortice and tenon' bricks dating from the Eastern Han period (25–220 AD). The bricks were designed to interlock and were primarily used for vaults.

Right The corbelling method of dome construction, which was increasingly used in tomb construction from the Tang Dynasty (618–907) onwards.

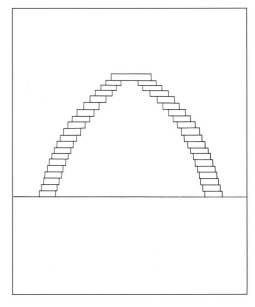

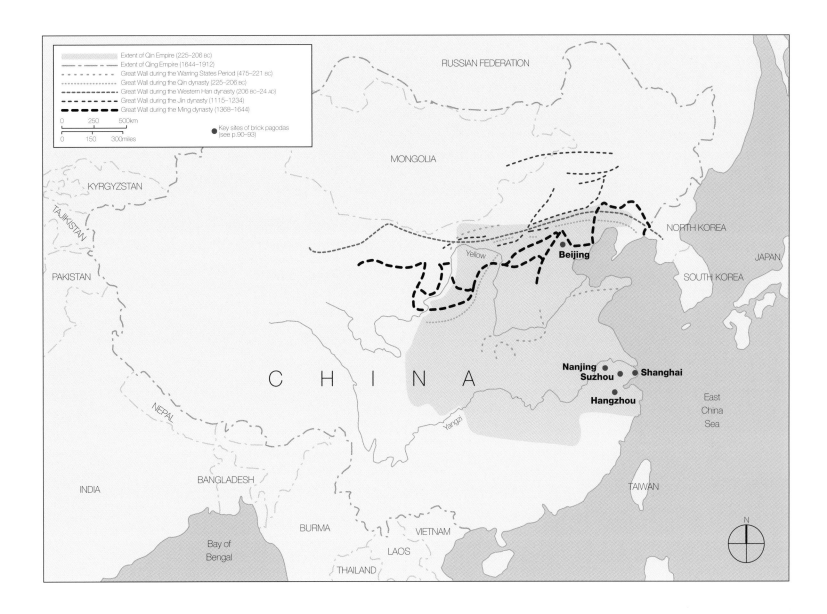

Map legend:

Extent of Qin Empire (225–206 BC)
Extent of Qing Empire (1644–1912)
Great Wall during the Warring States Period (475–221 BC)
Great Wall during the Qin dynasty (225–206 BC)
Great Wall during the Western Han dynasty (206 BC–24 AD)
Great Wall during the Jin dynasty (1115–1234)
Great Wall during the Ming dynasty (1368–1644)

0   250   500km
0   150   300miles

● Key sites of brick pagodas (see p.90–93)

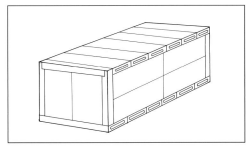

and gases and covering the whole with earth, or mud, a method which is called "clamp-burning" in the West.

Fired bricks were used economically in thin walls. Up until the Western Han period (206 BC–24 AD) all walls of fired bricks were only the width of a brick thick and were thus laid exclusively in stretcher bond. From the Eastern Han period (25–220 AD) onwards thicker walls were used, with alternating header on edge and stretcher courses, a type of bonding which appears to be unique to China. Other combinations such as matt-weave bond were also used. These were made possible by the use of large flat rectangular bricks. Economy was still a major factor and these were frequently used

to make hollow walls in a variety of ingenious bonds. The cavities were often filled with earth, broken bricks or rubble.

Surprisingly, these structures were built without an adhesive mortar. Lime mortar was occasionally employed in the Eastern Han period, but was not widely used for walling until the Song Dynasty (960–1279 AD). Before this, mud was used instead of mortar. Perhaps because of this, Chinese bricklaying laid great stress on the precise fitting of the blocks. It was not unusual from the Han Dynasty (206 BC–220 AD) onwards for the faces of fired bricks to be ground down and fitted together dry before being taken down again and rebuilt using mud mortar. In this way very fine joints could be achieved, which were often finished with paint or coloured powder. Early Chinese brickwork was rarely designed to be seen unadorned and was usually covered by plaster, daub or paint. In many areas of China even today walls of brick are plastered and the courses drawn back on afterwards in paint.

Left A hollow-brick tomb of the type built in the Warring States period (475–221 BC).

Above Map showing the extent of the Qin and Qing empire and the growth of the Great Wall.

Early Islamic brickwork (620–1000)

Talk of Islamic architecture usually conjures up images of brightly coloured glazed tiles covering onion domes and soaring minarets. In fact glazed tiles and onion domes were both later developments. Early Islamic architecture more closely reflected that of previous cultures.

The religion which Mohammed (c. 570-632) had founded in about 620 spread swiftly, conquering the whole Arabian peninsula by 644. By 732 most of modern Spain, North Africa, Persia, Uzbekistan, Afghanistan and parts of Pakistan were under the control of its ruling caliphs, forming an empire that stretched from the Atlantic Ocean to India. In the process it enveloped many cultures, absorbing their craftsmen and techniques. Among those conquered were the Sassanids, who had ruled Persia for 250 years, and whose capital at Ctesphion (near the modern city of Baghdad in Iraq) contained a palace built entirely of brick which was considered one of the wonders of the ancient world. Only a fragment of the massive building survives today, but even this is impressive, including as it does the largest unreinforced brickwork vault (span 25.3m) in the world. Where the materials were

available, major early Islamic buildings were built of stone, but where this was not the case the techniques of Sassanid and Byzantine brickmakers and bricklayers were widely employed.

The greatest brick buildings to survive from this period include the Palace of Mshatta in Jordan (743-744), the Palace of Ukhaidir in Iraq (c. 750–800) and the Great Mosque of al-Mutawwakil in Samarra (848–852). Following Byzantine and Sassanid practice, the bricks used in these buildings were typically square. Both mud and baked bricks were laid in thick walls and the overall appearance was one of strength and grandeur.

From the outset Islamic builders sought to cover the sacred buildings with patterns. Islamic law decreed that such decoration should not contain the images of any living beings, an edict which encouraged an

interest in abstract patterns of great intricacy and complexity. Before the adoption of ceramic tiles, the translation of pattern into architectural form created many difficulties. Stone was not easy to carve and was not always available, while in most Arab countries timber was in short supply. One solution was to cut or mould patterns in gypsum or lime plasters, an example of which can be seen in façade of the Magok-i Attari Mosque in Bukhara. Another alternative, also employed in the same façade, was to use moulded or cut brickwork. The Tomb of the Saminids in Bukhara is one of most remarkable and imaginative examples of this type of decoration.

Above and opposite
The façade of the Magok-i Attari Mosque in Bukhara.

The elaborate decorations are made using a combination of cut bricks and plasterwork.

The Tomb of the Saminids

The Tomb of the Saminids is one of the earliest surviving Islamic mausolea and one of the finest brick buildings ever built. It survived in an immaculate state of preservation largely because for much of its existence it had been buried under sand and other buildings. It was only discovered and rescued in 1934 by Shishkin, a Soviet archaeologist. Local legend has it that during the Mongol invasion of Bukhara in March 1220, the barbarian aggressors were so taken aback by the beauty of the building that they spared it even though they burnt the rest of the city.

The Prophet Mohammed is said to have preached against any form of tomb, prescribing that a Muslim should be buried, head towards Mecca, covered by a simple mound or the grave marked only by a stone or sticks. No doubt in the early years such a method of burial had a particular significance to the Arab nomads and played an important part in marking Islam out from Christianity and other religions. However, in the long term such an interdiction was to prove unsustainable because many of the cultures absorbed by Islam's rapid expansion had a long history of glorification of monarchs in funeral monuments which was not easily ignored. At first the solution was to limit such tombs to the caliphate, beginning with the burial of Caliph al Muntasir in Samarra in 862, but gradually and inevitably the trend spread through all Eastern Islamic countries.

It is now generally accepted that the Tomb of the Saminids was built in the reign of Ishmail, the Saminid king who ruled from 862 to 907. Documents show that Ishmail purchased land in this sector of the city for the tomb for his father, Ahmed b. Asad. In the end three sarcophagi were placed within the mausoleum, one for Ahmed b. Asad, one for Ishmail himself and a third for his grandson Ismail-Nasr II b. Ahmad (who ruled between 914 and 942).

The building he constructed is surprisingly small, each side being 10.8m, the whole being roughly cubic in proportions, and constructed of sand-coloured square bricks measuring 220–260 x 220–260 x 40mm, set in 10-mm joints. Standard bricks are mixed with specially moulded bricks and larger moulded elements such as twisted columns, and close examination reveals that many of the bricks were cut to shape after firing. Each element in itself is relatively simple. What is impressive is the way in which the architect combined a small number of different shapes to produce an effect of the utmost complexity and delicacy. The basket-weave patterns of the external brickwork catch the light and appear to move with the changing angles of the sun, the play of light and shadow creating an almost magical effect.

The building is also important as an early example of a new approach to the problem of putting a circular dome on to a building that is square in plan. The corners of its dome are supported on four arches. This 'chortak' (four-arched system) was revolutionary at the time and often copied in later monuments. The transition is concealed externally by a gallery of ten windows on each side which provide the only light to the interior. Symbolically the dome represents the heavens, while the cube refers to the *Kaaba* in Mecca and to the earth, together signifying the universe.

Opposite The Tomb of the Saminids, Bukhara, Uzbekistan (c. 900).

Above Detail of the squinch arch supporting the dome.

Following pages Details of the patterns employed in the façade.

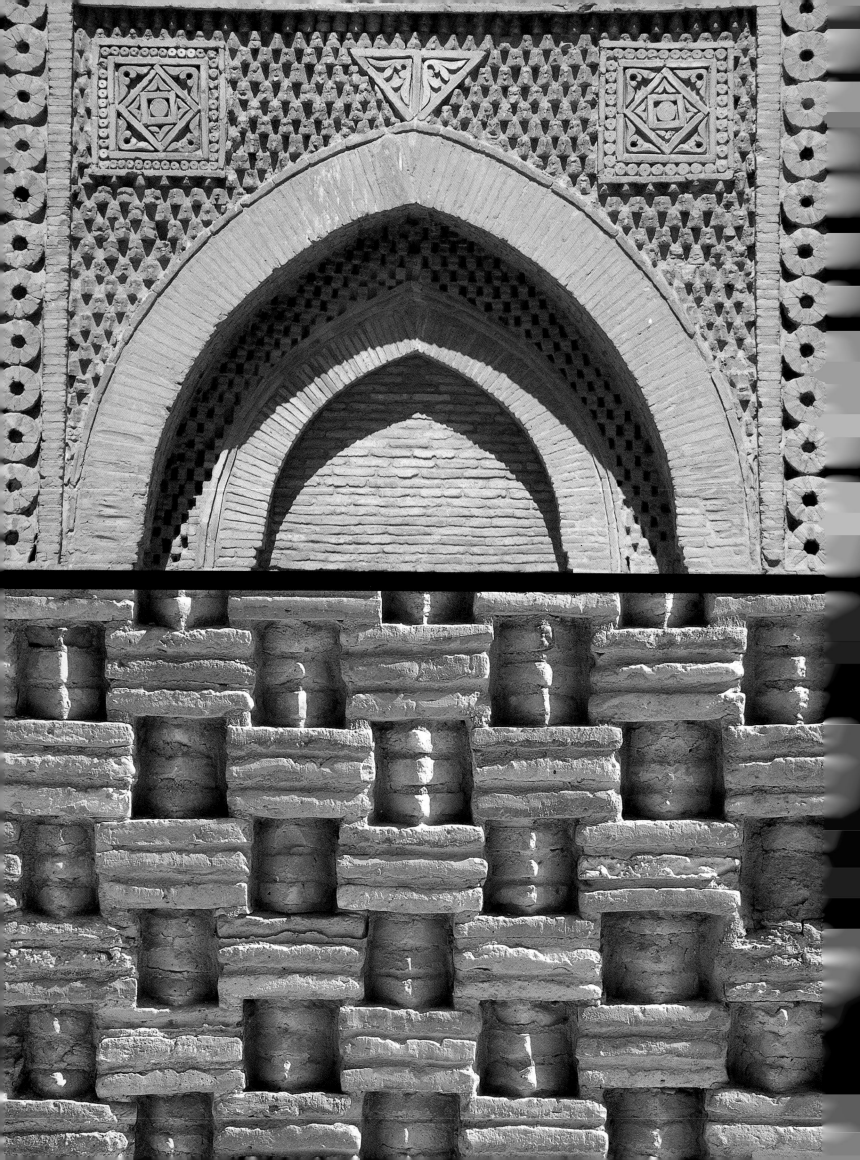

CHAPTER THREE

THE MEDIEVAL WORLD 1000 – 1450

The Middle Ages is a convenient term which admittedly is usually only applied to Western Europe. However, all over the world the period between 1000 and 1450 represented an age of unprecedented religious power. It was not only the age of the Catholic Church in Europe with its Gothic cathedrals, but also the rise of Buddhist temples in Asia and pagodas in China and the great Islamic mosques, palaces and tombs of the Middle East, North Africa and Spain. These great religions had very different aims and beliefs but all shared a common understanding of the importance of architecture in establishing a lasting and central presence for political and religious power in society, and all had a part to play in the history of brickwork.

The end of the period covered by the last chapter saw the development of brickwork in widely dispersed areas stretching from China to Western Europe. This chapter opens with the spread of brickwork into a new region where it had been previously unknown: the tropical forests and plains of South-east Asia.

The first section looks at Pagan, which was for 400 years the centre of a great kingdom in Myanmar (Burma). In that time its citizens constructed thousands of Buddhist shrines, many of which survive intact to this day and which together form one of the most remarkable collections of religious monuments in the world. The architecture of Pagan influenced much of South-east Asia but each culture produced subtle variations according to local requirements, beliefs and building traditions. An example of the complexity of these local variations can be seen in the next section, which looks at the development of brick construction in Thailand, where control was vested in a number of tribes and races during the period in question.

China was undoubtedly an influence on South-east Asia yet the exact extent to which this is true is again open to interpretation. Those searching for causes and effects might suggest that fired brick technology itself spread to this region from China, but it could equally be argued that it arrived from India via Ceylon (Sri Lanka). However, the nature of this kind of technological development is complicated and it is probably safer to suggest that each region developed its own technology inspired by others. As for China itself, early developments in Chinese brickmaking were set out in the last chapter, but few buildings survive from that era. The situation is better for the period 1000–1450, which is the focus in this chapter. In particular it saw the rise of pagoda construction, a building type that was unique to the

region. The evolution of the pagoda and its influence on brickwork is thus examined in its own section.

The chapter then returns to Western Europe, picking up where it left off, by tracing the development of the continuing tradition of brickwork in Italy. In northern Europe the situation is less clear. The Romans had conquered large parts of northern Europe, leaving behind dramatic brick buildings (such as the great basilica at Trier), but Roman brickmaking in the provinces had been carried out by the army. It was thus never understood by the local populace and when the troops retreated so the technology by and large went with them. With a few isolated exceptions (such as the basilica at Steinbach near Michelstadt in Germany, consecrated in 827) there are virtually no brick buildings constructed in northern Europe between the retreat of the Romans and the beginning of the 12th century. A number of explanations have been suggested for the sudden re-emergence of the technology in this period and its rapid spread across northern Europe, which are examined under the heading of the 'Riddle of northern brickmaking'.

What is certain is that once re-introduced brickmaking and the use of brick quickly became established across a wide area of northern Europe. The bricks produced there were different from those of the Roman or Byzantine tradition. They were of the rectangular thick type first seen in Europe in Ravenna and by the Middle Ages already well-established in northern Italy. Five further sections deal with various aspects of bricks and brickwork in the European Middle Ages. The first looks at developments in brickmaking. Sources for medieval brickwork include illustrations, guild records and building accounts but there are no first-hand descriptions. However, from what does remain it is possible to suggest how bricks were moulded, the types of kilns that were operated

and the changing status of the brickmaker throughout the period. The next section looks at the role of the guilds and town councils in regulating both brickmaking and bricklaying, and the effects of these regulations on the form and laying of bricks. The use of brick in buildings and its effect on architecture is then discussed in three sections. The first looks at Backsteingotik, the name given to the style of brick architecture that predominated in a region encompassing northern Germany and Poland in the Middle Ages, which saw a particularly high degree of interaction between the brickmaker and bricklayer, to produce large buildings with sophisticated moulded and glazed brickwork. The next section looks at the role brick played in fortification and castle design in the period. Finally a single building, the cathedral of Albi, is selected for detailed examination as a particularly unusual example of medieval construction, combining the functions of religious architecture and fortification in a single structure.

The chapter closes with two sections that examine some of the advances made in Islamic brickwork during the period. The first looks at advances made in decorative brickwork in the Middle East. The great tomb towers of this area boasted intricate bonding, producing patterns that included, in the most elaborate examples, letters spelling out passages from the Koran. The period also saw the development of glazed wares. Initially these were glazed bricks, but soon tiles began to be made in increasingly complex and colourful patterns that began to replace the more expensive and time-consuming decorative brickwork. The last section looks at one of the greatest buildings of the period, the magnificent mausoleum of Oljeitu at Sultaniya in northern Iran. Oljeitu set about building a new capital for his kingdom, centred on a great Mausoleum. This was covered in decorative glazed brickwork and intricate plaster and was surmounted by a huge dome. The structure of the dome is of particular interest as it is the largest of the double domes, a type of structure that had been in use in the Middle East since the 11th century and was to be the forerunner of the great domes of the Renaissance in Italy.

Opposite Palazzo Pubblico, Siena (1297–1310).
View from the courtyard.

Bersi Ta or Bo'en pagoda, China

Pagan, Burma

Roskilde Cathedral, Denmark

Mausoleum near Sultaniya, Iran

Stepped gable, Lübeck, Germany

Medieval timber-framed houses in Albi, France

Detail from Pagan, Burma

Holstein Gate, Lübeck, Germany

Dome of Chelebi Oghlu, Sultaniya, Iran

Detail from Saint Bendt's Church, Ringsted, Denmark

Siena, Italy

Holstein Gate, Lübeck, Germany

The Palazzo Pubblico, Siena, Italy

Longhua pagoda, Shanghai, China

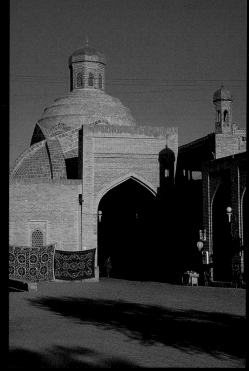
Taq Sarafan, Bukhara, Uzbekistan

Detail of the cathedral of Albi, France

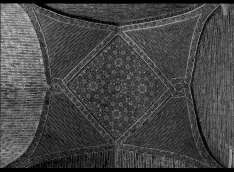
Interior vault, Mausoleum of Oljeitu, Sultaniya, Iran

Medieval brickwork, Queens' College, Cambridge, England

Castle of Malbork, Poland

Detail of the temple of Htilominlo, Pagan, Burma

Pagan, Burma

Mausoleum of Oljeitu, Sultaniya, Iran

The forgotten temples of Pagan

Few sights in the world are more breathtaking than the sun rising over the ancient city of Pagan. Situated in the north of Myanmar (Burma), the ancient city once acted as a crossroads between India, South-east Asia and China. Here, at a bend in the great river Irrawaddy, Buddhists from India mixed with the indigenous peoples, the Mons and Pyu, to form a new civilization that lasted for over 300 years. The houses of the city that once covered the fertile plain were made of timber and have long since disappeared, but the temples, which were made of baked brick, remain. The larger monuments rise majestically above the plain. Climbing the outside of these, one can sit above the tree tops and take in a panorama of temples ranged as far as the eye can see. It is thought that there were originally about 5,000 temples in this plain. Today some 2,000 remain, together forming one of the largest collections of ancient brick monuments in the world.

Under Anawrahta (1044–77) Pagan settled most of what is today called Myanmar or Burma through a series of military operations mounted against the existing Mons and Pyu tribes. Thus by 1100 Pagan had become the capital of a significant kingdom.

There are two main types of religious structure surviving in Pagan: the stupa and the temple. While the types themselves may not have been new, they soon developed in ways that are peculiar to the place.

Stupa
Of the two, the stupa is the first and perhaps most important building type. The stupa was the most basic form of Buddhist architecture. Buddhism pre-dated Christianity by five centuries (Siddhartha Gautama lived from approximately 563 to 483 BC) and started as an ascetic movement in India. The stupa, an image of the sacred mountain, Mount Meru, was adopted from Vedic Brahminism. The earliest surviving Buddhist stupas date from about 250 BC. Virtually all the early stupas were made from earth and stone where such materials were available. The largest brick stupa, the Jetavana Dagoba in the ancient city of Anuradhapura in Sri Lanka (Ceylon), was constructed by King Mahasena in the 3rd century AD. Anuradhapura had been founded in the 4th century BC and the Jetavana Dagoba is only the largest in a series of stupa. It is 123m high and was constructed in 500mm x 250mm x 50-mm bricks set in mud mortar, the mud containing a high proportion of silt and gypsum.

From 1060, Pagan had trading links with Ceylon and Burmese architecture was no doubt influenced by the older tradition, but, while the Ceylonese stupas were relatively simple, the Pagan stupas and temples became steadily more numerous and complex. They were designed with concealed rooms which contained holy relics. The stupa was then built around and on top of the treasure room, with the sacred objects buried at its heart. In a finished stupa there was no door, no inside that could be entered, only an exterior.

Although the walls were extremely thick, they were not solid but penetrated by a complicated series of inaccessible spaces and interconnecting vaults. In the case of the temples, the vaults were often not just single, but double or treble structures, with voids between, forming a series of interlocking shells.

All vaults in Pagan, whether accessible or inaccessible, were built using voussoired arches, with the faces of the bricks cut to shape and the bricks laid on edge. Voussoired arches of this type were not new in South-east Asia: they had been employed in buildings in the Be-be and Lei-myet-hna gu temples of the old Pyu capital of Sri Ksetera, dating from the 7th or 8th century, which had been invaded by Pagan in the 11th century. It is possible that captured Pyu craftsmen moved to the capital to work on the new monuments. The vaults are either barrel-shaped or constructed with pointed arches. The latter are common throughout Pagan architecture from at least the 11th century, if not before, but the cross vault (where two arched vaults join at right angles), which is a key feature of Western medieval architecture, does not seem to have been used. The rooms inside the temples were normally entered from small tunnels or doorways in the walls and do not interconnect, a method of planning that simplified both setting out and construction.

Bricks in Pagan are rectangular and average in size between 370 and 400mm long x 180–225mm wide x 50mm thick. They do not appear to have been inscribed or stamped and were made from alluvial clay using moulds. Clay deposited by water naturally settles out with the finer clay being left on the surface and this property accounts for the high quality of the bricks which are very dense and finely grained. No kilns have been discovered, suggesting that the bricks were probably burnt in temporary clamps. This has certainly been the method used for subsequent restoration works. The present clamps are relatively small and burn palm roots and charcoal, yielding about 50,000 bricks per firing. The resulting bricks were remarkably uniform and were laid in lime mortar. The fine river clay created hard bricks with sharp arises that could be laid with great precision and joints of as little as 5mm are not uncommon.

Externally Pagan stupas came in many forms, but the typical ones had three or five terraced levels linked by staircases. Around these terraces glazed terracotta plaques were set in the walls on each level depicting

the previous 550 lives of the Buddha so that the faithful could contemplate them during a ritual circumambulation or *pradakstina*. The whole stupa was surmounted by a convex or concave *anda* which was originally covered with plaster lotus petals and brightly coloured and surmounted by a tall metal spire. The smallest surviving stupas in Pagan are only 4 or 5m tall, while the largest Mingla Zedi is over 50m high.

Temples

The second major structural building type in Pagan is the temple or *gu*. Like the stupa it often held a secret treasure chamber at its heart, but the temple also had other internal rooms which were intended to be accessible by the faithful. The simplest form of temple

Top and opposite View of the temples of Pagan. Some 2,000 survive in the plain.

Overleaf A group of smaller stupas.

Above Large stupa with tiers of walkways.

Top An ordination hall, Pagan.

Above left Pagan at dawn, the temples rising out of the mist.

Above right Typical temple showing the entrances to the spaces within.

Opposite Close-up of the temple of Htilominlo, one of the largest temples in Pagan, built in 1211 for King Nantoungyma.

was symmetrical like the stupa. A central solid core which contained the artefact chamber was surrounded by four statues of the Buddha facing outwards in each of the four cardinal directions, in shrines lit dimly from concealed windows. Stairs passed up inside the building to give access to roof terraces above while the whole was, like the stupa, surmounted by an *anda*. The other type of temple was similar but longitudinal. In this type there might be only one statue facing outwards in a shrine accessed from a longer chamber onto which was attached a porch. In both types of

temples symmetrical arrangements of stairs passed up through the structure to allow access to roof terraces, which functioned like those of the stupas and culminate in an *anda*.

The fall of Pagan

Pagan was invaded by the Mongol hordes in 1287, but it was not destroyed. The area continued to be occupied by small hereditary groups of *hpaya kywan* dedicated to the upkeep of the larger temples but the surrounding wooden buildings disappeared.

Left Phra Chedi (1487), Chiang Mai.

Below right Wat Phra That (1281) in Wat Kukut, Lamphun.

Below left Ratona Chedi (12th century), Lamphun.

Stupas in Thailand and South-East Asia

In the period 800–1500 brick architecture was found not only in Burma, but throughout South-East Asia. At the beginning of this era, the area which today forms modern Thailand was occupied by four different peoples: the Mon, the Khmer, the Srivijayan and the Tai. As a result of these different influences it developed a particularly rich architecture of its own.

Mon architecture

The Mon came from South-West Burma. Like the people of Pagan they were Buddhists, although they freely adopted Hindu ideas. Politically they were loosely organized into principalities and controlled the West and North of the region. As the ruling class of the Dvaravati in Cambodia/Vietnam, the Mon had a wide sphere of influence. Mon religious architecture included stupas that were similar to those of Pagan (and no doubt influenced by them) and made out of brick.

The foundations of Dvaravati monuments were made out of laterite. This material is stiff when first dug from the ground and can be easily cut into bricks or slabs but hardens to a stone-like consistency on contact with air. It is easily mistaken for brickwork but it can be distinguished from it by the fact that it is more porous. The upper parts of the monuments were constructed using bricks which were set in some form of vegetable glue instead of mortar. The bricks themselves are rectangular and very fine in texture so that they fit closely together. The whole monument was then covered over with a lime-sand plaster, again bound with vegetable glue. The Dvaravati built chedi, which are stepped monuments. They are either octagonal or square on plan. Two of the best preserved of these survive in Wat Chama Thewi (Wat Kukut) at Lamphun. Legend says that Queen Chama Thewi determined where they should be constructed by ordering one of her archers to fire an arrow to the north. The most impressive of the two was reconstructed in 1150 by King Athitaraja of Hariphunchai, who reigned from 1120 to 1150, to celebrate his victory over the Lopburi. The present structure is thought to date from a reconstruction in

1281 after the previous one was destroyed in an earthquake. It is square in plan and consists of five tiers, with three niches per side at every level each containing a Buddha statue.

Khmer architecture

The Khmer ruled their empire from the great city of Angkor using a complex system of administration. In contrast to the Mon they followed the Hindu tradition. By the 11th century they had conquered much of the area of southern Thailand previously occupied by the Mon. The Khmer produced a far more formal architecture based on the system established at Angkor. There the monuments had been constructed in laterite and stone rather than brick.

Srivijayan architecture

The Srivijayan occupied the upper part of the Malay peninsula which they governed from their capital in Sumatra from the 8th to the 13th century. Their architecture was influenced by Javanese styles rather than those of the north. Like the Mons they constructed their monuments using bricks and vegetable mortar.

Tai architecture

The last group, the Tai (from whom Thailand would eventually take its name), seem to have originated in eastern China around 2000 BC and gradually migrated to live in small independent settlements across much of South-East Asia. The original Tai tribes were animists but they later adopted Theravada Buddhism. They first formed a kingdom called Lanna Tai in the north of the region, which existed from the late 13th through to the mid-16th century. To the south of Lanna Tai was the kingdom of Sukhotai, said to have been founded in 1238, which dominated the central areas of Thailand until it was overthrown in 1438 from the south by a Tai kingdom based on Ayuthaya. Ayuthaya conquered Angkor in 1432 and became the centre of a large empire which retained power until it was finally captured by the Burmese in 1767. Sukhotai and Ayuthaya were great cities, built of laterite and brick, much influenced in forms by the architecture of the cultures they had absorbed. Although now in ruins, they remain as an important reminder of one of the great brick architectural traditions that once dominated South-East Asia.

Top Wat Chedi Luang, Chiang Mai, built between the 12th and 14th century. An example of Lanna Tai architecture, the base is constructed of laterite, the upper part is brick.

Above A close-up of Wat Jed Yot, Chiang Mai, which is built entirely of laterite, showing how easily the material can be mistaken for brick.

China and the rise of the pagoda

The Chinese adopted the stupa and gradually developed it into the pagoda: a new form which was peculiar to them. The period 1000–1450 saw the greatest advances in this building type and as such formed a critical period in the history of Chinese building construction. Pagodas were built in stone and timber as well as brick, techniques and forms from both materials being directly reflected in the brickwork.

The stupa was introduced into China, along with Buddhism, in the Three Kingdoms period (220–280). The earliest pagodas, all of which have long since disappeared, followed the Indian stupa form, that is they had a base surmounted by a large inverted-bowl shaped body, topped by a spire or *cha*. Quite soon after their importation, the builders began to elaborate the base, transforming it from a single-storey structure into an elaborate multi-storey tower, the bell of the stupa becoming the roof, which ended in the timber spire or *cha*. The *cha* itself was further transformed into series of multi-tiered stone lotus leaves. While Indian stupa were not intended to be climbed, these new towers (pagodas) frequently had stairs inside, enabling the worshipper to ascend to the top. The view out from the upper parts gradually became increasingly important and the pagoda itself often took on additional functions as a watchtower, lighthouse or observatory. Verandahs were added allowing religious circumambulations at each level and leading to the structure familiar today.

It is thought that timber pagodas may have been an early innovation but that they have disappeared

through lack of maintenance. What is certain is that the oldest surviving pagodas are of masonry construction and commonly in brick. Brick pagodas came in four types: solid brick pagodas; hollow brick pagodas with a cylindrical central void; brick pagodas with brick staircases; and composite timber and brick pagodas.

The most basic, the solid brick pagodas, typically feature a large ornately carved plinth-like lowest storey, surmounted by a tower decorated by a large number of closely spaced projecting eaves. There is no internal access to any of the floors. The internal brickwork is often roughly constructed and simply bonded in mud mortar, the emphasis being placed on the external part of the wall which is more carefully laid in lime and sand mortar. This type of pagoda was particularly popular in the Liao Dynasty (916–1125 AD). The best known example is the Tianning Temple Pagoda in Beijing.

Hollow pagodas, as the name suggests, had a single large interior space running from top to bottom. This was typically subdivided by the insertion of timber floors at intervals. A series of ladders or stairs would allow the viewer to ascend to the highest level. Externally they appeared very similar to solid brick pagodas with large bases surmounted by many tiers of projecting brick eaves. The internal space tapered like the tower itself and the width of the internal space was limited by the length of timbers available to make the floors, which also played an important part in bracing the structure. The large internal void inevitably weakened the structure, limiting the height. Pagodas of this type were common in the Tang (618–907) and Song (960–1279) Dynasties.

The next logical step was the use of brick internal floors supported by internal walls, the staircases ascending in vaulted brick passages through the structure. Pagodas with brick stairways first appear in the Five Dynasties period (907–960) and were perfected in the Song Dynasty (960–1279). The passages that ran through the pagodas were created using corbelled vaults. Externally the pagodas closely resembled earlier types, that is they exhibited a base surmounted by tiers of projecting brick eaves.

Above The Yunyansi pagoda (929 AD), Suzhou, is 47.7m high with brackets in brick imitating timber.

Opposite The Liuhuo pagoda, Hangzhou. First built in 971 AD, destroyed twice, rebuilt in 1524 and restored in 1900.

Below left The Yunyansi pagoda (929 AD), Suzhou.

Below right The Longhua pagoda, Shanghai (977 AD), a typical brick and timber pagoda.

The problem with the pagodas up to this point was that there were no balconies: the climber had to view the countryside through the relatively small windows in the thick outside walls. The next and logical step was to add a series of timber verandahs to the outside, each covered by its own timber roof. This produced a pagoda that looked externally very similar to a timber pagoda but had the advantages of a brick core. One of the finest examples of this type of pagoda is the Liuhuo pagoda in Hangzhou.

The pagodas of the Song Dynasty (960–1279) are meant to represent the high point of pagoda construction. Larger ones would be built in the Ming Dynasty (1368–1644) but they would not match the quality of detail and craftsmanship of those in the Song. The details employed were extraordinary: the projecting brick or timber eaves were supported on brackets made of bricks especially moulded to imitate the multi-tiered timber brackets used in the carpentry of the period. This meant the brickmaker had to fashion a series of moulds in wood into which the clay could be thrown, and each special brick had to be carefully designed to fit with its neighbour, taking into account the shrinkage that would occur during the firing and drying processes.

By the Song Dynasty, brick production for use in pagodas and other building works had become sophisticated and standardized. Indeed strict rules for the 13 crafts involved in building work had been set down in a written building code, the Yingzao Fashi, which was issued in 1103 AD. It survives and is today one of the most valuable sources for the history of building construction. Among the crafts described is the practice of brick and tile making, including a list of the sizes of standard bricks which were to be used in all building works (see table opposite).

Bricks were often made with impressed decorative patterns. These and other special bricks were made in box moulds, while normal bricks were made using open moulds with ash as a releasing agent. Once moulded the bricks were set out to dry.

By the Song Dynasty bricks were being fired in kilns in brushwood-fuelled updraught and downdraught intermittent kilns. The Chinese were probably the first to use downdraught kilns for firing bricks. Yingzao Fashi includes instructions for a firing a kiln:

In the kiln the tiles and bricks are processed by complete combustion of firstly grass, then wormwood, later pine branches. For quinggun tiles, the pine branches are to be covered by a layer of goat/sheep dung, rice husks and heavy oil, [these acted as an emulsifying agent, allowing carbon particles to stick to the bricks during firing], burned under a limited supply of air to make a dense smoke.

The Chinese also used a particular technique for creating a reducing atmosphere within the kiln which produced the grey colour characteristic of many Chinese bricks. The method involved adding water at a late stage in the firing. This prevented oxygen entering the kiln, so that the iron in the bricks could not oxidize fully.

During this period Chinese bricks were typically laid in conventional lime and sand mortar although occasionally the mortar was strengthened by rice gruel, an additive that first appears in the Northern Song period (960–1127) and was used in the rebuilding of the Great Wall of China (1364–1644).

Opposite left The Liuhuo pagoda, Hangzhou, 59.89m high.

Opposite right The Bersi Ta or Bo'en pagoda. The earliest structure on this site was constructed in the 3rd century. The present structure was constructed in 1582, using 370 x 150 x 60-mm bricks.

Above The Twin Pagodas, Suzhou (982). One of the two towers which are 33m high.

Below left The Liuhuo pagoda, Hangzhou. The pagoda was used as a lighthouse.

Standard Brick sizes as set down in Yingzao Fashi (1103 AD) translated into millimetres

Building Type		Floor Bricks	Wall bricks	Bricks for steps
Base of multi-storey timber buildings of the grand (*diantang*) type	11 bay	640 x 640 x 96mm	416 x 208 x 80mm	672 x 352 x 80mm
	7 bay	544 x 544 x 90mm		
	5bay	480 x 480 x 86mm		
Bases of smaller timber buildings (*Tingtang*)		480 x 480 x 86mm		
Verandahs of *Diantang* buildings, pavilions and ordinary houses		384 x 384 x 64mm	384 x 192 x 64mm	
City wall		368 x 368 x 138mm 192 x 192 x 64mm	384 x 192 x 64mm 416 x 208 x 80mm	

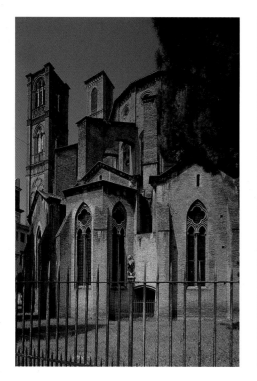

The continuing tradition of brick in Italy

Although the last vestiges of the Western Roman Empire in Italy were destroyed by successive waves of invasions from the north in the 6th century, the tribes that settled in northern Italy and embraced Christianity were far from the barbarians they were once thought to be. Indeed, as historians have begun to discover more about this period they have dropped the term 'Dark Ages' that used to be used and replaced it with 'early Middle Ages', which better expresses the continuity and the positive contribution it made. The churches and monasteries that the new rulers went on to build were heavily influenced by the construction methods of the conquered artisans ensuring that Italy remained at the forefront of brick technology in Europe for the next 600 years.

Above left San Francesco, Bologna (13th–14th century).

Above right The three churches of San Stefano, Bologna. The central octagon containing the Sepulchre of Christ was constructed in 1088–1160, the basilicas on the left and right in 400 and 737, with many subsequent additions.

Opposite Close-up of the decorative brickwork of the Sepulchre of Christ, San Stefano, Bologna.

Brick construction in Italy is closely associated with the Po valley. Although Italian brick stretches beyond this area, it is the great cities of Milan and Bologna that mark the centre of the great developments in brick building in the Middle Ages. It was of course the great plains of the river valleys, lacking stone but having alluvial clay deposits, that encouraged innovation in brick, although the material was to prove so popular in that it would eventually spread to hilly regions like Siena in Tuscany.

The tradition grew out of that which had flourished in Ravenna. Bricks were rectangular and thick rather than flat and square and were used in solid walls. The different types of clay found in the superficial deposits exploited produced different colours. In general the bright reds were preferred for normal walling purposes but the possibilities of using them in combination with other colours for decoration were understood and exploited. One of the finest examples of this kind of

work can be found in the church of San Stefano in Bologna.

Italian brick architecture developed its own language of architectural ornament particularly in the treatment of eaves. Below courses of saw-tooth bond and projecting mouldings, there would usually be series of terracotta or cut-brick blind miniature arches with pendants between standing proud of the surface of the walls, which are called 'corbell tables'. Later churches show more complicated versions of the same motif with the arches interlocking.

While this particular form of brick Romanesque architecture enjoyed a long history, northern Italy was slow to adopt the Gothic style that would come to prevail in northern Europe with its pointed arches, groin vaults and flying buttresses. The accounts of Milan Cathedral provide a fascinating insight into the resistance of local builders to the importation of new ideas although the clergy repeatedly sought outside

advice from northerners on the problems of designing the cathedral. Such a resistance was widespread and understandable. Much of it no doubt was just regional conservatism but there was a certain justification in doubting the suitability of the designs to the local materials for the Gothic of the French masters who were being consulted was predominantly an architecture of stone, while the churches of Milan were traditionally brick. Nevertheless Gothic churches were built and when they did appear could show a remarkable continuity with their stone equivalents. Such a case is the impressive church of San Francesco in Bologna, which sports something rarely found in brick Gothic buildings: a series of flying buttresses.

The riddle of northern brickmaking

While the brick tradition seems to have remained strong in Italy, in northern Europe it is usually said to have disappeared altogether with the withdrawal of the Romans. In these outlying colonies Roman bricks had tended to be made by the army, and of course, much of northern Europe had never been occupied by the Romans in the first place. But in those areas that were, such as Holland and England, brickmaking does indeed seem to have died out. The question is not so much how and why it died out, but rather how and why did it re-emerge in Denmark and northern Germany in the 12th century and spread with such speed across the whole of northern Europe? This has been long debated by academics and remains something of a riddle.

One theory, often repeated in one form or another, holds that northern Europe never developed bricks before the 12th century because its clays were unsuitable for making bricks using the Roman

solution was more mundane. For a start there is little need for a different method of making bricks. The clays of northern Europe are similar to those of northern Italy where the Romans succeeded in making bricks

techniques. The sort of large flat bricks the Romans used, it is said, could not be made using the clays available. The invention of a way of solving this problem is credited to the Cistercians, perhaps with information the Order of Teutonic Knights might have gathered during the crusades in the Holy Land. The technique suggested simply involved making thicker bricks. As the Cistercian monasteries spread across northern Europe it has been pointed out that they were in the perfect position to act as transmitters of the new technology.

This conspiracy tale of warrior knights and inventive monks is seductive but sadly the answer less than convincing in a number of ways. The most probable

in large numbers. Moreover, rectangular bricks were not an invention at all, being commonly found in northern Italy since at least the 5th century, as was seen in the last section. So at best one might credit the Cistercians with importing or reasserting an existing technology already at use in southern Europe. Likewise the claim that the Teutonic Knights brought back a brickmaking technique from the Holy Land is fanciful to say the least.

Nevertheless, there is no doubt that both the Teutonic Knights and the Cistercians did play a crucial role in encouraging and disseminating brick technology and that this role of dissemination was further supported by the trading links

created through the formation of the Hanseatic League.

Records of a Swiss monastery founded by the Cistercians have been analyzed in detail and provide many interesting insights into the way they used bricks. In particular it was clear that the material was seen as being appropriately humble in its origins for the piety of a religious order especially when used in an austere way which eschewed unnecessary ornament. All building projects for new monasteries had to be ratified by the headquarters of the order which encouraged the use of brick and a stylistic conformity.

Opposite, left and right
Cathedral of Roskilde (mid-12th
century). One of the earliest
medieval brick buildings, it
was built using three million
260 x 120 x 85-mm bricks.

Above Saint Bendt's church,
Ringsted (mid-12th century)
is one of the earliest brick
buildings in medieval northern
Europe. It was constructed in
270 x 130 x 85-mm bricks.

Left Exterior gables of the
Chapel of the Magi, Roskilde
Cathedral, constructed as a
royal mausoleum in 1462.

The mystery of medieval brickmaking

The exact way bricks were made in Europe in the Middle Ages is the subject of considerable debate because no illustrations survive from before the 15th century and there are no written descriptions of the entire process. Those records that do survive for brickmaking tend to be business accounts which tell us much about production costs and outputs, but little about actually doing it. A certain amount of information can be inferred from the bricks themselves, but this is in itself controversial. Nevertheless, what we do know seems to suggest that brickmaking throughout medieval Europe relied heavily on Roman precedents and Byzantine precedents.

Three types of brickyards were found in this period. The first of these were established for specific projects. The cathedral, monastery or noble would build on such a scale as to justify forming their own brickworks, which might, on completion of the project go on to supply bricks elsewhere but would more usually be abandoned. The second type of brickworks is that associated with a particular municipality. The running of such town brickworks no doubt had benefits in allowing the town to control the quality of the product even if they usually failed to provide a healthy income. The third type of brickworks was privately owned and run for profit.

The clay or brickearth for brickmaking material tended to be dug from superficial deposits and left to be attacked by the frost over the winter. The brickearth would then be trodden under foot and the stones removed by hand. The preparation of the material itself would then depend on the location.

Usually little in the way of sand needed to be added and when the clay was worked to a sufficient consistency with water it could be passed straight to the moulder.

The great medieval innovation was the moulding bench which records mention early on and which can be clearly seen in the surviving 15th-century and 16th-century illustrations. Open-bottomed moulds were used with sand or water as a releasing agent, the brick being carried in the mould to the drying ground and turned out individually. It is unclear whether bricks were also moulded directly onto the ground.

The drying grounds were usually fairly crude, being little more than areas of bare earth covered with straw, although in many northern countries some protection must have been provided from the rain. After two to four weeks the bricks were then ready for burning. Few kilns for bricks have survived although there are a large number of excavations of tile kilns and it seems likely that the same forms were used. They were very similar to the Roman ones, that is they had solid floors on which the bricks or tiles were stacked and under which the fire was stoked through one or more tunnels. They were fuelled with wood. Some may have had barrel-vaulted roofs but it is likely that most followed the Roman precedent and were open to the sky or covered by light temporary structures to keep off the rain.

Most bricks were probably burnt in clamps. These were essentially kilns made of unburnt bricks, the outside sometimes being covered in mud and the fire stoked in tunnels formed in the stacked bricks. Clamps have been probably been used throughout history for burning bricks but their temporary nature means that they leave little evidence behind them. Their exact form in the Middle Ages is not known.

The bricks that resulted from medieval brickmaking varied hugely in size. Some were quite large with sizes of up to 380 x 160 x 75mm being recorded while

Opposite Medieval, timber-framed house, Albi, France.

Left St Botolph's Priory church, Colchester, England (12th century), constructed with re-used Roman bricks.

Above 'The Brickmaker' in Hartmannus Schopperus's *Panopolia* (Frankfurt, 1568).

Below Brickmaking, from *Nederlandische Bijbel* (Utrecht, 1425).

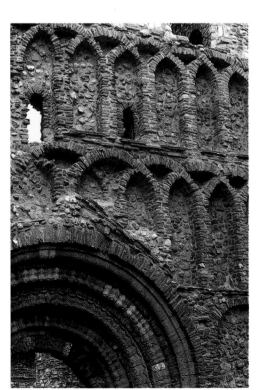

others were comparatively modest and closer to modern sizes. They also tend to be quite rough in appearance. Although some towns may have provided statutes setting out the sizes of bricks, for the most part it seems to have been left up to agreements between the builder and the maker.

Bricks and guilds: attempts at early regulation

Various parallels have been drawn between Roman *collegia* and medieval craft guilds. Both were organizations linking people working in trade and both carried religious and welfare responsibilities, but it is likely that it is there that the similarities end. Although their names and precise roles varied, craft guilds can be found in most major towns of both northern and southern Europe in the Middle Ages. These guilds were monopolistic by charter, that is the guild paid the noble, city or ruler for a monopoly so that all members of a particular trade had to join the guild to practise within the bounds of the town. In return for this privilege the guild paid dues to the town or city, saw that its members did not default on contracts and policed the standard of work undertaken. They also took care of those who fell on hard times and provided for the widows of those killed on site.

The importance of the existence of guilds is easily underestimated. Perhaps the most significant change they brought about was in training. Membership of the guild was restricted to those who had undergone a seven- or eight-year apprenticeship. In France this then had to be followed by the production of an examination piece ('the Master Piece', a term we now associate with painting but which then applied to all crafts) and by a further period travelling as a

'Journeyman' (the actual term Journeyman is probably derived from *jour*, or day meaning a person paid for by the day, rather than the act of travelling itself). On completion of all the requirements the apprentices would become 'free', allowing them to practise their trade and take their own apprentices. This system of apprenticeship not only provided cheap labour (apprentices were unpaid but had to be given board, lodging and instruction) but also ensured a reasonable

level of skill. Indeed the system of seven-year apprenticeships which it established would long outlast the guilds themselves and only declined in the 20th century.

Brickmaking probably escaped the guild system in most areas. Guilds operated only in towns within the town boundaries. Brickmaking was too polluting and too likely to cause fires to be allowed within most city walls and was thus predominantly a rural practice. However, both the number of guilds and their jurisdiction increased in the later Middle Ages and certainly by the 15th century guilds of kilnsmen are recorded in northern Italy allowing regulation of bricks at source. It was also possible to regulate the quality and size of bricks at the point of entry into the town and many towns seem to have had rules about minimum brick sizes. Models of statute bricks were displayed in public places.

Bricklaying was more obviously subject to guild regulation as it had to go on within the city boundary. Whether or not a particular town had a specific guild

Opposite The Campo in Siena, Italy. It occupies the site of the original Roman Forum and was first paved in red brick and marble in 1327–44. Since 1310 ten of the seventeen districts have competed in the famous Corsa del Palio horse race around the square.

Below Medieval brickwork in Siena.

Below left The façade of the Palazzo Pubblico (1297–1310), Siena.

Right Aerial view of the Campo with the Palazzo Pubblico on the left. Its tower 'the Torre del Mangia' built by Minuccio and Francesco di Rinaldo in 1338–48 is, at 102m high, one of the tallest brick structures ever built.

Below right The town of Siena, which traces its roots back to Roman times when it was called Saena Julia. Siena became an important building centre in the 13th century. The surrounding clay hills provide the raw material for the bricks out of which it is built.

of bricklayers depended on the availability of local building materials and on the population. Towns like Oxford in England, for instance, had ready supplies of stone and never needed a separate bricklaying guild. In such cases or in small towns any bricklayers there were joined the masons' guild. In England, where brick was a late development, separate bricklayers' guilds are comparatively rare before the 16th century.

Despite their monopolies the average bricklayer was not highly paid and worked long hours. In the winter when bricklaying had to cease in northern Europe to avoid the frost which destroyed the setting mortar, they could find little or no work and had to turn to alternative sources of income.

The guild system undoubtedly had advantages in regulating the craft and improving standards and can take some of the responsibility for the high quality of much surviving late medieval brickwork.

Backsteingotik: brickwork in northern Europe

Backsteingotik is a German term, meaning literally 'baked-stone Gothic', that is generally applied to the style of brick architecture that prevailed in what is now northern Germany and Poland from 1200 to 1600. It is a period and a style that has suffered great losses over the intervening centuries. At its height it saw the creation of some of the greatest masterpieces of the bricklayer's art that the world has ever known.

The influence of the Cistercians on northern European brickmaking has already been discussed. There is little doubt that they were instrumental in spreading the technology across the northern plains. For much of this area good building stone was in very short supply. Their involvement was crucial in demonstrating the suitability of brickwork as an alternative for the production of architectural works of the first order. Once established as a material that could combine a sense of piety and poverty with displays of virtuosity and wealth, brick quickly became adopted by towns and overlords seeking similar overtones for secular works using the same craftsmen who worked on religious buildings. Thus towns such as Lübeck in northern Germany or Torun in Poland boasted guildhalls, houses and town gates richly decorated in fine brickwork, as well as great churches. The merchants of the Hanseatic League, which was loosely based in Lübeck, built their houses in the same material. Their trading interests stretched from Holland to the far reaches of the Baltic and they may have been responsible for spreading the technology to England in the 13th century.

The great Backsteingotik churches like the Cathedral of Gdansk in Poland, the Marienkirche in Lübeck or St Nikolai in Stralsund tended to be of the hall type: that is, they boasted naves and side aisles under the same roof. Flying buttresses which were designed to arch over low side aisles were unnecessary and the emphasis was on maximizing the internal height. The disadvantage of this design is that there are no clerestory windows to light the upper parts of the nave. The windows in the side walls may have been very tall but they also tended to be rather thin and the light from them was obstructed by the piers on each side of the nave, making the central aisle rather dark. To try to compensate for this, it was common to paint the interior of the church white, sometimes with black lines imitating the mortar joints as if the building were constructed of large stones.

Externally the churches were their natural brick colour, the great brick walls of the tall side aisles projecting like forbidding red cliffs from the sea of timber-framed houses beneath. Ornament was introduced sparingly at first, in common with Cistercian principles, although later examples tended to be more exuberant. The most common area for decoration was the window tracery (the masonry transoms and mullions that subdivided the windows). Early windows tended to be tall and narrow with little subdivision, but later examples became quite elaborate. Large areas of enclosed wall panels (effectively blind windows) were also used to break up wall surfaces, and were frequently finished in white lime render.

In secular architecture the most conspicuous development was the elaborate gable end. In patrician houses these would be stepped, often with blind windows and arcades giving the illusion of a far larger building behind. This effect was further exaggerated by making the gable towards the street much larger than the end of the roof it covered. The same device was used on public buildings, the largest being the town halls, the later examples of which were often decorated with the most ostentatious displays of overlapping and intersecting blind windows and arcades. Walls were further enlivened by the use of bands or patterns of glazed bricks.

All this was achieved through a combination of the skill of the brickmakers and the bricklayers. The use of glazed bricks around windows such as those in the Holstein Gate in Lübeck shows that many simple pieces of decoration and indeed the parts of whole windows were being moulded or sculpted by the brickmaker. Nevertheless, it was also the case that the more elaborate shapes were being carved out of rectangular bricks after they had been fired, as they were laid. The great buildings of Backsteingotik are thus indicative of a highly organized system of brickmaking and bricklaying that allowed for the design of elaborate pieces of decoration and their fabrication by a collaboration between the brickmaker and bricklayer working closely together on a single project.

Opposite The Holstein Gate, Lübeck (1477), has glazed bricks around the windows and terracotta panels, indicating a close link between brickmaker and bricklayer.

Top The Castle Gate, Lübeck, built in 1444 by Nikolaus Peck. The Baroque 'hat' was added in 1685.

Above St Mary's Church, Gdansk, Poland, constructed between 1340 and 1502, is the largest brick church built in the Middle Ages.

Castles, fortifications and the Teutonic Order

The master builders of the European Middle Ages were called upon to design and construct castles and city walls, as well as cathedrals. The provision of bricks for castles and city walls was thus an important source of employment in the Middle Ages. Indeed, castles were larger than cathedrals and of more immediate importance in terms of protecting the populace from attacks from outside.

The use of bricks in fortifications pre-dated the Middle Ages. The Romans had used fired bricks to face their city walls where ready supplies of stone were not available. Walled defences in the early Middle Ages in northern Europe were frequently crude and relied on earthworks surmounted by timber palisades. The most immediate problem with such a fortification was that it was easily attacked with fire. Many types of stone, although not immediately inflammable, could also be

was not readily available or where the brick technology was better understood, castles and town walls were built of brick and many survive to this day. The largest and most impressive of these is the castle of Malbork (Marienburg) in Poland (see next page).

The Order of the Teutonic Knights of St Mary's Hospital of Jerusalem were one of the three great military and religious orders formed during the Crusades (the others being the Templars and the Hospitallers). The Order was founded in 1198 and originally had its headquarters in Acre, but after the fall of that city in 1291 and a brief period when it was ruled from Venice, the Grand Master moved his court and administration to the Marienburg (or Malbork) in what is now Poland in 1308. Here the Order constructed a magnificent castle from which it could rule over a sizeable territory and provide a defence for Christian Europe against possible attacks from the Baltic states to the east.

The castle was no doubt influenced in its layout by the castles in the Holy Land, but in its decoration and elevations it was wholly a conception of the Backsteingotik master builders that constructed it. The walls were laid in Gothic (or Polish) bond and ornamented with diaper patterns of glazed bricks, the upper parts being enlivened with moulded and cut brick stepped gables and pointed windows.

In northern Italy, defensive structures were also often of brick. Brick towers were built by individuals, for defence, and subsequently for ostentatious display. In Bologna 180 towers were built, including the two towers of the Garisendi and Asinelli families erected at the beginning of the 12th century which were 47.5m and 97.6m high respectively. This period also marked the beginning of fortress construction. One of the most dramatic was the Castello Estense built by the Este family in the centre of Ferrara. Construction of the castle began in 1385, but it was greatly added to subsequently, particularly in the Renaissance. One of the popular ideas is that the moats of these castles provided the clay for the brickmaking. Whether this was the case in Ferrara is debatable but evidence does survive for the use of this method in England in the 15th century at Herstmonceaux. However, this was a late castle. Poorly sited in a valley, it was probably never conceived of as primarily a defensive structure. It came after the invention of gunpowder which was to change the design of castles forever. Instead Herstmonceaux is a fascinating example of a new type of building that appeared in the late Middle Ages: the imitation castle, built primarily for show rather than practicality. The real fortifications of the next era looked altogether different and belong to the Renaissance.

made to crumble or lose their strength by lighting fires within or next to them. Brick was completely fireproof, having already been baked in temperatures which far exceeded any that one could easily generate next to walls in an attacking situation. A castle or town wall built with tiled roofs and brick walls was thus immune to attacks by burning arrows and fires against its foundations. How far these factors were taken into account is open to question and no doubt depended on the individual circumstances. Despite its advantages it was stone rather than brick that normally replaced timber for most fortifications in northern Europe. Nevertheless, in areas where stone

Opposite Herstmonceaux Castle, England (15th century), a late castle built more for display than defence.

Top and above Castello Estense, Ferrara, Italy. Construction began in 1385 but the castle was much altered in the Renaissance.

Following pages The great castle of Malbork, Poland (mostly 14th century), once the headquarters of the Teutonic Knights and one of the largest castles ever built.

The Medieval World

The cathedral of Albi and medieval France

Medieval abbeys were usually surrounded by stout walls to keep out intruders. Some religious orders such as the Teutonic Knights even built castles. There was also a third type of structure, the fortified church, of which the cathedral of St Cécile, Albi is one of the best-known and most interesting examples.

In general the brickwork of South-western France is more obviously Roman-inspired than its northern counterparts. Long thin bricks laid in thick joints continued in this region well into the Middle Ages and can be seen in buildings such as the gatehouse in Perpignan. Whether this is evidence of a continuous tradition of brickmaking in the region or just the influence of surviving Roman remains on a revival of brickmaking in the Middle Ages is difficult to say. No major buildings survive from the early Middle Ages. The first significant brick structure to be built in France after the Roman retreat was the church of Saint Sernin in Toulouse, begun between 1075 and 1080, whose choir was consecrated by Urban II (Bishop of Rheims, Pope 1088–1099). This church (in a much altered and added to form) survives today. That it was built from brick can be put down at least partly to the fact that there was a lack of local building stone.

During the following century the area to the north of Toulouse became the centre of the Albigensians, believers in the great Cathar heresy. The Cathars believed in the Manichaean doctrine of good and evil, supporting the notion that everything on earth was by its nature evil. Paradise could only be obtained by renouncing everything worldly and becoming a 'perfect'. Fortunately the heretics believed that absolution and conversion could be sought on the deathbed, allowing the believer to enter paradise after a lifetime of immorality. The Catholic Church in the region at the time was largely corrupt, and the ascetic life and forgiving attitude of the 'perfects' offered an attractive alternative. The movement swiftly gained widespread support among the populace and nobility. Condemned by the Church, the region became the subject of a bloody crusade involving widespread slaughter under Pope Innocent III (1208). The religious motivation of this crusade was probably as much an excuse as anything, for it finally gave the north a justification for an attack on lands outside its political control. The attacks when they came were swift and brutal and the last vestiges of the heresy, were wiped out by a subsequent long running and equally bloodthirsty inquisition. The name of the heretics, the Albigensians, was derived from the town at the centre of the heresy which was called Albi.

Following the purge of heretics in 1276 Bishop Bernard de Castanet was put in charge of the diocese and set about constructed a cathedral in Albi designed ever to remind the populace of the might, severity and power of the church, paid for partly by yet another inquisition. The result was the awesome edifice that dominates the town to this day, a brutal 78-m high fortress of a cathedral which took

Left Albi Cathedral, looking up the west tower. **Below** The upper part of the tower with its octagonal belfry.

two centuries to construct and was still not complete when it was consecrated in 1480.

In plan the cathedral is deceptively simple, consisting of a nave without aisles surrounded by chapels set in between massive piers. Externally these are semi-circular, but on the interior they taper towards a more modest pier in the nave. In effect the buttresses have been moved inside the church and chapels formed between them. There are two sets of windows. The lower ones light the chapels while the upper taller ones light the gallery above, the ceiling and the nave. At a much later date the vaults were painted and the stone porch added, completing the cathedral as we see it today. The original church would have been dark and rather plain. It also had an undeniable defensive quality with its narrow windows set high up in the thick walls. The brickwork is in stretcher bond, the bricks presenting a 200–210 x 50-55 face on the outside and laid in 20-mm joints.

Externally the fortified character of the cathedral is most apparent. The parapet around the roof is a 19th-century addition. This part of the cathedral was never finished. It was possible that the whole cathedral was intended to be topped with castellations and if this was the case then it would have appeared even more like a castle than it does today.

The entrances were guarded by a drawbridge and a stout gateway, since replaced. The windows are deliberately placed high up in the walls, inaccessible to the attacker, and are heavily barred and the walls of the base are extremely thick to resist battering rams.

It is doubtful whether Albi Cathedral would have been able to resist a concerted attack by a well-prepared military force but it was more than capable of providing shelter for its occupants from any civilian unrest, at least until help could arrive.

Architecturally, however, Albi is fascinating. Its deep walls are forerunners of the diaphragm walls that were invented in the 20th century. These two thin walls are separated by a very wide cavity, braced by internal walls at intervals forming buttresses. In Albi the system is less refined. The structure is just a cathedral inverted, with the buttresses on the inside. The disadvantages of such an arrangement are that the buttresses block any side aisles and that they reduce the amount of light in the nave. Nevertheless, the effect of a single large internal space and soaring sheer walls on the outside is undeniably dramatic.

The system is not entirely new. Precedents for similar arrangements of buttresses can be found in the church of Santa Catalina in Barcelona (begun 1247) and the Franciscan church of the Cordeliers at Toulouse (1268–1305, destroyed in the 19th century). Albi was, however, more rigorous in its application and more dramatic as a result.

The cathedral was widely studied in the 19th century and the system of internal buttressing was copied by many English architects, most notably by J. F. Bentley in the design of Westminster Cathedral, by Giles Gilbert Scott in Liverpool Cathedral and in Guildford Cathedral by Edward Maufe.

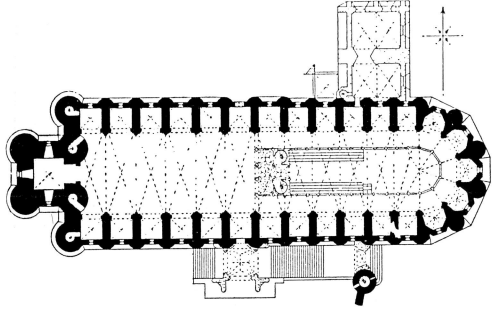

Left Plan showing the system
of internal buttressing that
supports the vault

Above Albi Cathedral from the
south-east (the town square).

Following pages The south
side of Albi Cathedral, west of
the porch.

Perfect patterns: Islamic brickwork in the Middle East

In the Middle Ages Islam continued to stretch from Spain to India and Islamic brickwork
was to be found throughout these regions wherever stone was difficult to obtain, but the
centre of Islamic brickwork continued to be in Persia, which covered what is Iran
and much of Iraq.

Between 1000 and 1450 three great dynasties held
power in Persia: the Seljuks, the Il Khanids and the
Timurids. The Seljuks, originally Turkish shepherds
on the steppes of Central Asia, ruled a great empire
established in a series of wars between 1037 and 1157.
As a clan they adopted Islam c. 960 and took their
name from one of their first great leaders, Seljuk.
Their empire, which stretched from Turkey through
Iraq, Persia, Afghanistan and Uzbekistan up to the
Aral Sea, was broken up by the Mongol hordes led
by Genghis Khan in 1220. The Il Khanids were the
descendants of Genghis Khan who took over ruling
an empire that stretched from China in the East
to Baghdad in the West. They ruled from the 13th
century to 1360 when they were conquered by
Tamerlane (Timur). The Timurids in turn ruled Persia
until they were defeated by the Shaybanids in 1506.
Thus the period 1000–1450 was a turbulent period in
Persian history that saw the capital moving many times
and shifting influences in architectural style,
yet throughout, brick remained the material
of choice in the region.

Brick sizes
Mud bricks continued to be used for common buildings
in the period. Fired bricks were only used for buildings
of significance. Following earlier precedent, bricks
tended to be square in the Middle East. Il Khanid bricks
in Persia were between 180–310mm square (most
being 200–220mm) and 40–70mm thick (most being
45–50mm). The large differences seem to be
determined by the source and the particular
brickmaker rather than the period so that brick sizes
cannot be used for dating and buildings will often have
bricks of many sizes from a singe phase of building
work. The Seljuk period used similar bricks with a small
number of bricks half that size. Special bricks for use in
ornament were commonly cut to shape using knives
and saws before firing, usually from standard bricks.
Very few buildings used especially moulded bricks and
where these were used the moulds appear to have
been made especially for that structure. Re-use of
bricks from older structures was also common.

In the Timurid period bricks became slightly larger
(averaging 240–270mm square and 40–70mm thick).

Special bricks were made using the methods described
above, but it became increasingly common to cut fired
bricks to shape as they were laid. Decorative brickwork
declined as brick gave way to tile as the chief method
of decoration.

Bricklaying
Bricks were laid in gypsum mortar (plaster of Paris,
called *gach* in Persia) made by calcinating hydrated
calcium sulphate in small rubble kilns. Both the
problem and advantage of this kind of mortar was
its quick setting time after the addition of water.
If the bricklayer was not careful the mortar would
set before the bricks were laid. Perhaps to delay
the set, the mortar was often mixed with clay,
sand, fine gravel and mud. However, the fast set
had great advantages in the building of corbels,
domes and vaults. In such a situation the bricklayer
could hold the brick in position until the mortar
dried, obviating the need for temporary
timber formwork.

In the Seljuk and Il Khanid period bricks were laid in
three ways: with equal (20-mm) horizontal joints,
with wide (20-mm) horizontal joints and minimum
perpends in the Roman manner or with horizontal
joints kept to a minimum and extra wide (20–60mm)
perpends. In the last arrangement it became common
to fill the joint with special insets of cured plaster
(called brick-end plugs) which were also made of
moulded, carved or glazed terracotta. The use of brick
end plugs is peculiarity of brick in this particular region
at this time and went out of fashion in the Timurid
period which reverted to 20-mm, slightly raked joints
of equal width. The care lavished on jointing in the
Seljuk and Il Khanid period also extended to pointing.
Most brickwork was flush pointed after the brickwork
was finished. Examples are also found of joints with
lines scored down the centre, a technique that would
become common in Europe in the 18th century where
it was called 'penny struck' pointing because of the
method of its execution there.

The ability of Islamic bricklayers to make intricate
patterns by cutting and laying bricks in ingenious
bonding patterns was demonstrated in the
last chapter in the Tomb of the Saminids.

Opposite The Kalan minaret
(1127), Bukhara, Uzbekistan,
thought to have been built as
part of the original Friday
Mosque.

Above and below The Ali
minaret (12th century), Isfahan,
Iran. The mosque itself was
rebuilt in the 16th century. The
47-m minaret is richly
decorated.

These techniques were further developed in this period in the construction of the so-called Tomb Towers some 70 or so of which seem to have been constructed throughout Persia, Central Asia and Afghanistan between the 11th and 13th century. The purpose of these towers is uncertain and may have varied from site to site, but architecturally they form a fascinating group. A common feature is the richness of their brick decoration, amply demonstrated by the richly ornamented surface of the Kalan Minaret in Bukhara. At their most intricate the decorative patterns were made to form letters spelling out passages from the Koran or dedications. The earliest surviving example of lettering made out of brick in this way is the tomb of Masud III at Ghazna (early 12th century). A fine late example can be seen at the tomb of Oljeitu at Sultaniya (1307–1313). There the letters are picked out from the background by being both in relief and glazed and it was indeed the process of glazing that marked the most important development of the period.

Glazed work

A common image of Islamic architecture is of buildings covered in brightly coloured glazed ceramic bricks and tiles. Simple single colour glazes were used in Seljuk work. The use of more complex multi-coloured glazed Islamic terracotta work can be traced back at least as far as the beginning of the 14th century and there are a number of fine examples from this period surviving in Sutaniya in northern Iran.

Complex glazes were built up on unbaked tiles pounced with charcoal dust. The patterns were incised and the divides between the colours outlined in manganese purple or the pattern was pounced on a clear glaze, the tiles were fired and after cooling a second (tin) glaze was applied before a second firing. This technique was known as majolica, *caverda seca*, or in Persia, *haft rangi* (seven colours). Normally the patterns were fired onto relatively large flat thin tiles which were applied with gypsum plaster onto the brickwork.

An alternative method of making decorative surface patterns from glazed ware was mosaic work. Tiles of single colours were painstakingly cut into small regular pieces which were assembled into intricate multi-coloured patterns. The technique seems to have come into use at the end of the 14th century. The effects of mosaic were more unified than tilework but much more difficult to achieve. Inevitably, in the long term, it was the larger, cheaper tiles came to prevail.

Glazed bricks were used in the construction of domes and in minarets but neither glazed bricks nor intricate brick bonding techniques could compete with the intricacy or the filigree patterns that could be produced using ceramic tiles. Although bricks continued to be the major building material in Persia and much of Central Asia, the invention of the glazed tile marked the turning point in its use as a decorative material. Thereafter it continued to play a crucial role in construction, but was increasingly hidden under other surface finishes.

Opposite Tomb of Chelebi Oghlu (c. 1353), Sultaniya, Iran. The dating of this tiny building near the Mausoleum of Oljeitu is uncertain. It has particularly fine brickwork with brick-end plugs constructed out of 200 x 200 x 50-mm bricks.

Above Small mausoleum, Sutaniya, Iran (date unknown).

Right Chashmeh Ayub Shrine (1379–80), Bukhara, Uzbekistan. Its conical dome is a typical example of the period.

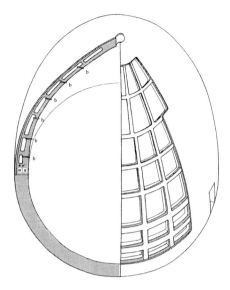

Re-inventing the dome: the Mausoleum of Oljeitu

On the first day of the 705th year of the Muslim calendar (in 1306) Sultan Muhammad Oljeitu Khudabanda founded his new capital at Sultaniya (meaning 'Imperial') in northern Persia. At its centre he built a magnificent tomb for himself surmounted by a great glazed brick dome that remains one of the most remarkable structures ever built.

Oljeitu, a brother of Ghazan Khan, inherited the Persian throne at the age of 23. As a child he had been baptized as a Christian and named Nicholas, but later under the influence of his wife he

converted to Islam, taking the name Muhammad Khudabanda. The fact that Oljeitu converted is important. He actively promoted Islam and under his direction non-Muslims were taxed differently and required to wear distinctive garments. Yet his own understanding of Islam changed many times throughout his reign and he was by turns a Hanafi, a Shia and a Sunni. As he altered his allegiances, he changed the buildings he was erecting.

The site of Sultaniya had been used for generations by the I Khans as their favourite summer camping ground and was known as Qunghurolong ('the falcon's hunting ground'). It is said that the idea to found a city here had been Oljeitu's father's but that he had died before construction could begin.

We are told that Oljeitu started his new city by building a citadel surrounded by a great wall of cut stone. He then erected a hospital and a college. His own residence was a palace consisting of a central pavilion surrounded by 12 smaller ones for the court. Soon the courtiers were vying with each other to build their own houses in the town. Within the walls Oljeitu had also begun the largest structure in the city, his great domed mausoleum.

Structure

The great mausoleum is octagonal with 7-m thick walls. Internally it contains a central space, surmounted by a great dome 26m in diameter. On the outside the dome is finished in a layer of bright blue glazed bricks. The structure of this dome is remarkable on two counts: first it is a double shell construction and secondly it was built without formwork or centring.

Double shell domes had been around for several centuries in Persia before the construction of the mausoleum. The earliest so far identified are a pair of tomb towers in Kharraqan, Iran dating from the 11th century AD. However, the domes of these earlier structures differed from the mausoleum at Sultaniya because they invariably involved two entirely

Top left Mausoleum of Oljeitu, Sultaniya, Iran (1315–25).

Top right Cutaway isometric of the dome (reproduced by kind permission of Rowland Mainstone).

Left The gallery which surrounds the building at the second floor level.

Opposite Mausoleum of Oljeitu (1315–25), Sultaniya, Iran. The tomb is an enormous octagon 38m in diameter, orientated cardinally with a 15 x 20-m hall on one side and a 50-m high dome.

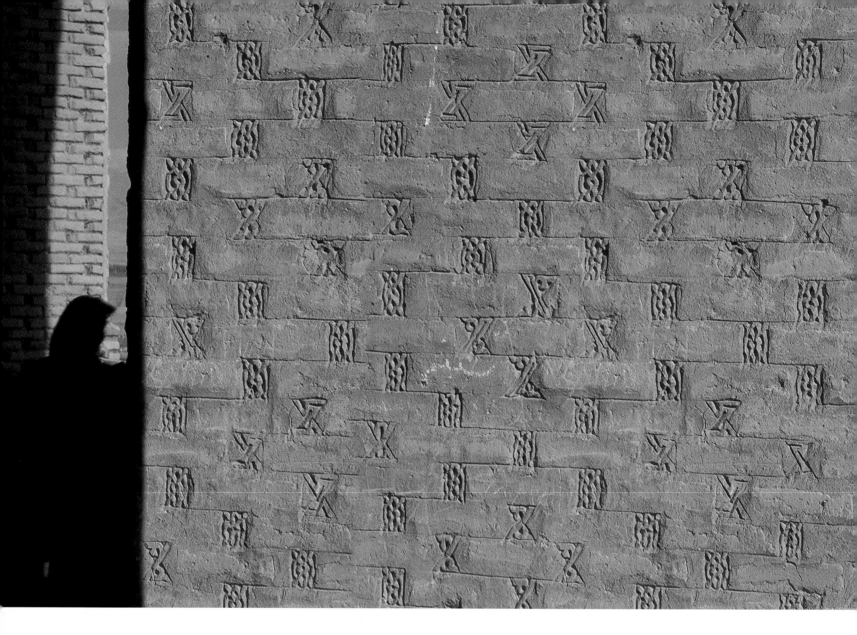

independent structures. It is thought that they were probably derived in form from the great timber double domes that had preceded them, such as those at the Dome of the Rock in Jerusalem and the Great Mosque

of Damascus. In timber, double domes make much more sense structurally because the space between the two skins can by used for structural frames to strengthen the outer dome against wind and support the inner dome from above. Timber structures of this kind would be used in Western European architecture from the Renaissance onwards. The purpose of the masonry Islamic double domes was aesthetic rather than structural and they tended as a result to be of limited span, while the use of gypsum mortar enabled them to be constructed without centering.

The Mausoleum of Oljeitu is enormous and structurally of an entirely different character. Its two brick domes are inextricably linked by a system of ribs that transfer the weight between the exterior and interior domes and directly onto the walls. To avoid the necessity of centering, each course of brickwork was laid close to the horizontal rather than leaning towards the centre of the dome. Internally, wooden scaffolding was supported on poplar spars set into the courses of brickwork below. This enabled the bricklayers to stand inside the dome on platforms cantilevered out over the void. The spars were

cut back to the surface on completion and covered with tiles. In addition a double ring of poplar timbers was placed into the brickwork at the base of the dome to act as a chain in resisting radial forces and the natural tendency of the bottom of the dome to spread.

Later Islamic domes became more bulbous, and the space between the domes became used for wooden ties to strengthen the external dome. This mausoleum thus represents a unique stage in the development of Islamic domes where briefly the two skins came together and acted as one structure. It was a form that was efficient and which would be later used by Renaissance architects to build much larger domes although whether they knew of or were influenced by the great mausoleum is open to speculation and remains unsubstantiated.

Brickwork

The construction of the mausoleum and the city around it must have required a considerable brickmaking industry, but no remains of kilns have been excavated. The bricks that were produced were square (200–210 x 200–210 x 50mm) with rectangular half-bricks (200–210 x 100–105 x 50mm), laid in 10-mm gypsum mortar joints laid in Stretcher bond/Common bond.

Staircases within the walls of the mausoleum give access to an upper gallery that runs around the complete exterior of the building. Here the original rectangular glazed bricks survive in parts, similar to those that covered the dome.

The internal wall of this gallery conserves a remarkable example of bonding using brick-end plugs. In places these are formed in the conventional way while in others they are made by covering the whole surface in plaster and carefully scoring the brick-course back in and incising imitation brick-end plugs.

Some of the vaults formed using decorative brickwork, but most exhibit intricate plaster decoration. Overall the gallery provides an insight into how brick was integrated within a range of materials. In places timber was used to support pendentives and other decorative brick structures which in turn were covered with plaster which was coloured or further decorated with tiles. In others the decoration is glazed brickwork which forms a structural function as well. For the builders, the importance was the final appearance and overall coherence rather than the method by which it was achieved.

Decline

By 1313 the great city of Sultaniya was virtually complete and the thousands of craftsmen who had been brought together to construct it, and had been its principal inhabitants, began to return back to their homelands. It was probably only then that the weaknesses of Oljeitu's choice of site became apparent. Sultaniya was a strange location for a city because it lacked any defensive advantage. Moreover, it was far from the trade routes that might have brought it commercial prosperity. When the Sultan died in 1316 at the age of 36, Tabriz again became the capital and Sultaniya went into rapid decline. Within a century much of the city was abandoned and by the end of the 17th century nothing remained but ruins. The Khanids too were in decline. They had started as proud Mongol warriors but had become softened by a life of luxury. The last Il Khanid sultan, Abu Sa id, who died in 1335, is said to have been poisoned, victim of a harem intrigue. A new horde was set to conquer and subdue what remained under the leadership of Tamerlane (Timur). Yet the architectural legacy of the Il Khanids was secure. Thousands of craftsmen carried back to their homelands from Sultaniya the decorative techniques and styles that had been established there and the great mausoleum continues to draw travellers from far and wide, as it still does today.

Opposite above A close-up of the brickwork in the upper gallery of the Mausoleum of Oljeitu, Sultaniya, showing the brick-end plugs. Some are real but many are just pressed into a layer of plaster covering the brick.

Opposite below The Mausoleum of Oljeitu, Sultaniya, showing the hall attached to one side.

Above The ceiling vaults of the upper gallery, Mausoleum of Oljeitu, Sultaniya. The rich patterns are thought to have been borrowed from book design, suggesting that the plasterers worked from paper patterns.

CHAPTER FOUR

THE BIRTH OF
THE MODERN WORLD 1450–1650

Between 1450 and 1650 the world changed dramatically. Moveable-type printing, which had been used in China since the 11th century, first appeared in the West, transforming books from expensive objects that could be only afforded by the very few into mass-produced objects that everyone could own. The Reformation split the Church in Europe into Catholics and Protestants. Italy was the birthplace of the Renaissance, creating a scholarly and artistic revival that swept through the rest of Europe. A new interest in knowledge for its own sake led to the birth of modern science and the realization that the earth revolved around the sun. European explorers reached America and the first colonies were founded.

The first five sections in this chapter are devoted to developments in Italy in the period which is generally called the Renaissance. At this time the Italian peninsula was still divided into many states which were openly hostile to each other. Despite this turbulent political climate, art, scholarship, and literature thrived, financed by the great ruling families that vied with each other for political and cultural superiority. In the building world this translated into a frenzy of building activity. As a result, the brickmaking trade prospered during this period and various cities applied increasingly stringent regulations to try to control it. In building the major change was the appearance of the architect. In the Middle Ages in Europe buildings had been constructed by master builders instructed by committees or informed patrons and working according to long-established principles. The Renaissance demanded a new level of uniformity in architectural detail and a scholarly approach. Perhaps more importantly architecture was seen as an art and as such the business of the artist, whose status was to be greatly increased during the period. Brunelleschi was one of the first of this new breed of men. A goldsmith by trade, he rose to prominence in the competition for the design of the doors of the Baptistery of San Giovanni (although it was Lorenzo Ghiberti who eventually received the commission). He studied the ruins of Rome and wrote one of the first treatises on perspective. He was a scholar and an artist rather than an artisan and operated as an expert advisor rather than a master workman. The addition of a new tier in the command chain was hugely important. The architect was not tied to conventions of Gothic practice and underwent no obligatory

apprenticeship. He used drawings and models to instruct the workmen and his expertise was in his knowledge of the rules of classical architecture and his ability to draw.

Architects, as they were characterized in the Renaissance, had a profound effect on the way the buildings under their control were produced. The craftsmen were required to follow orders and to produce work to the given plans and a budget. Perhaps more importantly in terms of brickwork there was a new division between the men responsible for designing the building and those actually building it. Decisions were made as much for artistic reasons as pragmatic ones. Brickwork had to adjust to the new forms required by classical and Baroque architecture. As a result the greatest technical advances in this period were in the production of terracotta. Italian craftsmen developed new techniques for making more elaborate forms and travelled all over the continent.

The chapter then moves from Italy to northern Europe, beginning with England. The period between 1450 and 1650 represents the flowering of English brickwork. The technology for brickmaking was slow to re-establish itself in England and even when it did re-emerge it was at first only in the eastern part of the country. No doubt its late appearance was partly to do with the relative geographical isolation of the British Isles, but the same insularity also meant that certain aspects of brickwork became popular there long after they had first appeared on the continent or developed in unusual ways. Thus England developed diaperwork at a late date, together with a fashion for extraordinarily ornate chimneys which had no direct parallel elsewhere. More interesting

still is the brief appearance of terracotta in the country.

The chapter then turns to Russia. Brickwork had flourished in Russia since early medieval times and developed its own distinct decorative style. The 16th and 17th centuries represent the high point of this tradition, exemplified by buildings such as the church of the Ascension at Kolomenskoe and St Basil's Cathedral in Moscow.

Islam had been gradually driven from the Iberian Peninsula in the 14th and 15th centuries, Granada finally falling to Castile in 1492. However, the Ottomans captured Constantinople and by the end of the 17th century controlled much of North Africa. In the East the Timurid Empire was divided into three. The new states formed were the Shaybunaid Uzbek Empire in Central Asia, the Safavid Empire in Persia and the Moghul Empire in India. The Uzbeks, under Muhammed Shaybani Khan (1500-1510) controlled an area which included Kazakhstan, Uzbekistan and Afghanistan. Under the rule of the enlightened Shaybanids and in particular Abdullah Khan II, Bukhara became the mercantile centre of Central Asia. The Safavids under Shah Abbas the Great (1587–1629) moved their capital to Isfahan, rebuilding the city with grand arcades, bridges, palaces, mosques and bazaars. The penultimate sections of the chapter focus on two of the most dramatic cities, Bukhara and Isfahan, tracing their architectural development and changing use of brick.

Finally the section turns to China. Between 1368 and 1398 Chu Yuan-Chang, a Buddhist monk, had led an uprising that drove the last Mongol emperor from Peking and established the Ming Dynasty (1368-1644), moving their capital to Nanking (to improve defence it was moved back to Peking in 1421). The Ming Dynasty saw a huge amount of building work but by far the largest project was the complete reconstruction of the Great Wall which guarded the northern border against re-invasion by the Mongols. Previous walls had been little more than earth ramparts. The Ming Wall, much of which survives today, was an altogether more permanent structure and was for most of its length constructed from brick or stone. It remains one of the largest building projects ever undertaken.

The entrance to
the monastery of
Corpus Domini,
Bologna (1477–80)

Florence Cathedral, Italy

Church of the Trinity, Ostankino, Russia

San Giacomo, Bologna, Italy

Si-o Se Pol Bridge, Isfahan, Iran

Santo Spirito, Bologna, Italy

St John's College, Cambridge, England

Masjid-i Shah, Isfahan, Iran

Church of the Decapitation, Kolomenskoe, Russia

Shah Mosque, Isfahan, Iran

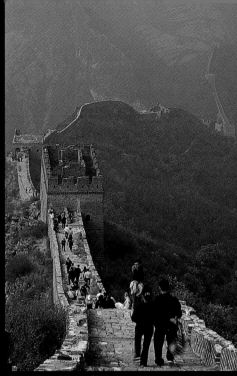

Great Wall of China, Simitai

Khwazi Bridge, Isfahan, Iran

Layer Marney Tower, England

St John's College, Cambridge, England

Church of the Ascension, Kolomenskoe, Russia

Brunelleschi's Dome

The building of the great dome of the cathedral of Santa Maria del Fiore in Florence, is one of the greatest achievements not only in the development of Italian Renaissance engineering and brickwork, but in the whole history of building construction. The story of the competition for its design and how it was won by Filippo Brunelleschi is one of the most entertaining in architectural history and has been retold many times.

Construction of a new cathedral in Florence began in 1294. The plan, which appears to have developed gradually, featured a long nave culminating in a large octagonal space (probably based on the Baptistery of San Giovanni). By 1400 the building committee was faced with the embarrassing problem of how to finish this focal part of the building, which demanded a dome far larger than anything than had been attempted since antiquity.

What distinguished Brunelleschi's solution from those of his rivals was his confidence that he had a method for constructing the dome without the need for centering. As we have seen, Islamic builders were already constructing large domes without formwork and had done so for centuries, but Persian bricklayers used gypsum mortar which set in minutes and were working on a more modest scale. The Florentine dome was far bigger than anything attempted in Persia since Ctesiphon. Moreover, gypsum mortar could not be used because it was not waterproof. Instead the dome had to be built with lime mortar, which took months, if not years, to harden.

Brunelleschi's solution to these problems was ingenious. Firstly he designed the dome to be built in two layers. It is not clear whether he had knowledge of this method from Persia. Certainly there had been not be resisted using masonry alone. But it is Brunelleschi's third innovation, the way he used bricks, which primarily interests us here and as far as we know it was entirely original. Following the typical Florentine building practice of the day, Brunelleschi had chosen brick as his principal structural material. It had a number of advantages: there was a ready supply, it was lighter than most stone and it was more easily shaped. Moreover, because of the time involved in carving it would have been more economic to use stone in large blocks than small ones but larger units would have been more difficult to lift up into the dome. Bricks solved this problem too as they tended to

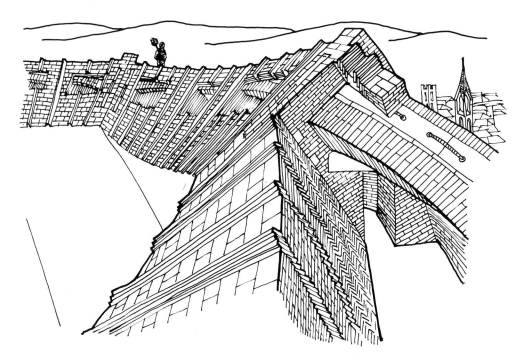

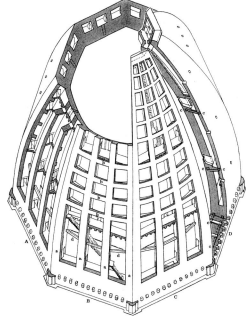

Above left A perspective after Rossi showing the so-called herringbone courses of the bricks on edge that prevented each new layer of bricks sliding into the void as it was laid.

Above right Cutaway isometric of the dome reproduced by kind permission of Rowland Mainstone showing the disposition of ribs in the structure.

strong trading links between southern Europe and Persia throughout the later Middle Ages so a transfer of information cannot be ruled out but no direct evidence to confirm such a hypothesis has so far come to light. Secondly, and perhaps also following Persian precedents, he devised a series of timber 'chains' around the base of the dome. These were important as they helped it resist hoop stresses (the tendency of the bottom of the dome to spread outwards) which could

be smaller and large size was not an advantage in their production.

Brunelleschi had to devise a way to lay the bricks in such a way that they acted like voussoirs in a giant arch. As the sides of the dome ascended the courses of the bricks would increasingly lean forwards. Somehow he had to stop the bricks (and for that matter the bricklayers) sliding down the slope and falling off the edge before the lime mortar had set and the next layer

could be laid on top. His solution involved setting bricks at intervals on edge to form vertical walls. These divided each course into segments each tapering inwards towards the centre of the dome. Because the space into which the bricks had to be laid tapered, the bricks naturally wedged themselves in place and the weight of the bricks behind them just wedged them more tightly. As the dome progressed it was still necessary to provide some scaffolding slung from above to allow the bricklayers to reach the inside of the walls without sliding off but no formwork was required. The resulting structure, which was completed in 1446, can still be seen today on the intricate brickwork as one climbs up inside the dome .

Above The great dome of the cathedral still towers over the city of Florence.

The brickmaking industry in Renaissance Italy

Manetti, Brunelleschi's biographer writing in the 1480s, claimed that Brunelleschi insisted on examining every brick that went into his dome. This is, of course, an exaggeration: it would have been physically impossible for one man to examine the millions of bricks required. A number of contracts which the building committee made with local suppliers survive to show that by 1421 the committee had already contracted four local suppliers to supply between 200,000 and 1 million bricks each. Tens of thousands of bricks were required each month during construction. As these figures show, brick manufacturing by the time of the Renaissance had become a large and potentially profitable business.

Brickmaking in Renaissance Italy has been the subject of considerable research providing a clear idea of the way it operated as an economic activity. One of the best sources is a report by Piero Pagni; he was one of a number of expert witnesses asked for advice in an inquiry into a complaint from kilnsmen that prices for bricks, which were fixed by law, had been set too low. Pagni examined two kilns, one with a capacity

of 10,000 and the other 17,000 bricks. He assumed that they could be fired 16 times a year (about once every three weeks) and estimated that they would thus produce 160,000 and 272,000 bricks respectively. He concluded that as a result the operators would make a profit of between 80 and 150 ducats a year. Both kilns also burnt lime (yielding a further profit), a requirement under Florentine law since 1325 (elsewhere in Europe lime was usually burnt separately in smaller kilns designed for the purpose).

Pagni's estimate is probably optimistic. Italian Renaissance kilns were of the Roman type fired with wood. They would have required time to stack, fire,

cool down and unload and the firing period was normally April to September.

In England, permanent kilns seem to have been less common. Bricklayers moved from site to site setting up temporary kilns. Only a few towns like Hull were constructed of brick and had municipal brickyards.

In Florence and elsewhere in Italy kilnsmen either owned the land on which the kiln was operated, or

rented it for an annual fee or percentage of the takings. The setting up of a kiln for a specific project in such a situation was unnecessary; there were more than adequate supplies available from existing kilns even for a project as large as the dome. Nevertheless, under such a system regulation was desirable to protect the consumer.

In Florence in the 15th century the responsibility for the enforcement of such regulations was entrusted to the Grascia, the communal office responsible for overseeing the public's interest in the marketplace. The regulations required a model mould to be kept in each brickyard, bound in iron and stamped with the official seal. The mould was to be larger than the fired brick to

allow for shrinkage during drying and firing, the size of the both the mould and brick being stipulated. Bricks were to be made in three sizes: *mattone* (290 x 126 x 73mm), *mezzana* (290 x 145 x 51mm) and *quadruccio* (290 x 102 x 73mm). Enforcement was in the hands of a guild agent. Kilnsmen were required to keep records of their products, prices and sales and to inform the agent four days before each firing to allow them to carry out an inspection. Prices of bricks were fixed by a special committee and each kilnsmen was allowed to operate no more than two kilns within ten miles of Florence.

All of these regulations were biased towards the consumer and placed a considerable burden on the

kiln operator, especially if the prices of other commodities rose. It was for this reason that Florentine kilnsmen asked for the inquiry that resulted in Pagni's report. Yet despite, or perhaps because of, the complexity of the records they were required to keep, kilnsmen seem to have been more literate and successful than might be considered possible for those engaged in what superficially appeared to be manual work. Some even gained senior positions in local government. Brickmaking was never pleasant work (Piovanni Arlotto, a Renaissance wit, famously joked that brickmakers were the cleanest of all Florentines because only they washed their hands *before* going to the toilet), but it was not without its rewards.

Opposite Plate from G. Ruscani's *Della Architettura* (1590) showing brickmaking. In the foreground on the right the clay is mixed with straw before being moulded. In the background the clay is prepared. A man is using a sieve to remove stones.

Above The cathedral in Florence still dominates the city skyline today as it did in the Renaissance.

The Birth of the Modern World

Brickwork versus stone in Renaissance architecture

From the general literature on the period, it is all too easily assumed that the buildings of the Italian Renaissance were all constructed in stone and that brick was relegated to second place. In fact, brick was one of the most important building materials of the time. Architectural history has traditionally focused on the works of a relatively small group of architects and on the outward appearance of the buildings they produced. If we look beneath the skin of those buildings or beyond this circle of architects, the story is entirely different.

Florence, often seen as the very centre of the Italian Renaissance, is a good starting point for a discussion of the role of brick versus stone. Architectural history typically depicts the architecture of Florence as being almost entirely of stone and indeed outwardly that is true. But in terms of volume of material used, stone was only of minor significance compared to brick. It is, for instance, well known that Brunelleschi built his dome in brick, but less appreciated that his Ospedale degli Innocenti is also a brick building clad in stone, render and terracotta. This is equally true of many of the other great buildings of the Renaissance. Often the outer render hides walls of hastily executed brickwork, with stone used only for dressings around windows and doors. Of course rubble stone was also used for such walls but brick was in general cheaper, easier to move and stronger. Many of Palladio's villas are brick buildings clad in this way.

The focus of the architectural history of the period has always tended to be on identifiable architects. In his great work *Lives of the Artists* Vasari depicted the patrons of art and architecture of his time as being

obsessed with the cult of the genius, which he was keen to encourage. Men like Michaelangelo were honoured in their lifetime and treated like the media stars of today. Architectural history has naturally tended to concentrate on the works of these individuals and their influence.

Another limitation lay in the architects and patrons themselves. They sought to recover the architecture of ancient Rome, when Italy was considered the centre of the world, and saw this as an architecture of stone. Brick in the Gothic period had begun to acquire a decorative language of its own, quite distinct from the detail to be found on classical buildings. Quite apart from the differences in colour, the texture and effect was totally different. It was not possible to fire bricks as big as the stone blocks used by the Romans. Thus they had to use brick, Renaissance architects wishing to emulate classical stone architecture were left with a problem which they solved in a number of ways. The simplest and most common was to cover the façade in stucco, scored to look like stone. Another was to lay the bricks with the same coloured mortar, to form a

uniform surface which at a distance would pass as stone. The Palazzo Farnese in Rome is so successful in this regard that few people realize it is brick. Another was to paint them, as can be seen at Santa Maria di Loreto designed by Antonio Sangallo the Younger. This is constructed in tiny bricks which are deliberately shaped to mimic Roman ones. On the ground floor the white trimmings around the doorways are marble, but on the upper storeys they are just limewashed brick.

In northern Italy the approach was different again. Here architects and builders continued to build in a Gothic style using the same brick details that had been used for centuries and when classical ideas did begin to appear they were interpreted in the existing language and materials, most notably in exuberant decoration in terracotta.

The Birth of the Modern World

Brick and the exuberance of Italian Baroque

In the late 16th century concern with producing an architecture that rediscovered
and obeyed the rules of classical architecture gave way to a new sensibility that valued
originality, complex shapes and richness in ornamentation. It was still classical in
inspiration but the elements were twisted into new shapes, deliberately distorted
and curved into ever more unusual forms. The name which would be later given
to this new style was Baroque.

Baroque architects played with surface in an original way. In Baroque architecture the façades were curved and contorted. Illusionistic painting on ceilings gave the impression that the room was open to the sky. Statues reached into the paintings and the division between painting, decorative sculpture and architecture was deliberately blurred. While High Renaissance architecture sought to instil in viewers a sense of repose, the architecture of the Baroque aimed to dazzle them with the richness of its ornamentation, continually drawing the eye from one intricate piece of decoration to the next. Architecture was seen as a stage set. But the price of this theatricality was the loss of a sense of materials.

Baroque architecture, where nothing was what it seemed to be and surfaces blended seamlessly into each other, was not easy to achieve in brickwork. Nevertheless the skill of the craftsmen, especially in northern Italy, was more than equal to the challenge, as can be seen in the façade of the church of San Carlo in Ferrara (1612-23), designed

by the great architect and mathematician Giovanni Battista Aleotti (1546–1636).

There are many examples of Baroque buildings constructed in brick. In Turin Guarini built Palazzo Carignano and the extraordinary cupola of the Chapel of the Holy Shroud in brick. Closer to the centre of the Baroque in Rome there is the curving façade of the Convent of the Filippini and in the campanile of Sant'Andrea delle Fratte by that master of the style Francesco Borromini (1599-1667). Many more could easily be cited.

Yet Baroque to a certain extent marked the end of a significant period of brick building in Italy. In seeking to create a continuity of material and ever more elaborate ornamentation the plasterers art was developed to an unprecedented degree. Plaster, and stucco in particular, had many advantages over brick, most notably in the finish that could be achieved and their cost. Moreover, unlike brick, plaster formed a continuous surface without any visible joints. Brickwork was always limited by the size of the unit of the brick and even when laid in

matching mortar the joints were still visible. Although brick could be cut and carved into elaborate shapes, to do so required great skill and was therefore expensive. Even the terracotta of the time could not match the effects achieved by the *stuccatori*. Brick was thus increasingly covered by renders and given a subservient and hidden role in construction. Terracotta fared even worse and the most of the great workshops which had decorated the buildings of Northern Italy eventually closed. The amount of brick used probably increased in the 18th century but the days of an architecture that was visibly brick and celebrated its origins were gone, replaced by a new architectural sensibility and style.

Opposite The church of San Carlo in Ferrara (1612–23) designed by Giovanni Battista Aleotti (1546–1636) and constructed using exceptionally fine-quality cut brickwork.

Above Palazzo Roverella, Ferrara (1508). Planes of flat limewashed brickwork with coloured mortar are contrasted with intricate terracotta friezes and cut-brick pediments over the windows.

Left Glazed terracotta roundel on the façade of Orsanmichele, Florence, typical of the kind of work that made the Della Robbia family's reputation.

Opposite Santo Spirito, Bologna (14th century). Tucked away in a side street, this tiny chapel has an exquisite terracotta façade.

Below The arcade of S. Giacomo Maggiore, Bologna (1477–81) with its moulded terracotta frieze.

The development of architectural terracotta in Italy

The rectangular repeated format and the coarse texture of the typical medieval brick placed definite limitations on what could be achieved in terms of mouldings and decoration. The solution was the development in the Middle Ages of what we now call terracotta. The acknowledged masters of this art were northern Italian craftsmen of the 15th century who produced a distinctive and unique form of ornamentation.

The term 'terracotta' is misleading because it makes it sound as though the material used in the Middle Ages was the same as that employed in the late 19th century, when in fact they are quite different. In medieval and Renaissance buildings the term is simply applied to work that is very similar to moulded brickwork but comes in pieces that are much larger and definitely not brick-shaped. The most important difference between this and 19th-century work is that the medieval and Renaissance examples are solid while 19th-century terracotta is hollow.

The material used to make medieval terracotta was very similar to bricks and tiles and often terracotta artefacts would be made on the same site. The differences lay in treatment. Clay for terracotta wares was more carefully washed and sifted to ensure the removal of stones and impurities, and little or no sand was added. The use of finer material created problems as the fired object could easily crack in the kiln. Such problems became more acute with size, which put a definite limit on the dimensions of terracotta pieces that could be fired. Large friezes and statues were typically made in sections then dried very carefully and for a much longer period than bricks. Fired or other materials such as ground burnt clay known as *grogs* would also be added to try to reduce shrinkage.

The clay was shaped in one of two ways. The first involved pressing the clay into carefully constructed box moulds carved with the inverse of the patterns to be produced. This method was appropriate for the production of friezes, sections of cornices and other repeated elements. Surprisingly complex shapes could be made in this way. The box moulds were carefully designed to come apart in the right way after the clay had been pressed into them. It was not uncommon for moulds to be made of two, three or even four interlocking sections that were removed one by one in the correct order to reveal intricate three dimensional shapes. The making of such moulds was time-consuming so a workshop would retain and re-use them where possible. It is possible to identify the work of a particular workshop by noting work produced by identical moulds on different buildings.

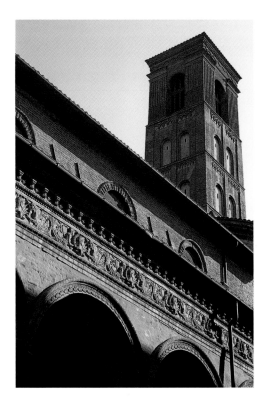

Above Terracotta roundel from the façade of Santo Spirito, Bologna, attributed to Sperandio di Bartolomeo.

The circular frame is composed of repeated moulded elements while the central figure was sculpted.

The second method of shaping the clay was more time-consuming and involved carving the shape directly in wet clay. Here the size limit became particularly apparent and much time and effort could be wasted if a larger piece cracked during drying or in the kiln. While some wastage could be allowed for in moulded work, sculpted work lost had to be started again from scratch.

The similarities between terracotta and medieval brickmaking are thus obvious and the two would be done together. Medieval terracotta and decorative brickwork are more or less synonymous. It seems likely that it was only during the Renaissance that workshops devoted entirely to the production of terracotta appeared, the most famous being that of the Della Robbia family in Florence.

The Della Robbia family are principally known for their work in sculpture and their glazed majolica-ware roundels which were occasionally used to grace buildings (the most notable being the frieze of the Ospedale del Ceppo in Pistoia). Like many workshops they kept their techniques a closely guarded secret and the art of glazed terracotta was lost with the death of the last member

of the family who ran the business in the mid-16th century. Many of the names of other great architectural terracotta makers of the northern cities have gone unrecorded. Nevertheless, the range of decoration and the imagination and skill that went into their works were considerable.

In medieval Italian buildings terracotta had been used for cornices to produce the distinctive 'corbel tables' (miniature arches beneath the eaves of a gable end). It was also employed in circular windows that were typical features of gable ends, and for decorative door and window surrounds. Such details are readily apparent on the façades of Saint Anthony in Padua (1232–1307 with domes added in 1424) and San Stefano in Ferrara (from 1450).

By the early 15th century some of the door surrounds were becoming more elaborate. The doorway of the monastic church of the Corpus Domini in Bologna (erected in 1456 and restored in 1478–81) is a fine example. Here the terracotta slabs are thin, large and moulded in high relief. Rasp marks used in making the moulds can be seen in the finished work.

Below Close-up of one of the figures from the doorway of the monastery of Corpus Domini, Bologna (1456).

Bottom The church of S. Stefano, Ferrara (from 1450). The windows are surrounded by moulded brick/terracotta.

Right Detail of the frieze and arches of the arcade of San Giacomo Maggiore, Bologna (1477–81) showing how the units are repeated and the dimensions of the overall design are co-ordinated to avoid cutting.

The Renaissance saw the re-emergence of the classical arcade. San Giacomo, Bologna has an excellent early example on the side of the street façade. The spandrels are plastered but the arches are picked out in crisp terracotta decorations surmounted by a deeply by a richly moulded repetitive frieze. A much later example incorporating elaborately decorated Corinthian pilasters and moulded window surrounds can be seen at the Palazzo Roverella in Ferrara.

The very nature of terracotta encouraged rich decoration. The sensibility of the more prominent architects was for an increasingly severe interpretation of classical antiquity and research into the rules that underlay the proportions of the orders. But the craftsmen of northern Italy were engaged in a seemingly uncontrolled and uncontrollable frenzy of architectural embellishment. In surface treatment this architecture was rococo before its time. Yet in this chaos there was great order. Perhaps the most successful example of this marriage between the freedom of the medieval school of terracotta and classical architecture is to be found in one of the smallest of buildings: the tiny chapel of Santo Spirito in Bologna. The exquisite façade of this building is tucked away in a narrow back street. It is made up entirely of moulded and carved terracotta which successfully creates a classical composition out of a relatively small number of repeated units.

The Birth of the Modern World

The English diaper-patterned Renaissance

The origin of diaper-patterned brickwork is obscure but early examples are found across
medieval northern Europe. The technique underwent a significant revival in England,
where it became a fashionable feature of 15th- and 16th-century brickwork, a large
number of examples of which survive.

Diaper patterns or diapering is the name given to the
technique of making patterns (particularly diamond
shapes) on the surface of a wall by using headers set
at intervals in a contrasting colour from the normal
bricks. The similarity of the term to the word used in
the United States for a baby's undergarments is not
coincidental as diapers and diapering share the same
origin in the diamond–weave cloth used at the time.

It used to be said that diaper patterns were
brought to England from France but in fact French
examples are later. The earliest diaper patterns are
found in Poland and northern Germany, where the
use of this technique was widespread from an early
date. All over brick diapering was used in the square
angle-turrets and curtain walls of the castle of
Radzyn Chelminski built c. 1300 and the later castle at
Malbork. Other patterns such as bands (the entrance
archway at Reszel Castle, Poland), zig-zags
(St Stephen's Church, Tangermunde, Germany),
spirals (on the Steinthor at Brandenburg-an-der-
Hayel, Germany) and v-shapes (the church of Corpus
Christi of the Lateran Canons at Krakow, Poland) were
also employed. The technique no doubt spread to
England via the trading links established by the
Hanseatic League as so much of English brickwork did.
Early (15th century) English examples can be found on
the gatehouses of Herstmonceaux Castle; on the
tower of Tattershall Castle, Lincolnshire; the Rye
House, Hertfordshire and on the Silver Street façade
of Queens' College, Cambridge. In some cases the
foreign influence is clear: the Rye House was built for
Sir Andrew Ogard who was born in Denmark, while
records show that the contractor at Tattershall was

one Bawdin 'Docheman' (meaning German). By the Tudor period the technique had become fashionable and was widely used.

The patterns were made using bricks of a contrasting colour to those in the main part of the wall. In England they were invariably darker green or black bricks but in northern Europe lighter bricks were sometimes used. It was originally thought that these darker bricks were simply bricks that had been too close to the heat and become over-burnt resulting in a glazed surface. Such bricks would otherwise have gone to waste so it was suggested that diapering might offer a way of using them in a constructive fashion. This may sometimes have been the case, but studies of Tudor buildings such as Hampton Court have suggested that there the bricks were being deliberately coated with a glaze before firing. Whatever the method of burning the headers, deliberate or otherwise, the essence of diapering was in the laying not the making. In England a number of patterns were used. The simple diamond network was common and could vary in scale. Solitary diamonds, usually called lozenges, were also used and could occur in repeated chains vertically or horizontally. Sometimes lozenges were placed within lozenges.

There was a large number of patterns which may have had some deeper meaning or may have just been left up to the bricklayers' imagination.

Despite the large amount of work that has been done on medieval and Tudor brickwork in England, there are still remarkable gaps in our knowledge. Recent research, for instance, has suggested that brick façades were often limewashed in a red colour so that the joints became invisible, but if that was the case it is difficult to understand why the bricklayers bothered to make diaper patterns at all. We know from surviving drawings that diaper patterns were designed to be seen but how would this have been possible if they were hidden under a lime wash? Then there is the problem that many patterns are intermittent. Was this deliberate or the result of later repair? Perhaps the darkened headers only acted as a guide and the patterns were actually painted on over top. Diapering thus presents us with a example of a technique that we observe but do not fully understand and an area where there is still much research to be done.

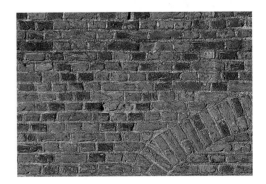

Top Hampton Court Palace (1514–1540), built for Cardinal Wolsey and heavily altered by Henry VIII.

Above First Court, St John's College, Cambridge (1511–21) showing the diamond-shaped diaper patterns and relieving arches.

English terracotta 1520–1545

The sudden appearance of a new type of decorative terracotta in England in the early 16th century was remarkable but more surprising was its rapid demise. As a style it seems to have lasted only about 25 years. From the modern point of view that may seem a long time but in the context of architectural history it was virtually overnight. As such it provides a useful example of the influence of politics on building construction.

The architecture of Tudor England is one of transition between the Gothic of the Middle Ages and the classicism of the later 17th century. It was a period when chivalry was admired and courtiers vied with each other to produce the most original buildings as symbols of their creativity and power. It was a sensibility which appeared to be very different from the humanism of the Italian courts. Yet it was almost certainly from northern Italy that craftsmen were imported in the first decade of the 16th century to produce decorative terracotta for some of the finest houses.

One of the most important was Layer Marney Tower. It was constructed between 1517 and 1525 for Henry, 1st Lord Marney (1457–1523) who was Captain of the Bodyguard first for Henry VII and then for Henry VIII. Marney rose, by virtue of his talents, to be a Privy Councillor, Knight of the Garter, High Steward of the Duchy of Cornwall and Lord Privy Seal. In the later years of his life he had started to build a great house for himself and his family, with a church beside it, and on his death his son, John continued the building work. Unfortunately he too died in 1525, leaving only the gatehouse and church complete. Thus what was meant to be the gate tower of a massive house stood rather incongruously alone.

Layer Marney Tower as it stands today is eight storeys high. The two main rooms over the gate itself are each two storeys high, but the turrets at each side contain intermediate floors. It is built of brick made locally, presumably on land owned by the Marney family. However, what makes the building remarkable is its terracotta detail. This includes the delicate window tracery and the decoration of the parapet. The terracotta is buff-coloured to resemble stone, which is rare in this area and correspondingly expensive. Even as terracotta it cannot have been cheap.

More remarkable still is Henry's tomb, which survives intact in the church he had constructed beside the house. It is made from large pieces of cream terracotta like the house but of exceptional quality and it remains one of the finest examples ever produced in England.

Layer Marney is not alone in using terracotta of this type and style. Other examples include early ranges of Hampton Court Palace, Sutton Place near Guildford in Surrey, and a group of tombs closely related to Marney's in style, all in East Anglia. The tombs have been shown to be the work of a single group of craftsmen and more recent research has demonstrated that the Marney moulds were also used in London.

It seems likely that there was a small number of workshops providing all the terracotta for these works. That they were Italian in origin is highly likely, firstly because Italians are known to have supplied terracotta for Wolsey's Hampton Court Palace and secondly because of their sudden disappearance. In 1534 Henry VIII broke off relations with Rome and soon after it became illegal to employ foreign workers. Any foreign terracotta workers would have been forced to gather up their moulds and leave. The Renaissance in England was not forgotten, but a very different transformation, the Reformation, had begun.

Opposite Layer Marney Tower (1517–25).

Below left Terracotta tomb of Henry, first Lord Marney, in the church at Layer Marney.

Above The top of a turret, with moulded brick corbel-table and flamboyant terracotta crenellations.

Below The main façade of Layer Marney Tower showing its ornate terracotta window mullions.

The twisted chimney

The twisted and flamboyant moulded brick chimney is a particular feature of English architecture in the Tudor period. The addition of a chimney to a house was expensive and as such it was something to be celebrated. Indeed the number and size of chimneys in a dwelling signalled its importance.

Fire for warmth was an important part of any English dwelling, but it was also a dangerous luxury. The walls of most houses in the Middle Ages were constructed of stout timber frames infilled with wattle and daub (simply basketwork covered in mud or plaster). The buildings themselves were often roofed in thatch of reed or straw. Everything about their construction was highly flammable. In larger houses the kitchen was usually in a separate building to try to reduce the risk of it setting fire to the main house. In the house itself the fire was set in a central brazier in the middle of the largest room (the hall), the smoke escaping through a lantern in the centre of the roof or through special vents at its ends.

The earliest chimneys were in castles and grand houses. It was only with the decreasing cost of the brick that chimneys began to appear in normal dwellings. In England the brick chimney is a 16th-century innovation, often inserted on the side or in the middle of existing timber-framed buildings. The fireproof nature of brick construction made it ideal for the construction of fireplaces and chimneys. Kitchens, which previously had been housed in separate buildings, could now be attached to the house. Smoke became less of a problem and the rooms could be lower. Ceilings were often inserted in the old halls, making smaller spaces that could now be heated more effectively.

Far from attempting to conceal chimneys, in the Tudor period English owners vied with each other to produce the most outlandish examples leading to ever more exuberant ornamental brick stacks. Sadly, centuries of sulphuric acid from coal-burning fires have done irreparable damage to virtually all of these great Tudor chimney stacks. Most of those we see today are merely faithful reproductions.

Each flue in a Tudor chimney was celebrated by a separate stack (often each being in a different pattern). Hampton Court Palace has several hundred stacks. Most were built using bricks made in special moulds. Some were moulded, the designs being carefully worked out to repeat in order to reduce the

number of moulds required, but many were simply cut to shape by hand.

This style of decorative chimney design was short-lived. As the classical style became popular in the 17th century, stacks became more austere, usually being simply octagonal, round or square. Whereas the Tudor chimneys had been as tall as possible for display, those of the 17th and 18th centuries were only as high as they needed to be and where tile replaced thatch they could be lower still. By the 18th century many chimneys were grouped into single large rectangular stacks, placed symmetrically along the ridge, sometimes grouped for architectural effect. The days of the elaborate moulded chimney were over.

Left and opposite Church of the Ascension, Kolomenskoe, near Moscow, built in 1529 to celebrate the birth of Ivan the Terrible.

Below Church of the Trinity at Khoroshevo, which has multiple tiers of brick arches termed *kokoshniki*.

The Birth of The Modern World

The isolated world of Russian medieval brickwork

Russian architecture does not fit neatly into the story of Western architecture, having few obvious precedents in the West, and through its isolation, little obvious influence on Western traditions. However, this very isolation resulted in an architecture that developed a rich language of its own. It was one which relied heavily on brick.

The early inhabitants of what is now Russia had a strained relationship with the Byzantine world. In the 10th century the Kievan Rus accepted Christianity as its official religion and this became the Russian Orthodox Church. Most buildings of this period were undoubtedly made of timber and indeed continued to be so, but archaeological evidence suggests that at least some of the early churches copied Byzantine building techniques and plans. Sadly, nothing survives to suggest how closely the very earliest resembled Byzantine churches in external form. The church of the Tithe (989–96) at Kiev was razed to the ground by the Mongols in 1240, but excavations in the early 20th century showed that its walls were made of *opus mixtum*, that is of stone alternating with flat brick lacing courses laid in lime mortar mixed with brick dust, a technique that Byzantine builders had themselves inherited from the Romans. Elsewhere solid brick walls were used. The Byzantine bricklaying technique of using flat bricks and wide joints can be seen in the cathedral of St Sophia at Kiev (c.1050). The recessed brick technique was used in the 12th-century church of the Saviour, at Berestovo, Kiev, and the Byzantine use of decorative patterns was similarly copied.

Yet for all the similarities in building techniques, by the 11th century the early Russian churches had already began to mark themselves out from their Byzantine forebears in external appearance, most notably by the use of towers. The Russian churches were covered in towers and domes of all shapes and sizes. The walls were thick and relatively solid. Most of the light in the interior thus came from the windows in the drums in the roof, dimly illuminating the rich frescoes within. This was an architecture that had a continual development from the Middle Ages to its highpoint in the late 17th century.

Nowhere can the central importance of the tower in Russian architecture be more clearly seen than in the church of the Ascension at Kolomenskoe. It was constructed by Vasilii III in 1529 in a commanding position overlooking a bend in the Moscow River. The centre of a larger palace complex, the church of Kolomenskoe consists of a single hollow shaft of space, square on plan, with high windows in the conical vault above. Its walls are 2.5–3m thick and rest on massive brick cross vaults reinforced with iron tie rods. The internal space is surprisingly small in area (a square 8.5m a side) but very tall

Above Church of the
Decapitation of St John the
Baptist at Diakovo, near
Kolomenskoe, 1547. The
architect was probably Barma,
who designed St Basil's in
Moscow.

(58m high from the ground to the cross) and is
reached by three sets of stairs leading to an external
platform. The central tapering spire or *shatyor* is
made of brick with limestone ribs and dressings
and sits over three layers of ogival *kokoshniki* or
tiers of arches.

Close to the church of the Ascension is the
equally extraordinary church of the Decapitation of
St John the Baptist. Here too there is a central tower,
whose walls enclose the central internal space,
vaulted in brick and this time covered by a timber
onion dome. In this case, though, the tower is
presented in a more traditional arrangement
surrounded by others, each enclosing a single chapel.
As at the church of the Ascension, the church of
the Decapitation is built of rectangular bricks
(270 x 130–160 x 80mm) set in 25-mm lime mortar
joints and whitewashed.

The towers on the church of the Decapitation
and the central *shatyor* of the church of the
Ascension both sit on tiers of arches called *kokoshniki*.
These strange arrays of blank arches seem to have
developed from the multiple arched gable ends
which characterized early Russian churches.
They begin to appear in the 15th century and

by the 16th have become a standard feature
of Muscovite architecture. Many tiers of arches would
be stacked up on each other, an effect that can be
seen most markedly at church of the Trinity
at Khoroshevo.

Another common feature was the corbel table. This
can be seen in the façade of one of the most dramatic
of Russian churches ever constructed, the Cathedral of
the Intercession of the Moat (popularly known as
St Basil's) in Red Square, Moscow (1555–61). Corbel
tables were used from the 12th century and seem
to have been adopted directly from the Western
medieval tradition. In St Basil's the brick is exposed
although heavily repaired. The bricks are large
(300 x 140 x 70mm) and set in 25–30-mm joints.
The ornament, usually made from moulded brick,
is so rich that there are few panels of flat brick but
where they do exist Flemish bond is used.

The progression to ever denser and more complex
ornamentation reached its apogee in the late 17th
century with works such as the church of the Trinity at
Ostankino. This church was built for the Cherkassiki
family on their estate north of Moscow between 1678
and 1683 by Pavel Potekhin, a master builder. Potekhin
used moulded and cut brick, limestone and lime

render to produce his detailed polychromatic designs, employing for normal walling 300 x 135 x 80-mm basic rectangular bricks set in fine 12-mm joints to no particular bonding pattern.

Just as Potekhin's brickwork represents a high point of the art it also marks an end. The 18th century saw the rise of a new architecture inspired by Western European Baroque. Brick would still be employed but covered by render. In the most fashionable parts of Russian society brick was required but not to be seen.

Left St Basil's, more correctly called the Cathedral of the Intercession of the Moat, Red Square, Moscow.

Above and above left The church of the Trinity at Ostankino (1678–83) is a virtuoso display of decorative brickwork.

The fall of the Timurid Empire and the rise of Bukhara

In the East, between 1500 and 1530, the Timurid Empire was divided into three. The new states formed were the Shaybunaid Uzbek Empire in Central Asia, the Safavid Empire in Persia and the Moghul Empire in India. The Uzbeks, under Muhammed Shaybani Khan (1500–1510) controlled an area which included Kazakhstan, Uzbekistan and Afghanistan. Under the rule of the enlightened Shaybanids and in particular Abdullah Khan II, Bukhara became the major mercantile city of Central Asia. The wealth that flowed in financed a great building campaign that endowed the city with a wealth of splendid mosques, madrassah and markets, many of which have survived intact to this day.

The largest building complex in Bukhara from this period was constructed around the existing Kalan Minaret (see page 114). The old mosque beside it was demolished and replaced with the much grander Kalan Friday Mosque (completed in 1514). Twenty-one years later the Mir-I Arab Madrassah was constructed

Mosque and the Mir-I Arab Madrassah are very large buildings with grand symmetrical plans. Gone are the intricate bonding patterns that had enlivened the Tomb of the Saminids. Instead architecture is made up of bold spaces and large masses.

to face it, forming an urban square. This complex is collectively known as the Pa-yi Kalan. The spacing of ornament on the façade of the Mir-I Arab Madrassah is typical of buildings of the period. The central entrance is richly decorated, not with bricks or mosaic but with large glazed tiles. However, the sides and rear of the outside of the building are exposed brickwork, with some areas plastered. The inside is similar. Tiles are employed for key areas but much of the interior is finished in white plaster. Here, as elsewhere in Bukhara in this period, the emphasis changed from a concentration on the decorative scheme to an obsession with scale. Both the Kalan Friday

Nor was this great revival of building construction in 16th-century Bukhara limited to sacred buildings. The rise in prosperity of the merchant also gave rise to new building works, this time in the form of covered markets. Much of the commercial activity in Bukhara was transacted in street markets and the streets were laid out roughly in a grid pattern. Crossroads were thus particularly important and the *taqs* were built at these points. They consist of covered arcades with shops on either side leading to a central domed hall at the meeting point of the four streets. The exact plan of the shops off these halls differed according to the goods being sold. The simplest surviving example is the Taqi Sorrafan (Moneychanger's Dome) which

consists of a central octagonal dome formed by four brick arches. The more complicated and much larger Taq-i Zargan (Goldsmith's Dome) is similar but has a dome made by eight intersecting arches. In both cases the brick domes were constructed on elaborate formwork. Each is only single shell but the arches act like ribs in a vault and do much of the work, particularly during construction. The webs between the arches are laid in horizontal courses, the outside being covered by large flat fired clay tiles to help shed the water. The external appearance of the structures is thus highly deceptive.

Opposite The Great or
Kalan Mosque (15th century),
Bukhara, Uzbekistan. This
130 x 80-m mosque is one of
the largest constructed in
Central Asia. It is directly
opposite the Mir-i Arab
Madrasa.

Above Mir-i Arab Madrasa
(1535–36), Bukhara, Uzbekistan.
A classic example of a madrasa,
a public school for teaching the
doctrine of the Koran and
Islamic law. The system was
established by Nizam at Mulk
(1018–92). The façade of the
Mir-i Arab Madrasa has been
recently restored.

The Birth of the Modern World

Safavids and the Persian Renaissance

The Safavids came to power under Shah Ismail, conquering Iraq in 1507, but they were continually at war with the Ottomans until the reign of Shah Abbas the Great (1587–1629). He settled with the Ottomans and re-organized the army. After a series of successful campaigns he succeeding in winning back all the lands that had been lost and in recapturing Iraq. However, his real successes were in domestic policy. The resulting stability and prosperity enabled him to build a court in his capital Isfahan that was even the envy of Europe.

Isfahan had been the capital of Persia under the Seljuks in the 11th and 12th centuries. In the early 17th century many of the buildings from that period

were still standing. Shah Abbas relocated the centre of the city to the south-west, laying out palaces and building great gardens and avenues down to the river. At the heart of his new city he built a great rectangular square (the *maidan*) 512m long and 159m wide. This was called the *Naqsh-I Jahan* (Design of the World). Built between 1590 and 1595, it was originally conceived of as a grand space for ceremonial and state displays, but in a second phase in 1602 the sides were developed to incorporate two storeys of shops in long covered brick arcades, with further arcades of shops running behind. During the day the square itself was also used for trading, but it was designed to be multi-

functional, doubling up as a military parade ground and as a ground for the Shah's favourite sport: polo. Architecturally this great square, covering over 8 hectares, was larger than any comparable space in Europe and unique in having façades that were constructed to form a single unified whole. As such it was often mentioned by the foreigners who flocked to Abbas's enlightened court.

The *maidan* was linked to the old city by a new covered bazaar which is important for its scale and the complexity of its brick vaulting. This market consisted of hundreds of brick vaults stretching not only the 2 kilometres north to the old Friday Mosque and the original city centre, but also providing a large market immediately north of the *maidan* itself. The bazaar contained shops, baths, factories and caravanserai allowing merchants to trade in comfort all year round. The entrance to the bazaar was in the centre of the north side of the *maidan*. Three other buildings occupied the centres of the other three sides: the great mosque, the smaller Lutfullah Mosque and the entrance gateway to the Shah's palace, the Ali Qapu.

Opposite the Lutfullah Mosque is the Ali Qapu, an extraordinary building which acted as the window of the palace and gardens behind onto the ordinary life of the square beneath. It started as an atrium in 1590 and gradually built up in a complex series of vertically stacked halls and chambers . On the front of these facing the square a balcony was constructed and covered by a towering canopy.

The great Mosque that formed the focus of the square was a huge structure, which reports say required 18,000,000 bricks and 475,000 tiles. Both interior and exterior are covered in tiles made using the *haft rangi* method, where all seven colours are put on and fired at once.

Bridges

The last surviving parts of the Shah's vision were on the river itself. Crossing the river was crucial to the success of the merchant city. The Shah and his successors did not just build ordinary bridges but created massive yet elegant structures that allowed the travellers to cross the river without descending from the level of the avenues down the sides of the banks. These bridges are two-storey high viaducts. On the top level, the width of the road allowed caravans to pass, beneath a second pedestrian passage contained shops and tea rooms as a refuge from the camels and horses above.

The first bridge was erected in 1597–98 by Abbas's general Allahvardi Khan. Called the Si-o Se Pol (the bridge of thirty three arches), it is over 300m long. It stood at the bottom of the main avenue in Isfahan.

A second much larger and grander example, the Khwazi Bridge was built downstream in 1650. It contains large sluice gates and is part dam, part bridge. Like the older bridge it too had several levels and included shops. Here there were six pavilions. The upper road went between these down the centre of the upper level. On either side facing outwards, covered arcades allowed pedestrians to cross the river without facing the dangers of caravans passing down the middle.

Bridges with houses or shops were common in Europe in the Middle Ages but tended to be stone with timber-framed upper sections. As rivers in towns in Europe acted as open sewers, both bridges and buildings facing onto the river tended to be less desirable properties. Because of this, inhabited bridges in Europe tended to be ramshackle affairs with little architectural merit. The bridges of Isfahan thus stand out as being designed as great buildings

Top The Lutfullah Mosque (1603–19), Isfahan, Iran. Built on the side of the *maidan*, the entrance portal features an exquisite *muquarnas* vault.

Above and opposite The Great or Shah Mosque (1611–30), Isfahan. The dome is 52m high and double-shelled, the external one rising 14m above the interior.

The entrance to the Lutfullah Mosque (1603–1619) takes its name from Sheikh Lutfullah Maisi al-Amili, a distinguished scholar and teacher who came to Isfahan at Abbas's behest and took up residence there. Its entrance portal is richly decorated in large multi-coloured glazed tiles and features an important *muquarnas* vault.

Muquarnas vaults developed in the 10th century as a development of the squinch (the arches employed to carry a dome over the corner of a rectangular space). It was discovered that the face of the squinch did not carry any load and could thus be safely carved into elaborate shapes. Sometimes these were made out of brick but more often they were constructed from timber and plaster covered with tiles.

in their own right, conceived as symmetrical structures in keeping with Islamic design principles.

The last of the Safavid Shahs lost power in 1722 when Isfahan fell to Afghan invaders. For a century, Isfahan had been one the most important centres in the Islamic World, described as the 'Pearl of Islam'. It was said that if you had seen Isfahan you had seen 'half the world'. With the fall of the Safavids

the Islamic world turned its back on brick as a facing material. Later Islamic buildings would still be built of brick but would tend to be faced in other materials. The Taj Mahal is a brick building with a double dome but is faced in marble. More commonly brick structures were covered in tiles or render. Brick had ceased to be a respectable finishing material.

Opposite, top and following pages Khwazi Bridge (1650), Isfahan, Iran. Part dam, part bridge, the Khwazi Bridge has sluices that allow the water levels to be controlled. The pavilions were designed to hold tea rooms although they are presently empty.

Above Si-o Se Pol (the bridge of thirty-three arches), constructed between 1597 and 1598, is one of the busiest in Isfahan. The lower section still contains tea rooms.

The Great Wall of China

The Great Wall of China we see today predominantly dates from the Ming Period, but the Wall itself has a much longer and more complex history. Indeed it would be more accurate to use the plural for over the ages many different Great Walls protected the north of China from invasions from Mongolia. The earliest were constructed in the Spring, Autumn and Warring States periods (7th and 6th centuries BC). These were linked and greatly extended by the first emperor of China, Qin Shihuang (259–210 BC) who constructed a wall some 5,000km long, usually referred to as the First Great Wall. This wall was strengthened, extended and rebuilt in the Han Dynasty, forming the Second Great Wall. The rebuilding under the Ming Dynasty is correctly called the Third Great Wall. The earlier walls had been made of the nearest materials to hand and were often little more than mud. The Ming Wall was a much more substantial structure made predominantly of brick or stone.

The Ming Wall stretched from Bohai Bay in the east to Jiayugan Pass in the west. There is a tendency to imagine it as a continuous single wall, but in fact it contained many branches and loops where more than one wall guarded a particular pass so that the total

length was far greater than a line from one point to the other (see the map on page 71).

Where possible the wall uses the terrain and is built over the top of the steepest ridges and mountains. This made construction extremely difficult but had great advantages in terms of defence. Its height and width also varied with the terrain. When it perched on top of a ridge with a sheer drop on either side it tended to be narrow and only 2–3m tall, but on more open terrain it was between 7 and 8m high. The width also varied. The Ming Wall was made with battered (tapered) walls for strength and was thus wider at the bottom that at the top. At the branch at Badaling, guarding one of the passes to Beijing, it was 6.5m wide at the base and 5.8 metres along the top. In other places it was only a few

metres wide and in certain places along the steepest mountain ridges narrows to a single wall. Guard towers were placed at regular intervals, their doors high up above the top of the wall. They are entered by wooden ladders that could be removed in time of attack. The walls acted as elevated roads between these towers.

Even in mountain areas the Ming Walls were commonly made out of brick. Along the length the bricks vary in size. Some were very large measuring 600 x 240 x 120mm but more conventional bricks of 440 x 210 x 160mm, 450 x 220 x 200mm and 370 x 180 x 100mm were also used. Those at Simitai near Beijing are of 370 x 180 x 100mm laid in 20-mm joints. Bricks were only used for the outside of the

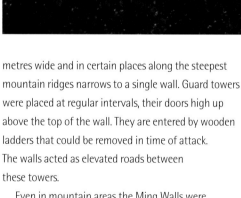

walls, the interior being filled with whatever material was to hand. In the mountains this would be rubble while in other places it would commonly be rammed earth.

Most of the bricks for the Great Wall were made and laid by the army. It was standard practice in the Ming period to stamp each brick with the date and the maker's mark. Most of these are the names and numbers of the military units involved.

Restoration of the walls has led to investigation of the techniques involved both in their construction and in the process of brickmaking. Bricks for the restorations are burnt using 'horsehoe kilns', which are claimed to be similar to those used by the original builders. These are a form of simple bonfire kiln.

The bricks were burnt using a reduction technique where oxygen was excluded during firing, resulting in brown or grey bricks. The bricks were then laid in lime mortar mixed with rice gruel, which is thought to have given it greater strength. It is certainly true that although the wall has crumbled in many parts, it has survived remarkably well and remains one of the most outstanding structures ever built, attracting many thousands of visitors every year.

Opposite below A stamped brick. Bricks were commonly stamped with the name and number of the army unit responsible for their manufacture, allowing faults to be traced back to the maker.

Above and opposite top The Great Wall of China dates from the Ming Period (1368–1644). Much of the work was carried out under Yung-Lo between 1403 and 1424 when he also moved the capital back to Peking.

CHAPTER FIVE

ENLIGHTENMENT IDEALS 1650–1800

In the 17th and 18th centuries the countries of northern Europe became more powerful than ever before. Through trade and imperialism they gained an influence in every continent across the globe. In Britain new political ideas were forged alongside radical changes in manufacturing processes and the beginnings of the Industrial Revolution. In the New World, the American colonies had created their own architectural heritage. New techniques were introduced into brickmaking and bricklaying which allowed increasingly complex forms to be made with accuracy and precision, in order to meet the increasing demands of the latest fashions.

The Low Countries, a term which generally covers Flanders (much of which is in modern Belgium) and the Netherlands, had been a centre of brickmaking and bricklaying throughout the Middle Ages. This chapter opens with a brief examination of this tradition and how it influenced 18th-century architecture at home and abroad, particularly in the form of the shaped gable, a motif that originated in this area and spread across Europe. An alternative style of brick architecture was propagated in France which mixed stone and brick in a closer accordance with the rules of classical architecture as set down in various architectural treatises written in France and Italy from the Renaissance onwards.

Both of these architectural styles called for increasingly precise standards of brickmaking. The problems involved in reconstructing medieval methods have already been touched on, but the situation is much simpler for this period because for the first time there is a wealth of written sources. Some of the earliest relate to brickmaking in England. Early in the 17th century the writer Francis Bacon had called for a study of the various techniques used by manufacturing trades which he saw as being conservative and inefficient. Bacon argued that if these techniques could be written down and studied by the great minds of the day, rather than kept as jealously guarded trade secrets, then improvements could be made that would be for the good of all. Bacon never managed to make such a study himself, but it later became one of the stated aims of the Royal Society, founded in 1660. It is thanks to various of its members that we have some of the earliest written descriptions of both brickmaking and bricklaying. Four sections look at the 17th-century developments in Britain and how the improvements in brickmaking and the ideas of style from the Low Countries and France

changed brick architecture in England in this period. The use of brick in the construction of new types of fortification that had been developed in the Renaissance is also briefly discussed.

The chapter then turns to developments in 17th-century Colonial North America. There the early settlers generally sought to construct homes resembling as closely as possible those from home, and each region soon developed its own vernacular. Much research has been done on brickmaking in these early years and it seems clear that although by the middle of the century some areas had developed active brickmaking centres, the shortage of skilled craftsmen (both brickmakers and bricklayers) always remained a problem. One thing is clear, however, that in the early years, at least, very few bricks were imported. Where they were used they were made locally. Many fine examples of early Colonial brickwork remain.

While the first half of the chapter concentrates on the 17th century, the second half of the chapter looks at the 18th. The same kind of thinking that had motivated the Royal Society to investigate the trades subsequently gave rise to the great Enlightenment encyclopaedias. Some of the earliest of these were compiled in England, but undoubtedly the finest were French and it is in French books on the trades that we find some of the earliest illustrations of kilns and brickmaking. Despite this, it is in England, and particularly in the construction of London – which expanded rapidly in this period – that the most obvious advances are made in brickmaking and bricklaying. The first of these was a new way of burning bricks by mixing the clay with ashes. The second was the imposition of a strict set of building regulations that set down parameters for many aspects of building construction

and led directly to the Georgian townhouse. The third was the perfection of rubbed and gauged brickwork. The fourth was the emergence of a new type of architectural terracotta called Coade stone.

London became a city of brick. The material became so fashionable that it was even used for country houses such a Holkham Hall in Norfolk. Inevitably, however, the fashion eventually changed and by the end of the century England turned to a technique, that already pre-dominated on the continent of Europe, of covering buildings in render. Although this seemed straightforward, there were great difficulties in producing renders that stayed on the brick walls beneath and the search for alternatives produced a number of innovations which were later to become useful in the 19th century when it was realized that they would make stronger waterproof mortars.

The chapter closes with one of the greatest Enlightenment architects, Thomas Jefferson, American President and author of the first draft of the Declaration of Independence. There seem to have been few things to which Jefferson could not turn his hand and his appreciation of architecture was no doubt influenced by the long period he spent in France. He oversaw the brickmaking and construction of his own house, Monticello, which he continually changed and adapted over his lifetime. But it was the construction of the University of Virginia which most successfully embodied his political, architectural, social and intellectual ideals in a single composition. Although it was not finished until the early decades of the 19th century, with its clean lines and immaculate brickwork it perfectly captures the atmosphere of the 18th century and its Enlightenment ideals.

Bedford Square, London, England

Cumberland Terrace, London, England

Brouwersgracht, Amsterdam, Netherlands

Groombridge Place, Kent, England

Tilbury Fort, Essex, England

Bacon's Castle, Virginia, USA

St Luke's Church, Isle of Wight County, Virginia

University of Virginia, Charlottesville, USA

The Old South, Boston, Mass., USA

Townhouse, Amsterdam, Netherlands

Kew Palace, Surrey, England

Place des Vosges, Paris, France

Old State House, Boston, Mass., USA

University of Virginia, Charlottesville, USA

William and Mary College, Williamsburg, Virginia

Bulmer Brickworks, Suffolk, England

Holkham Hall, Norfolk, England

Brick and the shaped gable in northern Europe

Renaissance humanism in Italy encouraged a concern for understanding and then re-interpreting the rules that governed the design of Greek and Roman architecture. Renaissance Italians saw themselves as rebuilding a new Rome. Not surprisingly, Protestant northern Europe had a much more complex relationship with antiquity. Perhaps nowhere was this more conspicuously evident than in the elaborate designs of gables that came to dominate northern architecture in the 16th and 17th centuries.

The Low Countries (Holland and Flanders) were major centres of brick building in the 16th, 17th and 18th centuries. The Dutch had developed a highly sophisticated brickmaking industry using huge kilns capable of firing over 500,000 bricks at a time. In the neighbourhood of Leiden in the 17th century, for instance, there were 30 kilns, each burning 600,000 bricks and fired between three and five times a year. It has been estimated that the total annual Dutch production exceeded 200 million bricks a year. In towns building in timber was forbidden. All new houses were constructed of brick and brick-paved roads became increasingly common. Dutch bricks were exported to neighbouring countries and to the West Indies.

While most Dutch houses were constructed wholly of brick, it was used in conjunction with stone for larger Dutch buildings. Only the most lavish were constructed with façades made entirely out of stone. The most common method of construction on prestigious buildings was to employ stone for decorative elements and use brick for the wall areas between. Thus the façades of the wealthy were bichromatic, the white decorative elements standing out against a darker background. In towns the houses had only narrow street façades and long deep plans as they had done in the Middle Ages and following medieval precedent the presence on the street was announced by prominent brick gables. The development of these gables into a

Subsequent outlandish shaped gables can be found on the Metselaerhuis (1526) and Vrijeschippershuis (1531) in Ghent, the Wewershuis (c.1541) in Antwerp and the Griffie in Bruges (1534–37). However, all of these examples were built in stone. Most innovations in style take time to move down the social scale. By the late 1530s examples of shaped gables were already beginning to appear in brick with stone dressings.

Four books were to have a significant influence in promoting the use of scrolled decoration and the type of ornamentation that accompanied shaped gables in northern Europe. These were *Trumphe d'Anvers* by either Cornelis Floris or Pieter Coecke, published in Antwerp in 1550; Floris's *Veeldeley Niewe Inventien*

Above Illustrations showing the development of the gable in Amsterdam townhouses from A. W. Weissman, *Het Amsterdamsche Woonhuis* (1885).

Opposite Townhouse with decorative shaped gables, Brouwersgracht, Amsterdam, Netherlands.

complex set of shapes and patterns is a defining feature of the northern European style architecture of the 16th and 17th centuries which is often called Northern Mannerism.

Shaped and scrolled stone gables first appeared in the Low Countries around 1520. The earliest identified use of the motif is in the gables of the extension added to the Palais de Savoie (now seat of the *Gerechstof* or Courts of Justice) in Mechelen in Brabant built for Margaret of Austria in 1517. Emperor Maximilian I (1459–1519) acquired the Low Countries through his marriage to Mary of Burgundy in 1477. He made Margaret stadholder of the Netherlands in 1507 after the death of her brother Philip the Fair through her young nephew Charles, who had been born in Ghent and became titular ruler.

van Antycksche Sepultueren (Antwerp, 1557); Jan Vredeman de Vries's *Architectura* (Antwerp, 1563) and Wendel Dietterlin of Strasbourg's *Architectura*, which appeared in the late 1590s. Floris's works showed a type of strapwork ornament that was widely copied. The influence of this on the gable designs in de Vries's book are immediately apparent.

The most obvious examples of the sort of designs that these books encouraged can be seen in the development of gables in Amsterdam townhouses surviving from the period 1600–1800 and in buildings such as the Vleeshal, Haarlem (1602–03). In the latter the brick is used more openly to complement the stone. Corner stones (quoins) and window mullions are picked out in stone which is also used in horizontal decorative stripes to break up the gable and façade into horizontal

bands. Later Amsterdam house façades tended to use less stone and more brick. The horizontal stripes disappeared and the centre section of the gable became elongated into a neck.

In Holland the shaped gable in its various guises remained popular up until the beginning of the 19th century, but the shaped brick and stone gables had an influence well beyond the Netherlands. Perhaps the two most notable buildings to use the motif beyond its borders were the Great Arsenal in Gdansk and the magnificent Frederiksborg Slot in Denmark. Both were started in 1602 and were designed by Netherlanders. The Arsenal was designed by Abraham van den Blocke and completed by 1605. The Frederiksborg Slot (Castle) took about 20 years to

finish and was on a much larger scale. Built for Christian II, it has survived largely intact except for a fire in the 19th century that destroyed most of the interiors. Like the Arsenal, it is a brilliant exercise in Netherlandish Mannerist composition, combining elements of romantic castle design with delicately drawn gables. It too is attributed to designers from the Netherlands, this time Hans I, Hans II and Laurens II van Steenwinckel, aided by Caspar Boegendt.

The influence of the scrolled gable also played an important part in English architecture of the 17th century although there the direct involvement of Netherlandish architects is less certain. Perhaps the earliest English examples are the stone gables on

the roofs of Kirby Hall in Northamptonshire, built between 1575 and 1583. Many, like those at Wollaton Hall, Northamptonshire (also in stone), were clearly inspired directly by books. From drawings by Inigo Jones and Robert Smythson dated 1616-17 and 1619, it is known that brick gables had begun to appear in London in the second decade of the 17th century, but the most notable surviving example, Kew Palace, dates from the 1630s. By that time, the English seem to have dropped the use of stone mouldings, building the gables entirely in brick. Examples of decorative gables are still found in early 18th-century small houses in rural areas.

Above Jan Vredeman de Vries, *Architectura* (Antwerp, 1563), plate 146. One of the books that influenced the forms of gables used in northern Europe.

Opposite Vleeshal, Haarlem, Netherlands (1602–03).

Above right and below Stepped gables, Haarlem, Netherlands.

Following pages Frederiksborg Slot (Castle), Denmark (1602–22).

Brick and stone classicism in France

It is a generally accepted convention of architectural composition that the corners of buildings should be made from materials as strong or stronger than the wall planes they bound . For instance, flint walls are bounded by brick, soft brick walls are surrounded by stone and the corners of rubble walls are finished in ashlar (smooth rectangular dressed stone). The harder materials enable the builder to produce a sharp corner which would not be possible in the softer wall material and protect the edge of the wall against erosion from weathering or accidental damage. When the joints around the corner stones are exaggerated, they are called quoins. If the stone or flint is a different colour from the stone or brick which it bounds, a framing effect is created. Its migration to northern Europe was gradual. Although examples could be found throughout northern Europe by the end of the 17th century it was particularly common in France.

In the Middle Ages most French buildings were timber-framed with lath and plaster infill. Brick was only used to build whole buildings in particular regions (such as around Toulouse) and even there it was generally restricted to the houses of the wealthy. It was used for infilling between the timbers (when it is called brick nogging) but much of that which remains was probably a later replacement for earlier less permanent materials. The architectural historian Jean-Marie Pérouse de Montclos has shown how a house built at the end of the 15th century for the merchant Pierre Du Puy in Tours had both an elaborate brick staircase and a façade that had stepped gables. In Paris the Maison Coeur is one of the earliest brick buildings. Built between 1436 and 1451, it has been much altered since. Like the house in Tours, it uses brick panels strengthened with stone at the edges and the remains of diaper patterns can still be seen on the upper storey. However, it was only in the late 16th century that the technique of using brick and stone to make two-tone classical façades became popular.

The Château de Vallery constructed between 1548 and 1549 had all the characteristics of the new style, with a tall roof, and a façade of brick with prominent stone quoins and stone window surrounds. Illustrations of the building were published in Jacques Androuet Du Cerceau's *Les plus excellents bastiments de France* (1576–1579) and it may well have been from this source that the style was spread across France. Androuet Du Cerceau's son Baptiste may have been involved in the building of the most influential example of brick and stone architecture: the Place Royale (or, as it is now known, the Place des Vosges) constructed between 1605 and 1612.

The two-tone brick and stone classicism prospered in the following decades. Stone still predominated for those that could afford it; brick and stone were an acceptable alternative. Thus at Vaux-le-Vicomte, Nicholas Fouquet faced his magnificent château entirely in stone but constructed the ranges of outbuildings in the brick and stone of the new fashion. But apart from the Place Royale, perhaps the most influential brick and stone structure was Louis XIII's hunting lodge at Versailles, built between 1623 and 1624, which became the centrepiece of the later expansion of the palace under Louis XIV in the late 17th century. Paris was one of the great cultural centres of Europe and as such attracted visitors from all over the world. They included English architects like Sir Christopher Wren and his patrons in the 17th century, and in the 18th century American travellers like Thomas Jefferson, ensuring that French brick and stone architecture had an influence long after it had gone out of fashion in its native land.

Opposite, top and above left Place Royale (now Place des Vosges), Paris, built between 1605 and 1615.

Above right Maison Coeur, Rue des Archives, Paris (1436–51).

The rise of the bricklayer's art in 17th-century England

In 1678 Joseph Moxon, printer, official globe-maker to the King and Fellow of the Royal Society, started publishing the first Do-It-Yourself manual on the building crafts in monthly instalments entitled *Mechanick Exercises or the Doctrine of Handy-Works*. Using detailed descriptions and lavish illustrations, he set out the tools and techniques of the various building craftsmen. In so doing he was controversially revealing for the first time to any who cared to purchase a copy, the hitherto carefully guarded secrets or 'mysteries' of the bricklayer's art.

For modern historians studying the history of building construction Moxon's work has proved invaluable, but in their own day Moxon's pamphlets were not an immediate commercial success. In 1680 he collected together those that had already been prepared and republished them as a book which covered carpentry, ironmongery and joinery. Bricklaying was only added in a later edition in 1700.

The picture that Moxon painted of the world of the bricklayer in the late 17th century is revealing. For a start, he dealt with plastering, bricklaying and roof-tiling under one heading. In this period in England it

seems that these were crafts that were often carried out by the same contractor, although in the larger cities both plastering and tiling were gradually becoming separate crafts in their own right. Most bricklayers in the capital, for instance, concentrated on laying bricks and in London at this time there was more than enough bricklaying work to go around.

Mechanick Exercises details the different types of bricks available, the ways of mixing mortar and the methods of setting out more complicated work such as mouldings and arches. It also contains details of how to determine the correct thicknesses of walls and

depths of foundations. The detailed engravings show the tools that bricklayers used. Most would be familiar to a modern bricklayer. The trowel, for instance, is similar to the Roman one which had been in use in Europe throughout the Middle Ages. Likewise, the weight and line and the set square have remained virtually unchanged today. There are also implements used for specialist work which are now uncommon, such as the rubbing stone used in rubbed and gauged work (see pages 190–91) and there are others like the brick axe (used for cutting bricks in place of the modern bolster-chisel) which have disappeared altogether.

Bricklayers in this period were normally trained by serving a seven-year apprenticeship, although the guilds of late 17th-century England were no longer powerful enough to ensure that all those practising a craft had done so. Most English bricklayers were male, but that was not invariably the case. The records of the Tylers' and Bricklayers' Company in London list ten

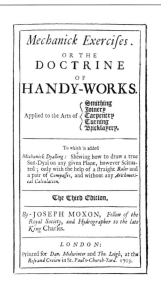

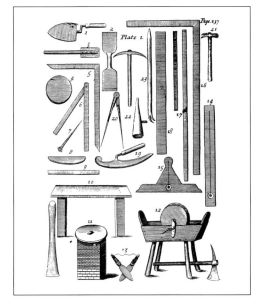

female apprentices between 1680 and 1780 and at least one husband and wife partnership operating the 1690s, but these seem to have been the exceptions.

In general, 17th-century England saw a great improvement in the quality of bricklaying. In the 16th century few walls had been laid in consistent bonding patterns. Where they were, English bond had predominated. In the 1630s, starting with buildings like Kew Palace, bricks were increasingly laid in Flemish bond with fine cut brick mouldings and shaped gables inspired by Dutch and continental architecture. With the growing demand for closer joints and better brickwork, bricklayers began to look for better bricks that were more consistent in shape and could be laid closer together.

Opposite Kew Palace, Kew, Surrey (1631).

Above left Frontispiece and plate showing bricklayer's tools from the 1703 edition of Joseph Moxon's *Mechanick Exercises or the Doctrine of Handy-Works*.

Above Kew Palace, detail of the façade showing the elaborately carved brickwork.

Refinements in brickmaking

Moxon's work on bricklaying has already been noted. Another Fellow of the Royal Society, John Houghton, wrote a report on brickmaking, providing perhaps the earliest written description of the techniques employed in England at the time.

John Houghton was an apothecary who dealt in tea, coffee and chocolate. In 1680, he became a Fellow of the Royal Society which had been founded in London in 1660 to study science (or, as it was then known, 'experimental philosophy'). From the beginning its members (or 'Fellows') took an interest in the trades and the ways they might be improved. Houghton's *Collection of Letters for the Improvement of Trades*, published in parts between 1681 and 1683, was an example of this kind of study and contained a detailed description of brickmaking at Ebbisham in Surrey based on the experiences of a workman there. In 1692 Houghton started publishing a weekly newsletter giving stock prices, confusingly entitled *A Collection for Improvement of Husbandry and Trades*. Each issue carried a short article on a different aspect of trade and between November 1693 and January 1694 these

again concentrated on brick, adding some new material and repeating much of the content of the previous *Letters*.

Two refinements in brickmaking appear for the first time in Houghton's descriptions. The first was the stock, a piece of wood which was nailed to the bench and which the mould fitted neatly over. Early stocks were plain boards, although in the late 18th century they were shaped to produce an indentation in the middle of the brick which in England is called a 'frog'. The term is thought to derive from the indentation in a horse's hoof which carried the same name. The second innovation was the wooden pallet board.

In the method Houghton describes, which is still used today, the clay is thrown into the mould which has previously been dusted with sand. A wooden bat

termed a 'strike' is then used to removed the excess clay. Next the brickmaker lifts the mould off the bench turning the brick out onto a wooden pallet as he does so. Finally the bricks are transported to the drying ground. In the 17th century this was done a few bricks at a time but later special barrows were introduced.

Before the invention of pallets, the brickmaker would hand the whole mould with the brick still inside it to an assistant who would take it to the drying ground and tip it out. In doing so the suction from the mould often lifted the edges of the brick, producing a deformed brick. Occasionally these were tamped down by pressing the mould back onto the wet brick, creating characteristic marks on the brick known as 'sunken margins'. In this early process the brickmaker needed several

The process of moulding. Photographs taken at Bulmer Brickworks, Suffolk, England.

Top row Scooping up the correct amount of clay from the pile, throwing it into the mould, 'striking' the excess clay off the top of mould, dropping the brick out of the mould onto a pallet.

Bottom row Dusting the bricks with sand before taking them to the hacks, picking up the bricks between two pallets, placing them in the hacks.

moulds, as the assistant had to carry them away each time and the bench needed to be set up within a few yards of the drying area. In the new process, the bricks were carried between pallets. They could be carried several at a time, allowing the moulder to work in a shed some way from the drying ground. Using only one mould helped to ensure that all the bricks were identical.

While female bricklayers were uncommon, brickmaking was very much a family affair involving not just women but children as well. Throughout the 17th and 18th century in England, it was common for brickmaking families to move from site to site renting land from farmers to make bricks. The parents moulded the bricks while the children trod the clay underfoot to remove the stones and carried the bricks from the moulding bench to the places where they were stacked to dry. This practice only ceased with the introduction of laws against child labour in the 19th century.

Groombridge Place and architecture in England before Wren

While architects were well-established in Italy, they were a new innovation in England in the 17th century where the term was still used interchangeably with surveyor. Surveyors had risen to prominence after the Reformation when large tracts of land had transferred from Church ownership to private individuals and the demarcation of boundaries became essential. The land surveyor did not of course necessarily get involved in building. Most buildings were designed by the craftsmen responsible for building them as they had been in the Middle Ages. Timber-framed buildings were designed by the master carpenter while grander stone ones were drawn out by the master mason or, in the case of brick, the master bricklayer.

By the 17th century Italian ideas about architects were beginning to appear in England, mainly through books such as Palladio's *Quattro Libri* and Serlio's *Five Books of Architecture*. The most prominent self-styled architect of the early part of the century was Inigo Jones (1573–1652).

Jones rose to prominence as a set designer for court masques. He was made Surveyor of the King's Works in 1613. Having lived in Italy, he was fluent in Italian and he was a keen follower of Palladio, many of whose buildings he had taken the trouble to visit and experience first hand. The few buildings he managed to construct for the troubled court of Charles I were brilliant exercises in Palladian design. They were constructed in brick, but faced with stone or render. Jones's chance to change architecture radically came to an end with the Civil War in 1640 when court architecture was no longer required. What Jones had done, however, was to spread the notion of architecture as something that carried social cachet and required learning.

New architects began to appear, like Roger North and Roger Pratt, who were both educated gentlemen well-versed in foreign architectural literature and designed for themselves and for friends. They were very different from the artist designers of the Italian tradition. It became quite common for a client to design a house himself according to established models and then contract a builder to put it together.

The buildings that resulted from the various types of patronage thus can be distinguished. At one end of the spectrum were simple brick buildings erected by the bricklayer to his own designs which often conformed to local traditions. Such designs tended to be conservative, preserving shaped gables, for instance, well after they had become unfashionable. The second type were buildings designed by their owners working from books or buildings that they had seen abroad. Groombridge Place in Kent was probably designed this way. It was built by its owner in a fashionable style

inspired by French and Dutch architecture of the period, but constructed in an English way.

Groombridge Place was built for Philip Packer, who was a barrister at the Middle Temple in London, a founder member of the Royal Society and a friend of John Evelyn and Sir Christopher Wren. It was almost certainly Packer who designed the house himself although Evelyn may have helped lay out the garden. Architecturally it is a mixture of the old and the new. It has a hipped roof, red brick neatly laid in Flemish bond with brick quoins and flat arches over the windows all in the latest fashion, but, the H-shaped

plan is traditional, being only one room deep.

Finally there were the buildings designed by the small number of professional architects who made their living entirely from design. They were often from a building trade background, but were educated enough to be able to produce designs in the latest idiom. Unlike the patron trying his hand, they had a very strong understanding of the way buildings were put together. Such men, like Hugh May and John Webb were in the minority, but were growing in importance and would eventually supplant the tradesmen as designers. The most famous such architect in the England in the 17th century was Sir Christopher Wren.

Groombridge Place Kent, (c. 1670–74), built for and possibly designed by Philip Packer. The house is constructed entirely in brick with brick quoins at the corners.

Above Front view over the moat which surrounds the house.

Opposite, left Entrance façade. The porch is a later addition.

Opposite, right View down the hill to the side of the house.

Right The stable block creates a yard on one side of the house.

Enlightenment Ideals

The Great Fire of London and Sir Christopher Wren

The architecture of the late 17th century in England was changed irrevocably by a single event and one man. The event was the Great Fire of London, which started in Pudding Lane in the City on the night of 2 September 1666 and burned for four days. By the time it finally died down it had destroyed the whole of the old City inside the medieval walls including St Paul's Cathedral, 13,200 houses and 87 churches. After the Fire Sir Christopher Wren, a brilliant academic, who was at the time one of the leading scientists of the age, turned his energies to the problems of rebuilding the City, becoming in the process one of the most successful architects in English history.

Wren's contribution to the history of brickwork was twofold. Firstly he was heavily involved in the drafting of building regulations for the rebuilding of London. Secondly he was active in designing many of the great buildings of the age, creating a new architectural language of brick and training the next generation of architects and craftsmen in design practice.

The regulations laid down after the Great Fire changed the appearance of London and created an unprecedented demand for brick. Despite numerous attempts to reform building practice, London in the early 17th century had consisted of warrens of dark streets and tiny alleyways running between ramshackle medieval timber-framed buildings. It was clear in retrospect that such building methods had been responsible for the quick spread of the fire and the resulting devastation. A committee, of which Wren was a member, was therefore formed to draft new regulations. These set out the width of all streets and alleyways and determined that all buildings were to be built out of brick or stone and the

Opposite Hampton Court Palace, East range (1689–94), designed for King William III and Queen Mary II by Sir Christopher Wren (1632–1723).

Right St Benet, Upper Thames Street (also known as St Benet Paul's Wharf) (1677–83), one of the City churches built after the Fire by Wren's office.

Below top The Orangery, Hampton Court Palace.

Below bottom Rubbed and gauged niche, Hampton Court.

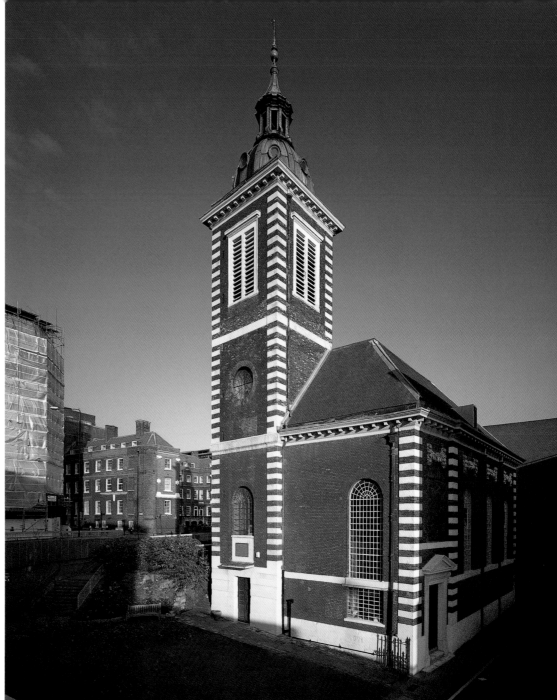

thickness of the walls and sizes of the timbers to be used in their construction.

Wren became immediately involved in the rebuilding, being appointed to design 50 new churches to replace those lost and to oversee the repair (and then redesign) of St Paul's Cathedral. In addition he was made Surveyor General of the King's Works, a post which made him the most important architect in the land and put him in charge of the maintenance and construction of all royal buildings.

Wren's architecture was heavily influenced by the 'brick and stone' style of classicism he had seen in France which he had visited in 1665. Thus many of his City churches were built in brick with prominent stone quoins at the corners. Others, like St Anne and

St Agnes, were entirely brick. Outside the city, perhaps his most adventurous exercise in this style was the new ranges he built for Hampton Court Palace for William and Mary. The accounts survive and show that the bricks for the building were burnt on the grounds. The round niches represent some of the finest examples of cut and gauged brickwork in the country. Hampton Court was an enormous project and a daring use of brickwork probably deliberately chosen to remind the King of his Dutch homeland. At the same time Wren remodelled Kensington Palace with a new front wholly in brick providing the royal couple with a useful residence closer to the centre of London.

Most of Wren's buildings were constructed in brick. Even where they were outwardly stone it was usually

only a veneer covering a brick wall underneath. The only exception was St Paul's Cathedral, where the ruins provided rubble for the core of the walls. Even in St Paul's, however, brick played a crucial role. The vaults were all constructed in brickwork as was the most important feature of the whole cathedral: the dome. In fact St Paul's has not one but three domes, one inside the other. The outer one is timber and lead. Inside this is a brick cone which supports the lantern. The third dome is underneath this. It is also made of brick and is the one that is visible when looking up from the floor of the cathedral.

Above Part of plate XIV from A. Felibien, *Des Principes de l'Architecture*, 3rd edn. (1699), illustrating an ideal fortification.

Left and opposite Tilbury Fort (1670), Tilbury, Essex, England, designed by Sir Bernard de Gomme (1620–85).

Enlightenment Ideals

Defending against enemy fire

The Renaissance marked a turning point in warfare. Although gunpowder had first appeared in Europe in the 14th century, it was not until the 15th that advances in cannon manufacture allowed it to be used effectively in the field. However, once the new cannons had appeared they proved devastatingly effective against traditional fortifications. Devising a system of defence against the new weaponry became one of the most pressing concerns of the age. The fortifications that were built in the 17th century were thus very different from their medieval equivalents and the particular properties of brick ensured that it played an increasingly important role on their construction.

When they first appeared cannons were too heavy to be moved. They were mounted on battlements and used for defence. It was not until Frederick I, Elector of Brandenburg, acquired some of the first cast bronze cannons mounted on wheels and used them systematically to defeat his rivals in a campaign from 1417 to 1425 that the problems in traditional fortress construction became evident. The traditional high curtain walls were structurally no match for the superior firepower of the cannons and actually provided an excellent target. Yet no significant advances towards a solution were made until the siege of Pisa in 1500, when the defenders held off a sustained assault by French and Florentine artillery and troops by building an earth rampart behind a breach in their walls. The second breakthrough was made by Fra Giocondo during the siege of Padua. He had the medieval walls pulled down and replaced by a ditch. These two features, the sloping earth rampart and the ditch, became essential ingredients of

fortification thereafter. They were laid out in increasingly complex polygonal plans generated by refining the form of the bastion.

Bastions were projecting parts of the fortification that could be used to fire along the walls in the event of attackers breaching the outer defences. They were deliberately designed to avoid any blind areas, giving them a strange polygonal form. A series of treatises in the 16th century set out increasingly elaborate designs for rings of ditches, ramparts and bastions which could be built around a town or castle to render it supposedly immune from attack. The greatest campaign for building such fortifications was initiated in France by Louis XIV in the 17th century and overseen by the greatest engineer of the age, Sébastien le Pestre Vauban (1633–1707).

Vauban's orders were to defend France from attack from the north. He commanded the Génie , the corps of engineers responsible for all defensive works and offensive operations. The models prepared for

fortifying the towns of northern France still survive in the Musée des Plans-reliefs at Les Invalides in Paris.

The Dutch also built many fortifications designed by Menno van Coehoorn. The English meanwhile had the sea for defence and restricted their fortifications to the coasts. The finest surviving 17th-century example is the fort at Tilbury, placed to guard the Thames, and designed by another Dutchman, Sir Bernard de Gomme, in 1670.

The sloping faces of the earth ramparts and ditches of these fortifications were constructed in masonry. Vauban advised that they should be built in either stone or brick but recognized that brick had a number of advantages. First was easy availability, second the cost and lastly, and most importantly, brick resisted cannon fire better than stone, chiefly because brick walls were made of smaller units. For these reasons brick was the primary material for fortification construction not just in France but throughout Europe in the 17th and 18th centuries. As these structures were enormous, requiring millions of bricks each, brickyards had to be set up specifically to build them. It was precisely these types of logistical problems that made the life of the fortification engineer such a challenge.

Enlightenment Ideals

Early brickwork in Colonial America

Some of the oldest buildings surviving in Colonial North America were built in brick.
Where suitable materials were obtainable the early settlers preferred to produce buildings
that reminded them of home. Transporting brick across the sea was unrealistically expensive
so it was not until bricks could be made locally that they could be used in any numbers.
The appearance and spread of brickmaking in the region was thus entirely dependent
on the development of facilities for making bricks.

The exact date of the first brickwork in the New World
is difficult to establish. Records are understandably
patchy. The first buildings were probably timber and
were not built to last. It seems likely that Spanish
settlers who built in the West Indies were the first to
use brickwork in the Americas. Their city of Santo
Domingo on the island of Hispaniola was begun in the
16th century and its major buildings (the palace, fort
and monastery) were all in brick, presumably burnt in
kilns locally. The first bricks used followed the Roman
fashion, being square and measuring 330 x 330 x
45mm. By the 17th century, however, they seem to
have moved to the rectangular European brick with
dimensions of approximately 260 x 120 x 70mm.

In North America, early brickwork has been found
in the settlements of the Dutch around the Hudson
River and of the English in Massachusetts, around the
Chesapeake Bay area and around Delaware at the
beginning of the 17th century. For instance, in 1611
Sir Thomas Gates brought brickmakers from England
to fire the bricks for the lower storeys of three streets
of houses in the settlement of Henricopolis on Farrar's

Island in the James River in Virginia. In 1619 the
church in Jamestown is reported as having been paved
with bricks and the idea of setting up a college for
training more brickmakers was actively discussed.

The development of early brickmaking in North
America was partly driven by the necessity for
providing fireproof chimneys. The idea that these early
bricks could have been imported, either as goods in
their own right or as ballast on ships, can be
discounted. 17th-century ships were relatively small
and the Atlantic crossing was hard and dangerous.
Only absolutely necessary and relatively expensive
goods could realistically be transported from Europe.
The small number of bricks or rocks used as ballast
in the average ship would barely furnish a modest
chimney. It was thus far easier and more economic to
import the tools and skills of the brickmakers than it
was to import the bricks themselves.

Following the establishment of brickmaking,
by the middle of the 17th century the first buildings
built entirely of brick began to appear. As bricks were
no doubt expensive, the earliest examples were

modest in scale. The Adam Thoroughgood House
near Norfolk, Virginia is a fine surviving example
of this type of building. Thoroughgood was English,
having been born in Kings Lynn in East Anglia.
He first visited Virginia in 1621 as a servant,
returning to England in 1626 after he finished
his agreed term of employment. Having married
well and having acquired a taste for the New
World he returned with his wife in 1628.

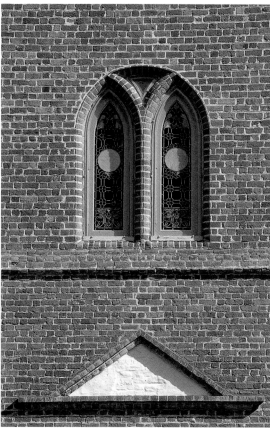

Above and left St Luke's Church, Isle of Wight County, Virginia (c. 1632). The top of the tower was added later as were the brick quoins. The church is built in 200 x 95 x 60-mm red bricks laid in Flemish bond in 20-mm joints.

Opposite Old State House, Boston, Mass. (1713), one of the oldest public buildings in the United States. Built in 210 x 90 x 55-mm bricks laid in 10-mm joints in English bond.

He prospered and 1635 he was granted 5,350 acres of land along the Lynnhaven River. For all his wealth, the present house which carried his name, is a fairly modest affair. It was probably constructed by his grandsons in the 1680s and may thus never have been his primary residence. It sits in a small garden running down to a tributary of the river. The front faced inland, a fact that can be determined by the use of Flemish bond on that façade (Flemish bond was the height of fashion in England at the time) but one that is surprising as most visitors would presumably have arrived by boat. The other three sides are laid in English bond. The bricks are 215–220 mm x 100 mm x 55–60mm laid in thick (15–20-mm) lime mortar joints. The settlers got around the problem of finding limestone for lime by burning oyster shells, mixing them with water, sand and animal hair as a binder. A similar mixture was used for the plaster on the interior of the houses.

A much larger and slightly earlier house, Bacon's Castle, survives not far away in Surry County, Virginia. The 'Castle' is actually a fine example of a two-storey farmhouse of the period, set over a basement. It was constructed in 1665 for one Arthur Allen, but took its present name from the part the house would play in young Nathaniel Bacon's rebellion of 1676 against the Governor, when he used it as a base. As a house, it cannot have been easy to fortify. Like so many Colonial houses, it was a direct copy of the architecture of home, in this case the mid-17th century farmhouses of Sussex, Kent and Surrey, in southern England. In England numerous examples of this type of house survive. The entry would have been through the typical two-storey porch on the front. The door has now been blocked up and made into a window, but the remains of a pediment can still be seen above. The ends of the house have prominent shaped gables of the type that were imported from northern Europe to England in the 1630s. With the exception of the basement, it is in every way a reproduction of an English house. The bricks were 230mm x 95–100mm x 60–65mm, laid in English Bond in 15–20-mm joints.

Both of these buildings show finely laid brickwork following the latest European fashions. Bricklayers to carry out such work cannot have been common in early Colonial America. The art of laying bricks to make walls could be learnt relatively quickly and might, with practice, have been carried out by an untrained worker, but the mixing and preparation of mortar would have required detailed instruction and the making of decorative details like shaped gables would have needed someone who had experience of working on such things. Skilled brickwork was extremely difficult to achieve without some form of apprenticeship. When Sir Christopher Wren was asked to help with the design of the College of William and Mary in Williamsburg (built 1695–99) such was the shortage of skilled labour that it was thought necessary for him to send some of his own bricklayers from England to supervise the work and no doubt to carry out the more difficult pieces of brickwork. Sadly, the building itself was destroyed in a fire in 1705 and the present structure is a replacement, but the story illustrates the lengths to which patrons were willing to go in order to find secure skilled craftsmen well-versed in the latest European fashions. This period was short-lived, for as the colonies grew an increasing body of craftsmen developed to fill the gap.

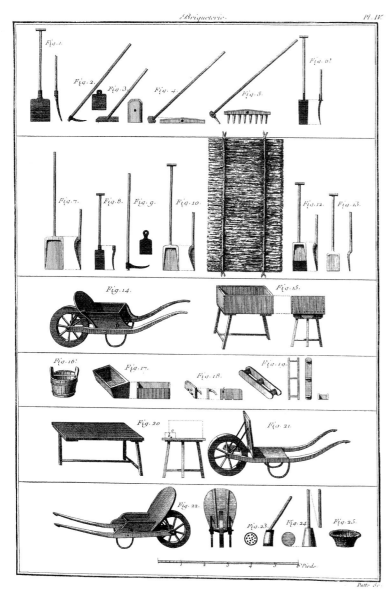

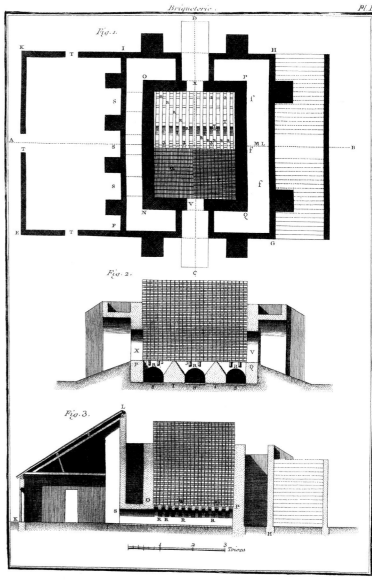

French encyclopaedias and kilns in the 18th century

The Enlightenment urge to explain and categorize was exemplified in the production of encyclopaedias, especially those produced in France in the middle of the 18th century. Diderot's famous *Encyclopaedie* was illustrated by volumes of large engravings covering key aspects of the various types of manufacturing and building trades. Surprisingly, though, Diderot did not provide pictures of brickmaking. A separate description was published later by the Academy of Science in 1763. *L'art du tuilier et du briquetier* (The Art of the Tilemaker and Brickmaker) provided the first images of clamps and detailed drawings of kilns and remains one of the most important sources on brick manufacturing before mechanization.

L'art du tuilier et du briquetier was compiled by Henri-Louis Duhammel de Monceau, Charles-René Fourcroy de Ramecourt and Jean-Gaffin Gallon. Duhammel was Inspector-general of the Navy and Director of the Academy of Sciences in 1743, 1756 and 1768. Fourcroy and Gallon were both Lieutenant Colonels in the Génie (the military corps of engineers which Vauban had commanded). Fourcroy and Gallon had first-hand experience of brick yards in the field. In 1767 edition a supplement was added entitled *L'Art de fabriquer la brique et la tuile en Hollande et de les faire cuire avec la tourbe* (The Art of Making Brick and Tile in Holland and How They Can be Fired with Peat) composed by Gabriel Jars the Elder. Neither of these works is long. *L'art du tuilier et du briquetier* only has 67 pages and nine full-page plates, while the supplement is only 11 pages long with one plate. Yet in this space the authors give detailed descriptions of three different ways of making bricks divided by the type of fuel used and thus the time .

The first section deals with bricks and tiles fired using wood using a traditional Roman kilns. Tile-making is dealt with in detail with plate I showing all the tools used in moulding and plates II and III showing two types of kilns. The first is a large kiln with a capacity of 100,000 bricks said to have been used at Le Havre while the second one is more modest with a capacity of 30,000–40,000 and said to be typical of the sort of kilns used in and around Paris. The tiles shown are released from the moulds using sand as a releasing agent, wooden pallets being used to carry the tiles to the drying ground.

The second section looks at bricks fired in clamps using coal as fuel providing the first illustrations of kilns. Detailed engravings show every aspect of setting out a clamp. The bricks are made using open moulds on benches with water as a releasing agent. They are then shown being carried in their moulds to the drying areas. They are first laid out flat and then turned on their edges before being stacked diagonally on top of each other and then finally stacked into walls. Instructions are given for the construction of a clamp to burn 500,000 bricks at a time.

The supplement contains details of techniques reported to have been used in Holland for firing bricks using peat as a fuel. The kiln shown is a Scotch kiln. In this type of kiln holes left in the bricks provide space for the burning fuel as in a clamp but permanent walls are provided, usually with doorways down the sides to allow the fire to be stoked. Scotch kilns may have been

used in Holland as early as the 15th century. They have also been excavated in Virginia dating from the early decades of the 17th century. The kiln shown in *L'Art de fabriquer la brique* has six-foot walls and measured 26–27 feet wide by 31–32 feet long and 18 feet high, holding some 350–400,000 bricks.

Plates from *L'art du tuilier et du briquetier* (1763).

Opposite left Plate IV. Tools used in brickmaking in six sections (top to bottom): (i) tools for digging, (ii) tools for preparing the clay, (iii) tools for carrying it to the bench, (iv) on the bench, (v) the bench and a barrow, (vi) tools for use at the kiln.

Opposite right Plate II. A large kiln said to have been used at Le Havre.

Above left Plate VIII. The construction of a clamp.

Above right Plate VI. The process of moulding the bricks. In the background the brick earth is dug from the ground. On the right the moulder works on a bench. At the bottom on the left is a diagram showing how the bricks are stacked. On the right is a small kiln.

Enlightenment Ideals

London in the 18th century: stock bricks, regulations and taxes

Between the Great Fire in 1666 and 1901, London's population grew from about 100,000 to 920,000. Only Paris rivalled it in size, yet unlike Paris, London was predominantly built in one material: brick. Regulations established following the Fire had decreed that all buildings had to be built in either brick or stone, but stone was expensive and brick predominated. As the cost of bricks rose one per cent for every mile they were transported by road, the outskirts of the expanding city became brickyards.

The London townhouse of the 18th century has many features which continue to make it popular today. Building regulations imposed after the Great Fire had sought to reduce the risks of fire while economy of means created relative uniformity. The houses were typically two or three windows wide. In the front, the road level was raised half a storey above the gardens at the back so that the basement opened directly into the garden but was below street level and the ground floor was raised. The fronts were relatively plain, the only ornament being applied in a cornice at the roof level and in an ornamental porch or door case.

The bricks used were what were called 'London stocks'. These can be identified by the black speckles visible in the clay that result from the way they were made. After the Great Fire it was discovered that the London clay could be more efficiently burnt if mixed with ashes (called 'spanish'). The Company of Bricklayers and Tilemakers, writing in 1714, claimed that the discovery had been made when bricks that had been produced from fields had been covered in burnt ash from the fire. The spanish which was subsequently collected as rubbish by cart and sold to brickmakers contained combustible material, reducing the amount of fuel used in firing the bricks and making the clamps more efficient. At the same date it was estimated that the reduction in cost was from 14 shillings a thousand to 12 shillings and sixpence. However, there was a temptation for the brickmaker to use too much spanish which resulted in poor bricks that quickly fell apart.

The first London stocks were red in colour and before the 18th century that colour was preferred throughout England. Unfortunately, much of the clay in the London area had a high lime content and was low in iron. It thus burnt to a yellow colour, gradually weathering to brown after a number of years. These were called 'grey stocks'. Initially they were thought of as inferior but fashions change and by the 1750s yellow stocks seem to have been more popular. In 1756 Isaac Ware wrote in his *Complete Body of Architecture* about red bricks: 'The colour is fiery and disagreeable to the eye: it is troublesome to look upon it; and in the summer it has a heat which is very disagreeable'.

It was not only fashion that affected the use of bricks but also taxation. It had usually been in the interest of brickmakers to make small bricks as they were sold by the thousand and small ones cost less in digging time and fuel. The situation changed in 1784 when the Prime Minister, William Pitt the Younger, introduced a tax on bricks to help meet the expense of the American War of Independence. The starting rate was two shillings and sixpence per thousand. The inevitable result was that bricks became larger to reduce the tax paid. To avoid this, the tax regulations were tightened in 1805 so that bricks above 10 x 5 x 3 inches would be charged double duty. Bricks became so popular that the 18th century saw the appearance of tiles made to look like bricks (mathematical tiles) which could be applied to existing timber-framed buildings to bring them up to date. Contrary to popular opinion, their introduction had nothing to do with avoiding the brick tax as they were actually charged at a higher rate.

Rubbed and gauged brickwork

The 17th and 18th centuries produced a new type of bricklayer whose skill in carving and laying bricks exceeded any that had been seen before. Such work would be used for window heads in virtually every house and to create sculpture in brick: Corinthian capitals, heraldic shields and cherubs, heads produced in exquisite detail and assembled with pinpoint accuracy. This technique was known as rubbed and gauged brickwork and it remains the very pinnacle of the bricklayers' art.

Special bricks were made for 'rubbed and gauged work' called rubbers or rubbing bricks. These were exceptional, finely made bricks for which the clay had either been sieved or left in a settling pond to separate out all stones. They were then carefully fired to produce a uniform red brick without obvious creases or deformities. These bricks were never used in the shape that they came out of the kiln, but always rubbed on a rubbing stone on at least five sides (the one inside the wall did not matter) to reduce them to exactly the dimensions required. Each brick was continually measured (or 'gauged')

until the bricklayer was satisfied that it would fit in its allotted place. In this way it was possible to preserve exact uniformity in the size of the bricks so that they could be laid with joints as thin as one millimetre. They had to be laid in lime putty rather than the normal sand and lime mix which was often coloured to give the wall a completely uniform appearance. If a flat wall was being built the final touch would be to sand down the whole surface of the finished brickwork using a rubbing stone to ensure that the surface was completely smooth.

The technique was also used for decorative details. Here again each brick was cut to size. However, this time the bricks were set out on a bench or board marked up with the position of each brick. Profiles were then cut with a brick axe. In the 19th century they were placed in a cutting box and cut using a wire saw guided by templates on each side.

The most common use of gauged work was for the construction of flat arches above doors and windows. In London these were required by law, exposed timber lintels being banned because of the fire risk. Normally flat arches were built with a slight camber so that they would drop into shape when the walls were built on top. A number of books were available explaining the authors' preferred methods for setting out both these and the more elaborate elliptical arches that became fashionable in London in the 18th century.

The finest craftsmen could make curved niches and sculpted figures by using a combination of brick axes,

saws, rasps and rubbing stones painstakingly to reduce each brick to the desired shape, while continually measuring and comparing it to the ones to which it had to relate on either side. Such works were beyond the ordinary bricklayer then as now and the very few who could carry out this sort of work must have been in great demand.

The very nature of rubbed and gauged brickwork, where every brick had to be individually cut to shape, made it far more time-consuming than ordinary work and the bricks themselves were also more expensive. It is thus not surprising that it carried a much higher price and was charged on a different scale. Normal brickwork was charged by surface area measured in 'square rods' (each equalling 272 sq ft, assuming brickwork of one and a half bricks thick). Rubbed and gauged work was measured in length of courses in feet. In the late 17th century rubbed and gauged cost approximately twice as much as normal brickwork.

The Secret of Coade 'stone'

The architectural style popularized by architects like Robert Adam in England in the second half of the 18th century created an unprecedented demand for classical ornament with which to decorate buildings both large and small. But carved stone was expensive. One person came up with a highly successful solution to this problem, providing catalogues of cheap but beautifully made sculptures and friezes that could be provided to order. Her name was Eleanor Coade and her product, called 'Coade stone', was so convincingly like real stone that it is still often mistaken for it today. It was actually a type of terracotta.

Quite how and why a young lady from a Dorset non-conformist Christian family came to be the founder of the most successful factory making architectural terracotta in late 18th century London remains something of a mystery. Certainly nothing of what little we know of Eleanor Coade's background and education provides any clues. She was born on 24 June 1733, the daughter of George Coade who until the 1750s ran a very successful wool-finishing business in Exeter. It was probably a happy childhood in a family without financial worries, but in the 1750s the wool trade went into decline and George was declared bankrupt. In the early 1760s the family moved to London and Eleanor became a linen-draper. Records show that she was a successful businesswoman and the value of her stock rose steadily. Her father meanwhile failed to regain his fortune and died bankrupt in 1769. In the same year Eleanor managed to raise the capital to buy a factory with her widowed mother in Lambeth and started manufacturing her artificial stone. 'Coade stone' was born.

It is easy to suppose that Coade stone was the first product of its type but this is not the case. A number of manufacturers in the mid-18th century advertised 'artificial stone' products based on various processes. The reason that these are not well-known is that they were of either of poor quality and have not survived or were not successfully marketed. Eleanor Coade's factory was in Lambeth on the site of one previously run by Daniel Pincot and it seems likely that she bought him out.

The method by which the Coade stone was made was a closely guarded trade secret. Some of the Coade stone sculptures were very large and thus presented the same problems of shrinkage and cracking to their makers as they had to earlier manufacturers of terracotta. Eleanor Coade solved these in two ways. Firstly the formula of the material used was specially designed to keep shrinkage to a minimum. She did so by mixing the clay with flint, crushed glass and grog (clay that had already been fired and then ground into

a powder) . Since the grog and the glass had been fired already, they did not shrink further. This enabled her to use white ball clays producing the characteristic stone colour, reducing their shrinkage from 20% to 8% on firing. The second crucial part of her method was the use of plaster moulds. The clay mixture was so rich in grog that it could not be sculpted directly (unlike medieval terracotta), so all the pieces, whether mass-produced or one-offs, had to be made in moulds, the clay being pressed in a relatively thin layer into the mould by hand. This method had three added advantages: firstly the sculptures were hollow, which meant that they could be fired evenly; secondly the surface of the plaster absorbed some of the water so that the clay naturally shrank away from the side of the mould; and thirdly, should further examples be required, the mould could always be used again.

It was chiefly Eleanor Coade's success in marketing her artificial stone that singled her out from her rivals. She ensured that her work was designed by the best artists, and used by the most fashionable architects of

Opposite Coade stone Lion from the Lion Brewery, London, which was demolished in 1950. Dated 1837, the lion was moved to Westminster Bridge where it stands today.

Above Bearded man keystone in Coade stone, from one of the houses in Bedford Square built around 1775.

the day. She held regular exhibitions of her products, produced beautifully engraved catalogues and made sure she never under-priced. When Eleanor Coade died in 1821 the secret did not (as is sometimes said) die with her, but it did transpire that she made few arrangements for the continuance of the firm. In the end it was brought by her manager William Croggan who had none of her business acumen and the firm finally went bankrupt in 1833.

By that time, however, Coade stone had been exported across the globe. The frieze of Buckingham Palace in London and columns of the Octagon (1799) in Washington are Coade stone and examples can be found as far afield as Rio de Janiero, Montreal, and Haiti.

Holkham Hall and the English Palladian country house

In 18th-century England, the Grand Tour became an accepted rite of passage for young members of the aristocracy. The returning gentleman was also expected to build himself a new country residence in the Italian manner in which the antiquities and works he had purchased on the continent could be displayed in an appropriate setting. One such man was Thomas Coke and the house he built for himself, Holkham Hall, was remarkable both for its size and because, despite first appearances, it was faced entirely in brick.

Thomas Coke (1697–1759), 1st Earl of Leicester, had taken a long 'Grand Tour' that lasted six years, returning in the spring of 1718. He had inherited the estate on the death of his parents in 1707 and now, laden down with manuscripts, printed books, paintings and statues acquired from his travels, he set about building a grand house in which to store and display them. He had met Lord Burlington and William Kent in Europe and with them acquired an enthusiasm for Palladian architecture. It was to Kent that he turned for the first designs for his great house.

The house that he started to Kent's designs was on an enormous scale. The state rooms, where the works of art were to be displayed and visitors could be entertained in style, occupied the whole of the main floor of the central block. Ranged around this were four large pavilions, each the size of reasonable country house in their own right, which it was envisaged would hold the living quarters for the family. In addition the design called for the complete re-planning of the park including the construction of a lake, raised formal gardens and obelisks and follies.

Not surprisingly, all this took a long time and a great deal of money to finish. That Kent's plan was extravagant to say the least and would be very expensive must have been obvious from the start. The first compromise, and the most important from our point of view, concerned the external facing material. Palladio's villas had been built of stone or brick faced with stucco. Most great English country were houses also built in brick but they were normally faced in stone. However, experiments in burning the local brick on the Holkham estate proved that it was rich in lime and burnt to a warm buff acceptably close in colour to Bath stone. It was thus decided that it would be suitable for use for the façade without rendering.

Unfortunately for Coke, the savings made in using brick alone were not enough to make up for the scale of the project or the huge amounts lavished on the interiors. Thomas spent some £90,000 of his own money and a similar amount was accrued in debts. It was not until the 19th century that the family paid off the last of these and the lack of funds thereafter largely explains how the house remained unaltered in later periods.

The cost cannot be blamed entirely on William Kent. Although his was the original plan, the building of the house and its garden was entrusted to Matthew Brettingham and proved a very lengthy process. Construction began in 1734 and took some 30 years to complete, by which time Thomas had died.

Holkham remains an extraordinary tribute to the bricklayer's art. The bricks are carefully laid with thin joints to produce a uniform surface that at a distance passes for stone. The effect is heightened by the rustication applied to the basement, where the bricks are specially cut to mimic large stones with chamfered edges. This detail is repeated at the corners of the building. The stone used for the window surrounds and details matches the brick so closely in colour that the transition is not obvious. The result is an extraordinary essay in brick masquerading as stone.

Above Side view of Holkham Hall, Norfolk (1734–64), showing the elaborate rustication of the basement storey and retaining wall in the foreground, all constructed in yellow brick.

Right Four pavilions are placed one at each corner of the centre block. Each provides living quarters for a separate branch of the family. The main block was reserved for state rooms.

Left Close-up of the entrance façade. Only the window surrounds, cornice and balusters are stone. The rest is brick.

Holkham Hall, Norfolk, England
(1734–64). The main entrance
front, including the two
pavilions on either side.

197

Nash and problems with stucco

Despite the fact that bricks were being produced in enormous numbers in the late 18th century and had become the dominant walling material in Europe, this is hardly apparent from a casual examination of the major works of architecture of the period. Even in England the success of brick in providing affordable houses for rich and poor alike gradually led to its being shunned in fashionable circles. Elsewhere in Europe the demise of brickwork exteriors was probably more to do with a wish to produce façades with apparently flawless surfaces and continuous decoration. The material that enabled this to be achieved did not replace the bricks; it was merely applied to their surface. It was called by various names, but in England it was (and still is) commonly referred to as 'stucco'.

Opposite The terraces around London's Regent's Park, which were designed by John Nash in 1811 and built between 1812 and 1828. Park Square (1823–25) forms a transition between Regent's Park and Portland Place.

Below left Gloucester Gate (1827), one of the terraces facing the park.

Below right Carlton House Terrace, The Mall, London, designed by John Nash in 1827–32.

The term stucco is Italian in derivation and was originally used to mean plaster mixed with marble dust. The *stuccatori* were the great Italian plasterers who created the extraordinary interiors of the Baroque. What the English call stucco is really nothing more than external render.

Buildings have been rendered since the beginning of civilization. Mud bricks are normally covered in a protective coat of mud painted with a lime wash. The purpose of these surfaces is partly aesthetic (to produce a smoother, more uniform appearance) but also partly practical as it prevented the bricks from being washed away. The Romans used lime-based renders and these were employed throughout the Middle Ages, usually consisting of lime mixed with sand and a binder such as straw or hair. As external rendering became more popular in the 18th century, so an increasing amount of research was carried out into new mixtures that would be easier to apply and last longer than traditional lime renders. In London the fashion for rendering the outside of townhouses arose in 1775 and lasted until about 1850.

When the architect brothers James and Robert Adam specified external render for their great Adelphi housing project on the bank of the River Thames, they purchased two different patents. One was for a render invented by a Revd David Wark but this obviously proved unsuitable because they subsequently bought the rights to produce another from Revd John Liardet. Soon the Adam brothers were not only using Liardet's stucco for their own projects but also dispatching it throughout the country. Both Liardet's and Wark's stucco's were oil-based cements, Liardet's being made with linseed oil. For ten years from 1774 these cements were all the rage. Unfortunately they were faulty and by the 1780s they had already begun to fall off the façades to which they had been applied, to the great financial embarrassment of the Adam brothers.

Finding a stucco that did not peel off the brick below remained a problem. A solution was provided in 1796 when Revd James Parker took out a patent on a cement which was subsequently known as Parker's Roman Cement. This was made from grinding nodules of clay and lime which were found naturally occurring in the bed of the Thames Estuary. The result was a strong hydraulic cement (that is, it set underwater) which proved perfect for rendering the outside of buildings. One of the first architects to take it up was John Nash.

Nash had specified Liardet's cement for his first project in Bloomsbury in the 1780s, which went wrong and forced him to flee to Wales to avoid his debtors. Twenty years later he returned to London, his enthusiasm for property speculation and stucco undiminished. In the early 19th century he was responsible for the creation of some of the largest and grandest property developments the capital has ever seen, including Regent Street, Carlton Terrace and Regent's Park. All were built of brick covered in stucco.

Today we associate Regency architecture in general, and Nash's name in particular, with white façades because they have long since been painted that colour. Painting them white was in fact a later development. Where finances would allow they were usually scored to imitate stone coursing and painted to look like weathered masonry. Nevertheless, such finishes needed to be regularly re-done and by the 1840s it had become common to simply re-paint in washes of flat oil colour, covering up any earlier work and providing the effect that survives today.

Thomas Jefferson and the architecture of Independence

If one man can be said to embody more than any other the spirit of the United States at the end of the 18th century it is probably Thomas Jefferson (1743–1826). Statesman, author of the first draft of the Declaration of Independence, President and man of letters, he was also a more than competent architect who left behind him two highly inventive works built in brick which have been a source of inspiration ever since: Monticello and the University of Virginia.

Jefferson started building a house for himself on his estate near Charlottesville, Virginia in 1768, the same year that he first stood for public office. Monticello, as he was later to call it, remained a building project for much of his life, for he was constantly adding new things to it or re-arranging the layout of its rooms. The building as he left it was a two-storey house disguised as a one-storey one. It was built in 190 x 85–90 x 67–70-mm bricks laid in Flemish bond with 12–15-mm penny-struck joints. The bricks were presumably burnt on site. Jefferson kept large numbers of slaves to work on his estate and they may well have been involved in making the bricks.

Jefferson was an avid reader and much of his knowledge of architecture came from books; he also spent five years in France, from 1784 to 1791. It is often said that he was the first architect to bring Palladianism to America. While this is almost certainly an exaggeration, it is fair to say that he was the most influential advocate of the style. Palladio's buildings, however, were not obviously built of brick. Jefferson's choice of brick as a visible material on the outside

of his buildings is thus out of step with his Palladian ideals.

Stonemasons were in short supply in post-Independence Virginia. In designing the Virginia State Capitol building in 1786, Jefferson changed the capitals from Corinthian to Ionic 'because of the difficulty of Corinthian capitals', by which he meant the inability of finding skilled craftsmen to make them. The same problem was evident in building the portico of the Rotunda in the University of Virginia, where the capitals had to be imported from Italy after the Italian craftsmen who had been hired to carve them gave up and went home. Nevertheless, Virginia had a strong tradition of brickmaking and the red and white style of architecture was well-established with brick walls and painted timber details. Jefferson adaptedthis, combining it with a sophisticated architectural sensibility derived from his knowledge of classical architectural sources.

Nowhere is the balance that Jefferson managed to achieve between the use of local craft traditions and new architectural ideas better demonstrated than in his final work, the designs for the University of

Virginia in Charlottesville. It was here that Jefferson brought together his political, philosophical and architectural ideas to produce a utopian vision of a university.

Jefferson was successful in defining a vision of what American architecture could be like and has been called the first professional American architect. While this is not strictly true, he was undoubtedly instrumental in shaping the idea of what such an architect might achieve. His brick buildings were constructed for the few, but by the time he died in 1826, huge technical changes were already underway which would mean that very soon brick would become an affordable method of building for everyone.

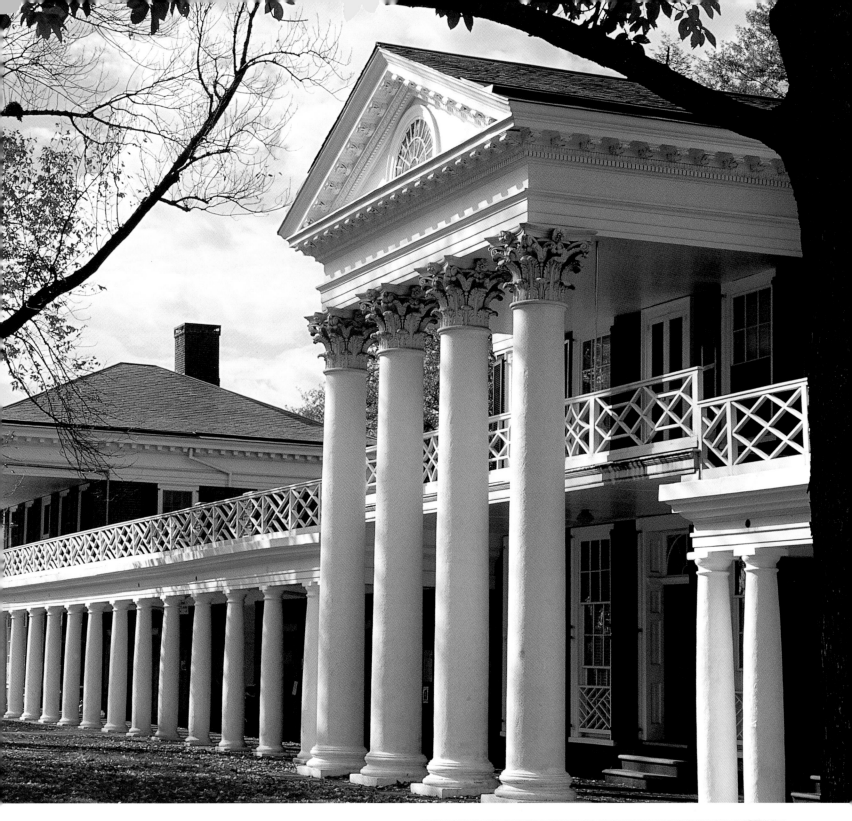

Opposite The rotunda (1823–26), University of Virginia, Charlottesville, Virginia, by Thomas Jefferson. Based on the Pantheon in Rome, the rotunda was at the centre of Jefferson's design and housed the library on the first floor under the dome. He had originally planned to incorporate a planetarium but died before the building was completed.

Above Pavilions around the Lawn (1817–26), University of Virginia, Charlottesville, Virginia. The students occupy rooms off the colonnades between the pavilions while each pavilion was designed to house a professor and his family, and provide space for classes. They were also practical demonstrations of the classical orders.

Right Monticello (1768–1826), near Charlottesville, Virginia, designed for and by Thomas Jefferson and altered many times during his life.

CHAPTER SIX

MECHANIZATION AND INDUSTRIALIZATION 1800 – 1900

The years between 1800 and 1900 saw the greatest changes in the brick manufacture in history. Brickmaking was transformed from a handicraft into a mechanized industry. Yet the greatest changes were happening outside the narrow world of brick manufacturing in the very fabric of the industrializing world. Huge expansions in population and changes in the way materials were made and transported led to a enormous growth in demand for bricks and great advances in the ways in which they were used. The railway tunnels, sewers, factories, houses and office blocks built in the wake of the Industrial Revolution were all constructed of brick and museums and churches were decorated with new types of terracotta. Brick was everywhere, and increasingly its presence was celebrated architecturally.

The drive towards mechanization in brickmaking occurred in all three of the stages of manufacture: clay preparation, moulding and firing. The chapter opens by examining these developments, first looking at preparation and moulding and then at the various types of new kilns which were devised to speed up the firing process and make it more efficient.

Changes in bricklaying were more subtle. By far the most important was the increased use of cements for mortar. Through the ages, bricks had been laid in a wide variety of mortars, but the most popular were those based on lime, often with various admixtures to add strength or speed up the setting process. Such mortars were comparatively weak. The holy grail for engineers was a quick strong cement that would dry under water and would continue to grow in strength after it had set. The great engineering projects for canals, sewers and railways produced the perfect testing grounds for the various cements that were being patented throughout the early part of the 19th century and most importantly for the discovery and development of the solution to these problems in the form of Portland Cement.

In addition to new types of mortar, Victorian inventors were also at work on the brick itself. Patent bricks of all shapes and sizes abounded. The most important were used in fireproof floors. Indeed it was the fireproof nature of the brick which accounted for the popularity of the material for factory construction throughout the century. Walls could be built using conventional bricks. Floors were initially constructed using low barrel vaults but these were slow and expensive to lay. By the end of the century a

bewildering array of flooring systems was available to solve this problem. One of the suggested uses for patent bricks was to produce cheap cottages for workers. Brick was used for the construction of mass housing across the world in this period but it proved more economic to use simple rectangular bricks.

Up the architectural scale, advances in the manufacturing of architectural terracotta made ceramics acceptable once more to those professional architects who had previously seen brick as being too down-market for major commissions. With the use of terracotta and brick in Germany and in Britain, in such buildings as the Albert Hall in London's South Kensington and the flexibility of new manufacturing methods, terracotta and brick once more became a fashionable combination.

At least as important were the reactions of various writers on architecture, such as Ruskin in England and Viollet-le-Duc in France whose influence on the Gothic Revival saw an increased use of brick in ways that could not have been dreamt of in the Middle Ages.

Spain had a long tradition of brick architecture dating back to the Moorish occupation of the Iberian peninsula and before that the Romans. One of its most important contributions to the art of bricklaying was a particular type of shell vault developed in the 16th century. However, it was almost invariably concealed under plaster within the structure and made little visual impact. It was only in the 19th century that it came to prominence in the work of one of the most eccentric architects of all time, Antoni Gaudí (1852–1926).

The last two sections of this chapter turn to developments in the United States. Brickmaking machines had caught on there more quickly than elsewhere and soon America was producing bricks in enormous numbers. Cities like New York and Philadelphia became renowned for their use of brick. Two architects, Frank Lloyd Wright and Henry Hobson Richardson, stand out from the rest for their use and understanding of brickwork. Richardson's Sever Hall is an elegant exercise in romantic revivalism, which sensitively reacts to its surroundings (Harvard Yard) and seamlessly blends historical motifs with modern invention. Wright's architecture too refers back to historical precedent but forms a fitting entry into the 20th century. Together Wright and Richardson mark the end of one era and the beginning of another.

Opposite Wharncliffe Viaduct, Hanwell, Surrey (1836) designed by the great engineer Isambard Kingdom Brunel.

Rijksmuseum, Amsterdam, Netherlands

Granary Building, Bristol, England

Housing, old Shanghai, China

Nathan G. Moore House, Chicago, USA

Rijksmuseum, Amsterdam, Netherlands

Arthur Heurtley Residence, Chicago, USA

Guëll Pavilions, Barcelona, Spain

Colegio Teresiano, Barcelona, Spain

Digswell Viaduct, Welwyn, England

Museum of History, Moscow, Russia

Keble College, Oxford, England

Guëll Pavilions, Barcelona, Spain

Sever Hall, Harvard, Cambridge, Mass., USA

Colegio Teresiano, Barcelona, Spain

Crypt, Guëll Colony Church, Barcelona, Spain

Central Station, Amsterdam, Netherlands

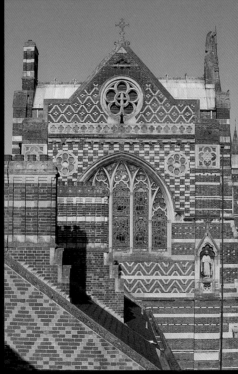
Keble College, Oxford, England

Prudential Building, London, England

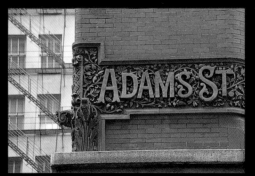
Rookery Building, Chicago, USA

Keble College, Oxford, England

Nathan G. Moore House, Chicago, USA

Keble College, Oxford, England

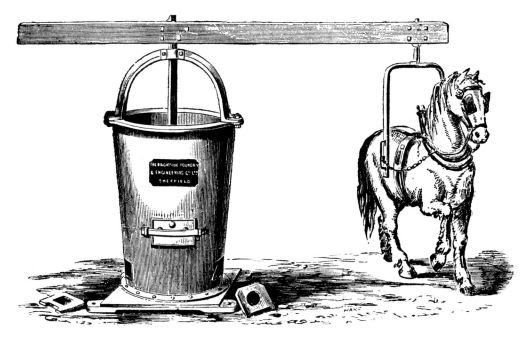

Left A 19th-century illustration of a pug mill which was used for mixing the clay.

Below Alfred Hall's brick press, patented in 1845. The machine incorporated a horse-driven pug mill which forced the clay into multiple moulds.

Opposite Two machines operating on the revolving table principle. A vertical plunger forces clay into moulds mounted in the table which revolves to put the next set of moulds under the plunger.

Mechanization and Industrialization

Brick moulding becomes a mechanized process

Up until the beginning of the 19th century virtually all bricks were moulded by hand in the traditional way, but, as other trades became increasingly mechanized, it was inevitable that engineers and manufacturers would turn their attention to brickmaking machinery in the hope of reducing costs and increasing production. By the end of the century, there was a bewildering variety of machines on the market, all claiming to produce the perfect brick.

One of the first machines to be introduced into brick production was the pug mill, a device for preparing the clay before it was moulded. It consisted of a barrel with a vertical axle in its centre from which a number of cutting blades projected. The axle was turned by a horse, causing the blades to rotate and slice up the clay fed in at the top. Clay mills of a similar design had been used in England in the 17th century in potteries, but do not seem to have been commonly used for making bricks until the end of the 18th century, when they were re-named 'pug mills'.

The pug mill did a better job of breaking up the clay than could be done by hand, but it did not solve the problem of removing the stones nor did it solve the more onerous problem of actually moulding the bricks. Moulding was just the sort of slow and repetitive work that appeared perfect for mechanization and even before 1800 a number of inventors had tried to come up with a workable mechanical alternative.

The earliest recorded brick-moulding machine is a British patent filed in 1619 by John Etherington for 'a certaine Engine to make and cast clay of alle sorte of earthern pipes..tiles and paving stones', the details of which have not survived. An account also survives from Robert Dowglass, a brickmaker in Belfast, Ireland, in 1660 for a 'slush' moulding machine (to use the

terminology of Q. A. Gilmore, a 19th-century writer on brickmaking machines). It worked by pouring very wet clay into wooden moulds with many compartments greased with pork fat. The bricks would then be left to

dry sufficiently for them to be turned out. Dowglass boasted that he could make 'forty-eight dozen a day' (i.e. 576 bricks). This was much less than the average brickmaker working by hand, who was generally

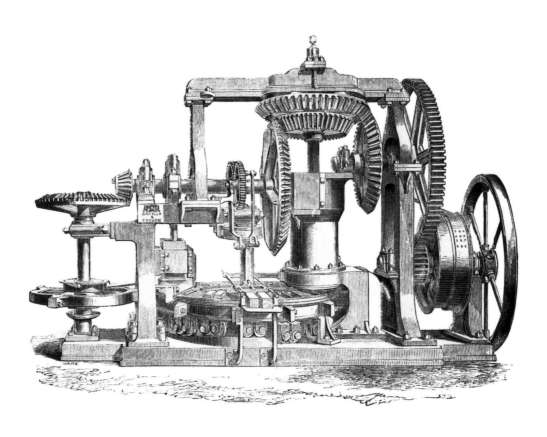

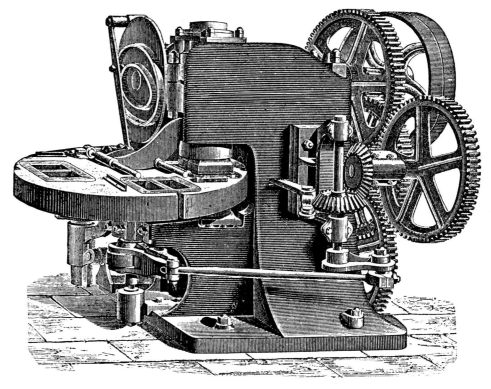

thought to be able to mould 1,000 bricks a day. The other obvious disadvantage was the number of moulds the process required. Neither machine seems to have been widely used and although slush moulding machines were made in the 19th century they were never successful. Most inventors concentrated instead on one of two methods: pressing or extrusion.

Early pressed bricks

The most obvious solution to the problem of making a brick by machine was simply to mimic the hand-moulding process by devising a machine that would push relatively stiff clay into the mould. The key problems were: feeding the clay into the mould, removing each mould and replacing it with the next one, and turning out the bricks.

Some of the earliest patents for brickmaking machines were filed in the United States. David Ridgeway in 1792 was granted a patent for 'an improvement in making bricks'. No description has survived but it is thought it was probably similar to one filed a year later by Apollos Kingsley of Connecticut whose 'essential parts were a charger which moved up and down, a revolving horizontal table which brought the moulds successively under

the charger which would then compact the clay in each'. A machine of this type with eight moulds was in operation in Washington D.C. by 1819 and produced 30,000 bricks a day. Bricks taken from this machine were said to be dry enough to be fired immediately. If this was the case, then it would be the earliest of what was later called the dry-press process. In this, dry clay is ground up and then pressed under enormous pressure into the mould. Many patents were filed for such machines during the 19th century,

but very few proved successful in solving the key problem of applying sufficient pressure to both sides of the brick to form it. More commonly the clay was used wet (called the soft-mud process) in much the same consistency as it would have been for hand-moulding. This meant that when moulded the clay had to go through a similar drying process before it could be fired.

The sheer number of patents filed and the poor descriptions in records of brickmaking factories make

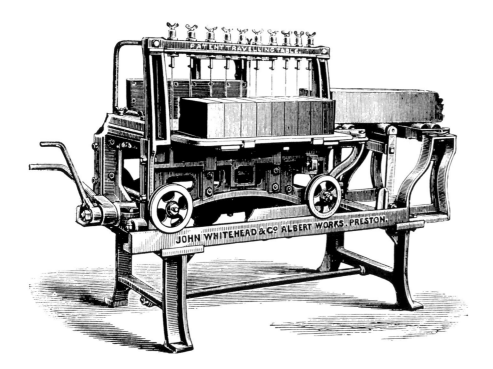

it very difficult to trace the development and success of individual techniques. Between 1820 and 1850 no fewer than 109 patents were issued for brickmaking machines in Britain alone. By 1820 repress machines were being used to compress previously hand-made bricks to improve their quality and finish. In the 1830s, moulding machines using the processes described above first seem to have appeared in Britain.

Extrusion machines

The much more successful stiff-mud or wire-cut process for brickmaking also appeared in the early decades of the 19th century. Here, too, tracing the success of individual machines is difficult. A patent was issued to Johann Georg Degerlein for a machine answering this description in Britain in March 1810. It used a plunger to force out a column of mud that could be cut into bricks. The use of a screw-threaded pug-mill to force the clay out through a die, creating a bar of clay which could be cut by wires was patented in November 1839 by the Marquis of Tweeddale and Thomas Ainslie. This type of machine produced a long extruded sausage of clay which then had to be sliced up into individual bricks. The earliest cutters were simple knives, but later examples employed large numbers of wires that would cut a number of bricks simultaneously, acting like a giant cheese-slicer. The slicing device also had to be designed in such a way as to cope with the continual movement of the clay, which created a considerable challenge.

When correctly designed both wire-cut and pressed-brick machines produced very smooth uniform bricks that could be laid with very fine joints. Although many 19th-century architects liked the uniformity of the product, others complained that the bricks lacked the texture and character of hand-made ones. A number of devices were thus added to extrusion and pressing machines to produce surface variations artificially.

In general, brickmaking machinery seems to have been more swiftly adopted in the Unites States where there was a shortage of labour, than in Europe where workers were opposed to mechanization. By 1847 there were 93 patents for brickmaking machines in the United States. In 1828 a machine in New York City was said to be producing 25,000 bricks a day. In 1890 a census showed that 5,828 brick and tile firms in the United States had invested $18,000,000 in machinery. England and Europe lagged behind and most English yards were still using hand-moulding methods in the early 20th century.

Top A steam-driven wire-cutting machine from the 1860s. Note that the bricks are cut by a hand-operated set of wire-cutters.

Above Whitehead's wire-cutting machine. The moveable carriage allowed the cutters to operate as the column of clay moved forward.

Opposite above A steam-driven stiff-mud (wire-cut) brickmaking machine dating from the 1860s. The column was sliced into long blocks before being transferred to the wire-cutters to be subdivided into bricks.

Opposite below Modern wire-cutting machine in use in contemporary Iran. It operates on a similar system but is fully automated and driven by electricity from a generator.

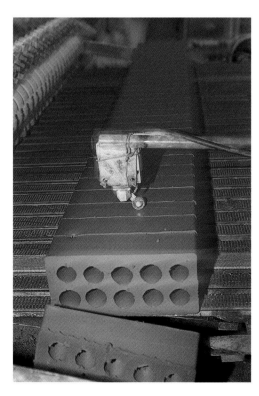

New types of kiln

Although considerable ingenuity was being applied to devising mechanical ways of moulding bricks, they continued to be fired in the traditional way. It was not until the middle of the 19th century that a series of patents began to appear in the United States and Europe for new and more efficient kilns. These were for downdraught and continuous kilns, types which are still in use in one form or another in brick manufacturing today. Their invention allowed bricks to be made more efficiently and in much greater numbers than ever before.

Downdraught kilns

Downdraught kilns were not invented in Europe. The Chinese had used downdraught kilns in the Ming Dynasty, if not before, but Europeans did not develop them for brickmaking until the 19th century. It is difficult to establish with any certainty the date of the first downdraught kilns used for brickmaking. The design was probably derived from Thomas Minton's patent for a porcelain kiln in 1793.

Before the invention of the downdraught kiln, all kilns were of the updraught type where the smoke was removed from the kiln through the top, usually through a serious of vents. The Roman kilns, Scotch kilns and clamps that had been used in 18th-century Europe were all examples of updraught kilns. The problem with updraught kilns is that the bricks at the bottom, where the fire is burnt, get too hot and over-burn, while those at the top are usually under-fired.

Downdraught kilns solve these problems by introducing the hot air at the top of the kiln and withdrawing the waste gases from the bottom through a series of grates in the floor. The most

obvious external difference which distinguishes the downdraught kiln from its predecessors is that it has a tall chimney. This is essential to draw the gases through the kiln efficiently and to stop the fires going out. The amount of wind blowing will have an effect on the downdraught kiln and the kilnsmen must carefully regulate the gases coming out of the chimney and the amount of fuel and air going in to maintain the correct temperature within the kiln.

Although there are a number of types, the simplest form of the downdraught kiln is the beehive kiln. It is circular with a shallow domed roof. The stoking holes are placed at regular intervals around the circumference with a space being left for a doorway for loading (traditionally called a 'wicket'). When the kiln is full, this doorway is bricked up. Typically sheds with tile roofs are built around the outside of the kiln to offer protection to those stoking the kiln and keep the fuel dry.

Downdraught kilns of this type can fire 12-100,000 bricks according to size. They have the advantage

that they can fire different shapes and sizes of wares simultaneously if carefully stacked. Because of their flexibility in this regard and the fact that they can produce small numbers of items, they are still used in specialist brickyards today where the emphasis is on producing particular types of product to order.

A downdraught kiln of this type is still operated by Peter Minter of Bulmer Bricks in Suffolk. His kiln holds 12,000 bricks and works on a two-week cycle. The 'setting' or correct placement of the bricks and tiles within the kiln must be done with care and takes four men two days. The wicket is then sealed and the fires stoked. It takes two days to get the kiln up to firing temperature. The bricks are then held at this temperature for thirty-six hours. Thereafter the flues are opened and the kiln is allowed to cool down, a process that takes another two days. Finally the wicket can be opened and the fired bricks removed, unloading taking two days. The whole process from beginning to end takes two weeks.

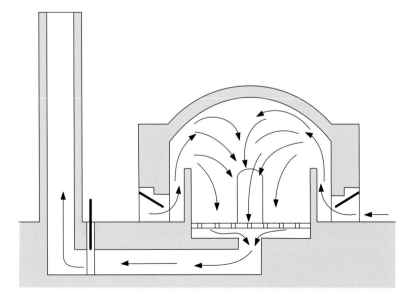

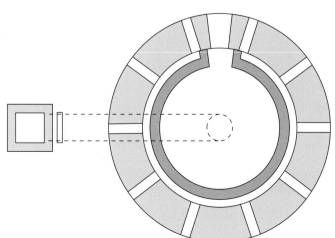

Opposite Plan and section of a typical beehive downdraught kiln showing the movement of the hot gases which fire the bricks.

Above The beehive kiln at the Bulmer Brickworks in Suffolk, England. The pantiles cover the timber-framed lean-to stoking shed which surrounds the central kiln. The fireplace in the back of the chimney is lit to draw the smoke through the fire from the kiln.

Downdraught kilns like the one at Bulmer together with clamps, Scotch kilns and Roman kilns are all termed 'intermittent kilns'. They all shared the same basic method of operation: the bricks were placed in the kiln when it was cold, they were then heated gradually to white heat, allowed to burn at this temperature for several days and the kiln was then cooled down to a temperature at which they could be safely removed. As the cycle took several weeks, the use of intermittent kilns put a strict limit on the number of bricks that could made. The alternative was the 'continuous kiln', the first example of which was invented by Friderich Hoffmann in Germany in the late 1850s.

The Hoffmann kiln

The Hoffmann kiln burnt continuously, 24 hours a day, 365 days a year. Indeed some kilns are said to have been continuously fired for over 50 years. This was achieved by building a large kiln in the form of a circle consisting of a number of segments each with its own door (wicket). These segments are usually confusingly referred to as chambers, but there were no walls between them. They are simply the areas that can be unloaded or loaded through a single door. At any one time bricks are stacked in most (but not all) the chambers. The free chambers are being either loaded or unloaded. The bricks stay in the same chambers, but the fire moves in a constant direction around

the kiln. Thus one chamber will be at white heat while those on either side of it will be either cooling down or heating up. When the bricks in that chamber are correctly fired, the heat will be moved to the next chamber. The gases from the hot chambers are directed to those to be heated up by systems of ducts which are regulated by valves. Fuel is poured in through vents in the roofs of the chambers.

Circular Hoffmann kilns were limited in capacity. A better solution that became common from about 1870 was to lengthen the kiln into an oval. A rectangular version called the Belgian kiln was also made. By using fuel in one chamber to heat bricks up in the next, Hoffmann kilns were more efficient, burning less fuel and cutting down pollution.

Friedrich Eduard Hoffmann was the son of a school teacher. He was born on 18 October 1818 in Gröningen near Halberstadt in Mid-Saxony. He went to school in his home town and at the age of 20 went to work as an assistant under his brother in Posen, East Prussia. He graduated from the Royal Building Academy in Berlin in 1845, becoming *Regierungsbaumeister* (chief engineer) for the Berlin–Hamburg Railway. In 1858 he received a patent in Germany for his new kiln, described at the time as being 'for use in making bricks, tiles, cement and mortar'. From then on he devoted his energies to working in the ceramic industry, producing designs for kilns, editing journals and subsequently running factories.

The Hoffmann kiln is one of the most successful designs and continues to be used in various forms throughout the world today. Writing in the 1950s, A. B. Searle compared Hoffmann kilns with downdraught ones:

> 'Eight downdraught kilns, each holding 28,000 bricks will burn 5,000,000 bricks a year, allowing for various contingencies. A continuous kiln with 18 chambers each holding 16,000 bricks, will cost no more, and will burn with less than half the fuel.'

The Hoffmann kiln was ideal for mass-production, but it was not good for firing objects of different shapes and sizes and it could not be run efficiently for small numbers. Indeed stopping and starting a Hoffmann kiln is particularly difficult, making them unsuitable for firing less than 2,000,000 bricks a year. Thus, although Hoffmann kilns and their variants came to dominate brick production at the end of the 19th century, smaller kilns still had an important role to play.

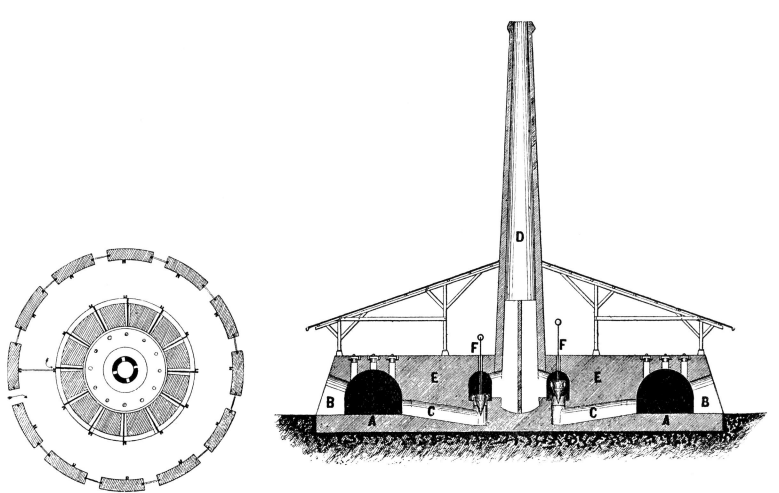

Opposite Unloading a chamber of a Hoffmann kiln in operation in Iran. Once empty, the chamber will be reloaded with green bricks and the next chamber unloaded.

Above Plan and section of the original Hoffmann kiln. The bricks are fired in the chambers (A) and unloaded through the wickets (B). Fuel is fed in through the holes in the roof while exhaust gases are extracted through the flues (C) controlled by valves (F) to the chimney (D).

Below Plan of the oval version of the Hoffmann kiln which is the same in section as the circular version.

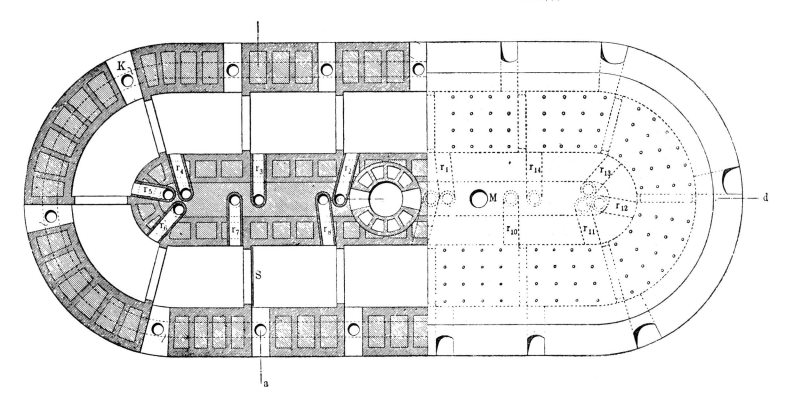

Above The Digswell Viaduct (1848–50), Welwyn, Hertfordshire, designed by Lewis Cubitt and built by Thomas Brassey. Cubitt also designed King's Cross Station in London.

Right Wharncliffe Viaduct (1836–38), Hanwell, near London, designed by Isambard Kingdom Brunel (1806–59), with its remarkable eliptical brick arches.

Civil engineering:
canals, railways, sewers and Portland Cement

The professional divide between architects and engineers was more marked in the 19th century than it is today. The design of public buildings was still the exclusive preserve of the architect who remained responsible for designing their structures. Professional collaboration between architects and engineers only began in the late 19th century when buildings started to use iron frames and architects felt uncertain of their design. Thus the 19th-century engineer designed all those utilitarian structures that were considered unworthy of the attention by the architect. As architects were not involved, these structures are usually overlooked in histories of the subject, although in terms of volume of construction they far outstripped architect-designed structures. More importantly from the point of view of the present study, they were very often built in brick.

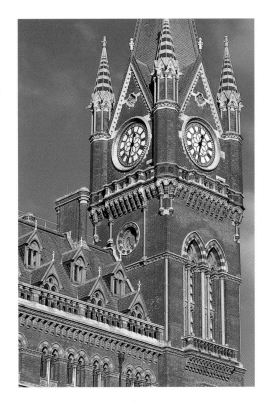

Above The Midland Grand Hotel (1866–77), St Pancras station, London, designed by George Gilbert Scott (1811–78). The hotel also houses the ticket office and waiting rooms.

Canals

Bricks were not only transported in massive numbers by canals and railways, they were also used to construct them. The earliest canals were constructed in China in the 13th century, but it was not until the 18th century that major construction programmes got underway in England. In canal construction, speed was of the essence and the sides of the canals were made out of local materials wherever possible to save on cost. When the Bridgewater Canal was opened in 1761 to transport coal from the Duke of Bridgewater's collieries at Worsley to Manchester a visitor observed that 'the duke, like a good chemist, has made the refuse of one work the material parts of another'. He was referring to the clay which had been dug out of the path of the canal and used to line the sides and make bricks for the roofs of the tunnels. In 19th-century England, bricks were preferred to stone for tunnel linings and the hard non-porous blue-black Staffordshire bricks were looked upon particularly favourably in this regard. By the 1820, there were 3,000 miles of canals in England allowing the transport of coal, bricks and other heavy materials with relative ease.

Railways

While the canals were important, they were soon superseded by the railways which first developed in England at the beginning of the 19th century, rapidly spreading across Europe and the United States. Railway stations and sheds were often made of brick, but the numbers involved were insignificant compared to those used for lining railway cuttings, for bridges, and for tunnels. Like canals these were often made from the clay removed in construction.

The most visible use of brick in railways was for the construction of viaducts, which attempted to reduce inclines so that trains could carry large loads more efficiently. These were not necessarily tall: one of the longest viaducts in the world runs between Bermondsey and Deptford in south London. Built in 1836, it consists of 878 stock brick arches and is only 40 feet high. In contrast, the Stockport viaduct (1841) is 1,800 feet long and 110 feet high with 22 arches. The Digswell Viaduct, at Welwyn, Hertfordshire, which still carries railway traffic passing north out of Kings Cross in London, is one of the most dramatic. It is 100 feet high, 4,560 feet long, consists of 40 brick arches. and was constructed in 1850 for the Great Northern Railway, using 13 million bricks made from local clay.

Although the numbers of bricks used for viaducts may seem large, far more were used in the construction of linings for tunnels. The great innovator in this respect and one of the greatest engineers of the period was Marc Isambard Brunel (1769–1849), the father of Isambard Kingdom Brunel (1806–59).

The elder Brunel, who had fled France to escape the guillotine, first attempted to make his fortune in America where he constructed the old Bowry Theater in New York, before he moved to London in 1799. He was knighted for a single project that made him famous at home and abroad. It was the first tunnel under the River Thames, indeed the first tunnel ever constructed under a navigable river. Brunel's great innovation was the tunnelling shield, an iron frame that supported the face of the tunnel, behind which the walls could be constructed in safety. To make it work Brunel needed a mortar that would dry underwater. For this he turned to a patent already discussed in the last chapter, Parker's Roman Cement.

In 1827 Brunel wrote a progress report on the Thames Tunnel explaining his methods: 'the bricks are laid in Roman Cement and no centering is used for the arch except a slight iron one which is moved forward with the work. Thus the excavation and the building of the tunnel keep pace with each other...The tunnel consists of a square mass of brickwork 37 feet by 22 feet containing in it two archways [carriageways]...The consumption of bricks is from 60–70 thousand per week with about 350 casks of cement....The bricklayers work night and day in shifts of eight hours'.

The work of the bricklayers was carefully supervised and if any brick was found to be loose the bricklayer was instantly dismissed. The tunnel finally opened in 1842 and later had a railway laid in it which remains in use to this day. During its construction Brunel used the tunnel yard to carry out some of the first tests on new materials. In 1838 he built an experimental iron-reinforced brickwork arch using Roman Cement creating a cantilever 60 ft long which required a counter balance of 62,700lb. However, despite its success in these ventures, the days of Roman Cement were numbered. Experiments which were to lead to its replacement for such works were carried out on another great engineering project of the 19th century: the London sewers.

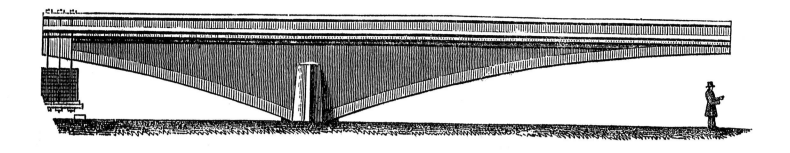

Sewers

The invention of the water closet in the 18th century had an unfortunate side effect: human waste, which had previously been stored in cesspits in back gardens before being carted away, now flowed into the drains and then into rivers. The earlier practice had hardly been hygienic, but the new one was proving disastrous. In London 6,536 people died in a cholera outbreak in 1831–32, 14,137 in a second in 1848–49 and 10,738 in a third in 1853–54. By 1858 the smell of the Thames had become so bad that Parliament could not meet. The hero of the hour was the engineer Joseph Bazalgette. Between 1858 and 1875 he supervised the construction of 1,200 miles of sewers under London that carried the drains 20 miles downstream where they could be safely discharged into the Thames Estuary well away from the city. Most importantly, he was one of the pioneers of the use of a new material: Portland Cement.

Portland Cement

On 21 October 1824 a bricklayer called Joseph Aspdin had taken out a patent on a new artificial stone, which he called Portland Cement because of its similarity to Portland stone. Roman Cement was brown while Aspdin's cement was white.

Ever since Parker's discovery that a superior cement could be made by burning the clay-rich lime nodules found in the Thames Estuary, inventors had been searching for a way of making a cement which artificially created the same effect by mixing clay and chalk in the correct proportions and burning them. This proved much more difficult than originally supposed. Today we call that replacement Portland Cement.

In fact Aspdin's first idea, recorded in his original patent, did not create what we call Portland Cement. His cement was no stronger than Roman Cement. It was his son William Aspdin who discovered by accident in 1842 that over-burnt waste from the manufacture of his father's recipe created a cement that retained its white colour, but had much greater powers of adhesion, creating the material we know today. Eighteen months later the same discovery was made independently by Isaac Charles Johnson who worked for John Bazley White. White already manufactured a type of stucco called Keene's Cement, but he soon started making his own Portland Cement. The Aspdins went out of business in 1855 and it was White's company who ultimately became the main supplier during the 19th century.

It was all very well for Aspdin and White to claim that their Portland Cements were stronger than their rivals, but it was more difficult to prove it. In December 1847 the first public compression tests of White's cement were carried out by Henry Grissel at the Regent's Canal Ironworks. They were witnessed by James Meadows, then President of the Institution of Civil Engineers. Nevertheless, English observers remained sceptical and White's company, then run by his son George White, had more success marketing their product abroad than at home. The Administration des Ponts et Chaussées in France carried out their own tests in 1847 and concluded that Portland Cement was far superior to any other product on the market in France. They put it to immediate use in the construction of Cherbourg harbour, using it not as a mortar but in the form of 45-ton solid blocks of

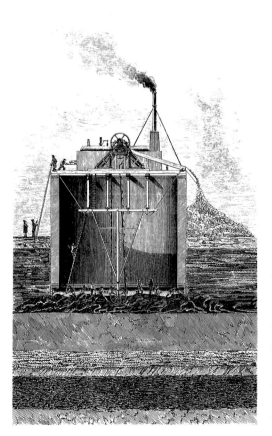

Above Marc Brunel's experimental cantilevered arch, which he constructed in 1838. The arch used Roman Cement and iron reinforcement.

Below One of the 15–25-m diameter vertical access shafts that Marc Brunel dug into the bed of the Thames from which he constructed the tunnel.

concrete. Thus by this time three uses had already been recognized for Portland Cement: stucco, mortar and concrete.

In brickwork, lime and sand remained the most common mortar. Roman Cement was used only where its water resistance was essential. In the London sewers, for instance, lime mortar was initially used for the roofs and upper half of the drains, while the lower halves (which carried the water) were made with Roman Cement. Portland Cement cost one and a half times more than Roman Cement and twice as much as lime mortar; nevertheless, Joseph Bazalgette was interested in the claims made for its superiority and directed an assistant engineer called John Grant to test it. Between January and July 1859 Grant carried out 302 experiments on the cement, concluding that Portland Cement was far stronger than Roman Cement and that it strengthened with age and immersion in water. As a result Portland Cement mortar replaced Roman Cement mortar on all new works on the London sewers. The results were later given as a paper delivered at the Institution of Civil Engineers in London in December 1865 together with details of how they had been used. By the late 1860s, Portland Cement had gone from being a material that engineers treated with suspicion to being an industry standard based on Bazalgette's seal of approval.

The acceptance of Portland Cement as a viable alternative to lime mortar was one of the most important in the history of bricklaying and was to have far-reaching consequences. Lime mortar was relatively weak. It kept the bricks apart and accommodated movement between them as they expanded and contracted as the temperature of the air changed. Mortar made with Portland Cement was much stronger; indeed it was often stronger than the bricks themselves. As a result, it glued the bricks firmly together. On the positive side, this allowed bricks to be laid in new ways, but the negative aspect, not initially understood, was that, once they were held rigidly together, brick walls expanded and contracted monolithically. This meant that, if movement joints were not incorporated into walls made with Portland Cement, the expansion and contraction could break the building apart. This was not initially realized because the difference in cost meant that such walls were rare. In fact, it was not until the middle of the 20th century that Portland Cement mortars became generally used for normal building work instead of lime mortar.

Left 'The New 4 per cent office' at the Bank of England, 9 June 1818. The Bank was designed by Sir John Soane. The vaults were constructed using hollow 'bottle bricks', first used in 1785 by the French architect St Far, for the Palais de Justice in Paris.

Opposite above Bonded warehouses (1908), Cumberland Basin, Bristol, built using brick façades and a concrete frame. Warehouses of this scale were a key part of Britain's Victorian industrial cities.

Below Two illustrations showing different types of patent floors of the many available around 1900. Floors like these used hollow terracotta sections spanning between steel joists.

Mechanization and Industrialization

Patents, pots and fireproofing

There is no doubt that the fireproof properties of brick were an important factor in its popularity in the 19th century. Factories were particularly prone to fire and all-brick construction offered an attractive if expensive solution.

Traditional brick building construction still relied heavily on timber for its structural stability. The floors and internal partitions were usually timber and these usually played an important part in bracing the structure as a whole. Timber lintels were used over windows and doors even on the inside leaf of the wall where on the outside of the building flat arches were on display. Timbers were also inserted into

the brickwork itself to strengthen it. These were known as bonding timbers. The practice was used at least as early as the 16th century in England and was mentioned in 18th century building manuals. It was eventually abandoned when it was realized that in time the timbers rotted, contributing to structural failures. The removal of bonding timbers from Georgian houses remains a problem today.

All these timber elements were flammable. It was, of course, possible to make the wall, ceilings and floors out of brick by using arched vaults, and such solutions were tried, but they used a huge number of bricks and as a result were limited in height. They were also costly and difficult to construct. Another solution was to use lightweight vaults. A French architect, St. Far, invented a vaulting system which he used successfully for the

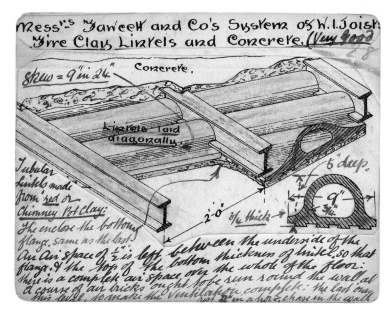

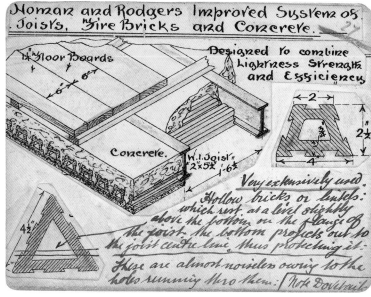

dome of the Palais de Justice in Paris in 1785 and employed by Sir John Soane in the construction of the Bank of England in 1818.

The invention of new and improved methods of smelting cast iron in 1709 by Abraham Darby meant that large members such as iron columns could now be produced. Uptake in England was slow, however, and it was not until the construction of the celebrated Iron Bridge at Coalbrookdale built between 1777 and 1781 that architects and engineers began to trust the material. The destruction of the Albion Mills by fire in 1791, only five years after they were built, led to an increased interest in fireproofing and led the designers to look again at iron and brick. The Derby Mill, constructed by William Strut in 1792, retained large timber floor beams but used brick arches with iron ties instead of planking and cast-iron columns. Strut's friend, Charles Bage took the idea one step further in a mill at Shrewsbury constructed between 1796–97 substituting iron beams for the wooden ones, the brick arches being supported on large flanges at the bottom of these beams. This type of construction, with larger beams creating greater spans, predominated in mill and barrack design in the first half of the 19th century in factory construction.

Next it was the brick vaults that came under scrutiny. The laying of a large number of bricks in shallow arching vaults required both skill and time. In the second half of the 19th century inventors set to work devising a bewildering array of solutions to this problem. By 1900 a huge range of patented pre-fabricated hollow terracotta bricks and beams were vying for a place in market. Typically these were designed to have concrete poured on top of them and it was only a matter of time before reinforced concrete floors replaced them altogether.

It was inevitable that the same sort of thinking should be applied to bricks. A number of patent brick systems were put forward in the 19th century, mostly based on the idea of larger hollow units which could be easily fitted together. An example exhibited at the Great Exhibition of 1851 is typical of this type of product. Simpler rectangular hollow bricks did find favour in Germany and northern Europe, where they are still used today, but even there the traditional brick is often used for facing. The size and shape of a brick had become so widely accepted and had proved so versatile that it was not easily replaced.

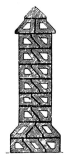

Above Hitch patent bricks as exhibited at the Great Exhibition in 1851, where they were used to construct a cottage intended as a prototype for future working-class housing. The exhibit was sponsored by the Society of Arts and Prince Albert.

Opposite 'Over London –
By Rail', a view of the notorious
Victorian slums from

Paul-Gustave Doré (1823–83)
and Blanchard Jerrold, *London:
A Pilgrimage* (1872).

Mechanization and Industrialization
Housing an industrialized world

As industrialization progressed, populations in Europe rose. In 1750 the population of England and Wales was about 6.5 million. By 1791 it was 8.2 million, in 1831 nearly 14 million and by 1871 22.7 million. In 120 years the population had increased threefold. What is more, much of that population now lived in cities, working in the factories. Similar figures could be quoted for other European countries as their populations exploded during the Industrial Revolution. Germany's population increased from 41 million in 1871 to 64.9 million in 1911 while America grew from 38.5 million to 91.7 million in the same period. Moreover the influence of European countries in the form of colonialism spread way beyond their borders. The increase in population created a demand for new dwellings.

In America much of the housing was constructed in timber. Elsewhere brick was commonly employed. Terraced houses were constructed in vast numbers in England, usually paid for by factory owners who then rented them back to their workers. The emphasis was on quantity rather than quality. Typically the houses were very simple in plan with different families on each floor, children and parents crammed in together in the minimum of space. Virtually all of these have now been cleared and it is the more salubrious and better built examples that tend to survive today. The latter typically consisted of two rooms on each floor: a kitchen and front room on the ground floor and two bedrooms upstairs. Toilets were in a yard at the rear. Initially houses were built using local materials but by the end of the century brick could be transported by rail, allowing brick of any colour to be used in any district. Houses no longer necessarily matched other buildings in the local area.

Of course, mass housing was not necessarily well-built. Horror stories abound in the late 19th century of greedy and unscrupulous builders skimping on materials and creating badly made, and at times positively dangerous, buildings. Georgian houses were often constructed badly too. Better-quality bricks were used for the outside while the ones on the inside of the wall might have been very poor with little or no bonding provided between the two layers so that the walls fell apart. In the 19th century the mortar was also a cause for concern. In December 1878 the *Builder* reported the case of a builder who had used building refuse and soil instead of sand and was duly fined by the magistrate. Elsewhere there were tales of bricks being laid in mud instead of mortar and of every attempt being made to reduce the amount of expensive lime employed. Despite these claims many of the buildings were sound and stand to this day.

By the end of the 19th century most European countries also had colonies abroad. Here they often built as they did at home, adapting their techniques only where absolutely necessary to take into account the local climatic conditions. Wherever possible the colonists baked bricks. For example, mile upon mile of brick terraced houses were built in Shanghai in this period. The grey bricks were burnt using traditional Chinese methods. However, the buildings which were used to house local labour working in foreign factories were Western in design, with details to suggest a local origin. In tropical areas brick was also used, but is less visible as it was typically covered in render because exposed brick was difficult to keep free of vegetation. By 1900 there were few corners of the globe that did not have some buildings constructed from brick, however alien and unsuitable it might be to the local conditions.

Above Streets in the old quarter of Shanghai. Only ten years ago, the city was almost entirely composed of labyrinth networks of streets like these still grouped around the state-run factories where the inhabitants worked. Most have now been cleared as Shanghai has developed into one of the most sophisticated cities in modern China. A small district is being preserved for tourism. The houses, most of which were built in the 19th-century, were small. No heating was allowed and small boxes on the front step held the cooking stove. Today they are supplied with electricity and still provide cramped accommodation for thousands of people.

The terracotta revival

The 19th century saw new techniques in the making of terracotta that allowed architects to incorporate detailed figures and reliefs at a reasonable cost. In so doing it was responsible for reviving an interest in brick as a building material.

Terracotta did not become fashionable in England until the 1860s and in America until the 1870s. Predictably, each successive revival was influenced by the previous one. Prior to this, however, its use had been promoted in Germany by the architect Karl Frederick Schinkel (1781–1841). In 1803 he had been on a tour of Italy and made detailed studies of the medieval and Renaissance brick and terracotta he found there. Inspired by what he saw, he later built a number of buildings in brick including a church, the Friedrich-Werder Kirche (constructed between 1824 and 1830). The best known and most influential of these was the Bauakademie (constructed between 1832 and 1835).

The Bauakademie (Architectural Academy), which stood next to the Friedrich-Werder Kirche in Berlin, housed a school of architecture and a public body responsible for art administration on the upper floors, with shops below. A skeleton of brick arches with iron tension rods provided the structure, leaving much of the external wall to be filled in with non-load-bearing brick panels. The brickwork itself was of exceptional quality to Schinkel's specification. Red unglazed bricks alternated every five courses with a band of lighter violet-coloured glazed bricks with fine lines of mortar between. Decoration was provided by allegorical terracotta reliefs in panels above the windows and around the doors, representing the evolution of

architecture and the balance between art and building technology, and by bands of purely ornamental work at the floor levels. The style of the building was termed *Rundbogenstil* (round-arch style). With its terracotta decoration, it combined Lombardic, Romanesque and Byzantine elements, but as brick architecture it could also be safely linked with the distinctly German *Backsteingotik* tradition. Its great technical advantage was the flexibility it allowed in façade design and it emerged as the style of choice for German institutions in the 1830s.

In England, national interest in the material was principally rekindled by the design for the Albert Hall (1867–71) and what is now the Victoria and Albert Museum (1859–71) in London's South Kensington, responsibility for which lay in the hands of the Secretary of the Science and Arts Department, Henry Cole. Cole was passionately interested in the improvement of the arts in general and terracotta in particular. As a young man he had toured England looking at how the material had been used in the early 16th century and later he travelled extensively in Italy. He was aware of recent developments in German architecture. It was thus hardly surprising that the style he chose for the buildings under his control was *Rundbogenstil*, which so successfully provided a way of articulating Italianate detail over large 19th-century

façades. Cole selected architects who worked in close collaboration with artists to produce the decorative details. Both the Victoria and Albert Museum and the Albert Hall could hardly have been more prominent yet they were achieved at remarkably low cost.

From the completion of the South Kensington buildings, terracotta began to appear throughout the country. Alfred Waterhouse (1830–1905) became the champion of the material in Britain in the following decades and his buildings remain a remarkable tribute both to his talent and to the material's possibilities. Like Schinkel, Waterhouse had originally considered a career as an artist and had travelled widely. He set up his own practice in Manchester in 1853, moving to London in 1865. His most famous design and one of his most dramatic was the Natural History Museum (1873–81), again in South Kensington. It was an enormous building, with a 680-ft (207-m) long main façade. Waterhouse distinguished it from its neighbours by setting it in the Gothic style. This married well with the contents of the museum. Instead of gargoyles, the front could be festooned with sculptural depictions of animals and every surface decorated with leaves or foliage, accurate in every botanical detail. The terracotta itself was unusual for its time both in colour (it was buff and blue-grey rather than pink) and because it was used for the entire wall surface (parts of the Victoria and Albert Museum had been made this way but not on such a scale). The complexity of the design and the scale of the operation proved too much for the contractors and the construction was dogged by problems, the building eventually opening five years late and considerably over budget. Despite this, it was generally admired by the public, who watched its progress through the sympathetic popular press. To this day it remains, both internally and externally, a stunning example of the use of the material and its possibilities. Waterhouse continued to design in brick and terracotta throughout his career, most notably in 17 of the branch offices he built for Prudential Assurance, his Victoria Building for the University of Liverpool (1887–92) and the headquarters of the Prudential (1898–1906) in London, but none of these rival the sheer exuberance and scale of the Natural History Museum, which remained his masterpiece.

Terracotta – the moral controversy

Waterhouse's enthusiasm for terracotta, which he called the 'material of the future' was not shared by everyone. Architects using terracotta tended to fall into one of two camps: those who used it as sculpted brick and those who used it as stone. The former tended to prefer the pink or red colours which the critics cruelly dubbed 'slaughterhouse red'. Those who used it as stone preferred the buffs and lighter pinks. These too were criticized, terracotta being rejected as an inferior poor man's substitute for stone. Part of the blame for that interpretation lay with the manufacturers themselves who, in the face of competition, had actively promoted their product as a low-cost alternative to stone and continually

attempted to undercut each other. In so doing they both lowered the status of the material and in their greed all too often drove their companies to the point of bankruptcy.

The more successful factories promoted the artistic side of product. In this they found an unexpected ally in the Arts and Crafts Movement. In theory, the supporters of the Movement were against mass production and factories of any kind, but they saw in terracotta a different kind of product. Although each mould could produce many copies, the sculpting of original models had to be done by hand and the creation of moulds themselves involved considerable skill. Terracotta workshops were thus perfect examples of craftsmen having

Opposite Royal Albert Hall (1867–71), Kensington Gore, London, designed by Francis Fowke, with its terracotta frieze illustrating 'The Triumph of Arts and Sciences'.

Above Terracotta details from the Victoria and Albert Museum (1854–71), London (left); the Prudential Assurance Building, London (centre); and the Rookery, Chicago (1885–86) by Burnham and Root (right).

Top Prudential Assurance Building (1879), Holborn, London, designed by Alfred Waterhouse.

a direct artistic input into the manufacturing process. The Art Worker's Guild promoted the material from its formation in 1884, particularly through the work of Charles Harrison Townsend, Edward Prior, Halsey Ricardo and Gilbert Bayes. But the most extreme example of Arts and Crafts terracotta was probably that of Mary Watts, wife of artist George F. Watts, who founded a village workshop called the Potter's Art Guild to build a memorial chapel for her husband in 1896 using only material dug up on the estate.

The flip side of the Arts and Crafts argument about the autonomy of the craftsman was that terracotta could be perceived as a threat to the architectural profession. Many manufacturers like George Jenning, Burmantofts, and J. C. Edwards produced catalogues of decorative elements available 'from stock'. At the very least this was seen to encourage lazy architects to assemble buildings from an unrelated jumble of pre-existing parts, and at worst it could be perceived as obviating the need for an architect altogether. In practice neither was the case. From the manufacturer's perspective, moulds were usually made of plaster and could not be re-used indefinitely. The catalogues were intended to provide ideas rather than actual stock details. While on the architect's side, even the most wayward designer still had to match his decorative panels to the size of bricks available, and in an age where there was no standardization of brick sizes this meant redrawing every detail to fit. Although there is no doubt that terracotta could and was used by mediocre architects to hide their badly proportioned designs under a forest of details, in the hands of the great architects, terracotta provided unrivalled opportunities for creating meaningful and co-ordinated decorative schemes for which detailed drawings could be provided to control every aspect.

Manufacturing

The manufacture of architectural terracotta has changed surprisingly little since the 19th century. Then, as now, it differed markedly from brickmaking or other pottery; greater accuracy was called for, the pieces produced were sometimes very large and shrinkage had to be taken into account. Victorian terracotta often relied on local clays, giving each manufacturer's product a distinctive colour. Thus the Ruabon works in North Wales produced the bright red terracottas which were widely used in North-western England, while the London-based Doulton factory provided the buffs and pinks more common in the capital.

The Natural History Museum (1873–81), South Kensington, London, designed by Alfred Waterhouse. The façade is decorated with terracotta animals, reflecting the contents of the museum.

Making terracotta

Top row 'Running' a cornice in plaster from which a mould will be cast in plaster in reverse; finishing the plaster mould; sculpting the clay by hand.

Middle row Filling the mould with clay (note the thickness of the layer applied); turning the clay out of the mould; removing any edges before firing.

Bottom row Empty moulds; a baluster being finished; various fired terracotta pieces ready for shipping.

For the architect too, terracotta imposed a new discipline. In stonework the final details could be worked out at the end of the project just before carving, but in terracotta all the drawings had to be completed early on in the process to allow for the eight weeks of manufacturing. When drawings were received in the factory the first task was to completely re-draw them at a size that took into account the shrinkage that would result from firing. After approval by the architect, these drawings were then taken to the modelling shop. Here a clay or plaster model of the piece would be made to the oversized drawings. This was then painted with a varnish so that a plaster mould could be cast around it. The design of this mould was no simple matter as it had to come apart to extract the finished piece. The clay itself was then poured into the mould as a slurry or pressed into it to the correct thickness by hand. The clay was left to dry and then extracted from the mould and finished by hand before entering the kiln for firing. In order to avoid cracking, the thickness of the terracotta was severely limited, which meant that larger pieces were always hollow. When fitted in place the hollows were filled with cement.

Manufacturers experimented with machine extrusion rather than moulding but it was difficult to control and unsuitable for most of the work required. The technique was more commonly adopted in America, most notably by the California firm of Gladding McBean. In England it was only used by Doultons.

The 1890s: faïence, glazed brick and Art Nouveau

Glazes had been used in pottery and tiles for thousands of years, but applying them to architectural terracotta in northern climates presented its own particular problems. The usual practice of firing the piece at a

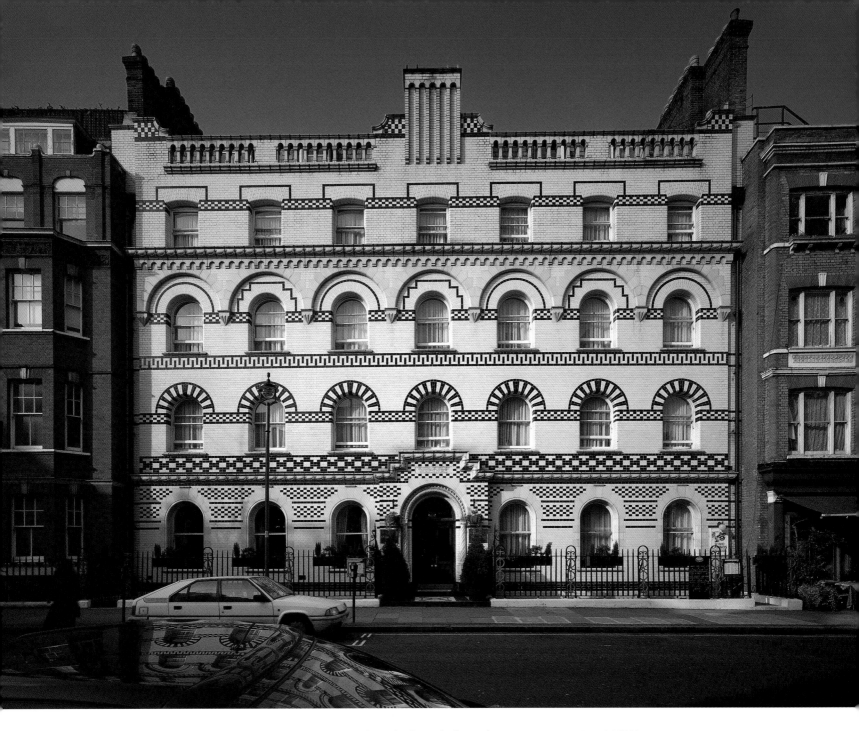

lower temperature, applying the glaze and then re-firing was simply too expensive for large scale architectural work, although smaller pieces (capitals, mouldings etc.) were produced in bulk in this way. More importantly the re-firing meant that early glazed works broke up in frost. They could thus only be used indoors. This problem was solved by single-fired glazing which was developed by the London firm of Doulton in 1888. The company of T. C. Booth went on to develop white glazed terracotta in America in 1894. Chemists specializing in glazes were in high demand, with glaze recipes remaining closely guarded secrets. By the end of the century, glazed terracotta (or faïence, as it was known in Britain) was available in a wide range of colours and heavily marketed for its wipe-clean 'pollution-resistant' properties.

The exuberance of natural terracotta was out of fashion in England by the end of the 1890s, but glazed ware in the form of tiles, glazed bricks and glazed terracotta were becoming increasingly popular. The older material represented a decadence and historicism that was unacceptable to the new order. Glazed terracotta, by contrast, was new, practical, economic and utilitarian. The finely wrought buildings of the 1860s and 1870s were now covered in a thick ugly black soot. Glazed terracotta, by contrast, promised always to look clean and new. Just as importantly the colours of the old material were mute and strictly limited while the new ones came in a bewildering range of bright and exciting hues. As a result, in Britain glazed terracotta began to be used for everything from banks to public houses, underground stations to cinemas.

Above Howard de Walden Nurses' Home (1901), now the Langham Court Hotel, London, by Arthur E. Thompson. A fine example of a façade composed entirely of glazed bricks and terracotta.

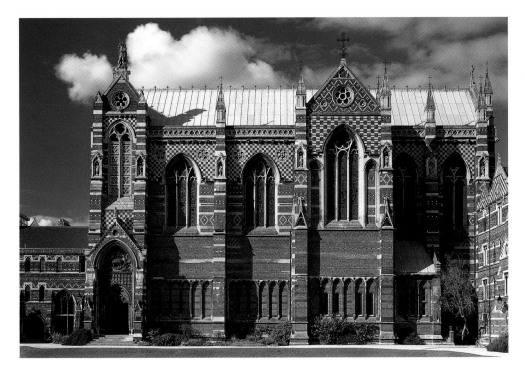

Opposite and left
Keble College, Oxford
(1867–83), by William
Butterfield (1814–1900).
Two views of the chapel.

Below All Saints Church,
Margaret Street (1849–59),
London, by William Butterfield.

Mechanization and Industrialization

Butterfield, Ruskin and English polychromy

By the middle of the 19th century, with the abolition of the brick tax in 1850, brick was becoming cheaper, and advances in transportation by rail meant that architects no longer had to rely entirely on local sources. Colour could be introduced into brickwork. It was suddenly possible to mix blue bricks from Staffordshire with yellow London stocks and lively Kentish reds or to build brick buildings in towns like Oxford where there was no local surface clay. That such a thing might be desirable, however, was a matter open for debate.

In the late 18th century in England it had become increasingly accepted that externally at least buildings should largely monochromatic. The sensibility came no doubt partly from the assumption that Greek and Roman buildings had been uncoloured, but it was applied with equal vigour to Gothic ones from which the colour had been removed at the Reformation and in the Interregnum.

Victorian England was riven by Protestant theological debate. On the one side were the growing bodies of new reformist Churches while on the other were those wishing to return to high-church Anglicanism with a close adherence to the Book of Common Prayer and a suspicion of everything new. The conservative Cambridge Camden Society produced a journal on church design, the *Ecclesiologist*. The first issue appeared in 1841 and it continued to be published until 1868, the society having ceased its Cambridge connection in 1844–45 and become the Ecclesiological Society. This journal became the main centre of debate on church design and thus of Gothic Revival architecture. Their attitude to colour was a telling reaction against what was seen as puritanical

austerity. 'We would have every inch glowing' they declared in 1845, while 'Puritans…would have every inch colourless'. Of course the reaction was to condemn the writers as Catholics. Thus the debate raged between those who favoured colour in architecture and those who saw it as aesthetic and moral decadence.

The great writers in favour of colour in England were the architect George Edmund Street, design reformer Owen Jones and the art critic and writer John Ruskin. Street put forward his ideas on polychromy and promoted the use of brick in his *Brick and Marble Architecture of the Middle Ages in Italy*, published in 1855. Owen Jones promoted the use of decoration in design in his *Grammar of Ornament* (1856), while Ruskin enthused about the importance of colour and pattern in his *Seven Lamps of Architecture* (1849) and *Stones of Venice* (1851–53). Architects like Street, Scott, Teulon and Waterhouse all exploited the possibilities of polychromatic brickwork, but the most famous and strident architect in this tradition was undoubtedly William Butterfield (1814–1900).

Butterfield's work is characterized by a strong use of polychromatic brickwork, most notably in All Saints Church, Margaret Street in London and Keble College, Oxford. Keble was highly controversial at the time because Oxford had no history of brick construction, of which Butterfield was well aware. When attacked, he declared his intention 'as long as I continue to work, to take the responsibility of thinking for myself, and to use the materials, whatever they may be, which locality and this age supply'. Despite this apparent

Left and top Keble College, Oxford (1867–83), by William Butterfield (1814–1900). Views of the chapel across the main quadrangle.

Above View of the hall.

modernism, however, like all Victorian architects he was careful to cite historical precedents. He thus justified the lively zig-zags and diaper patterns of the upper parts of the walls as references to medieval brick patterns although his were clearly more elaborate than anything that survived from the Middle Ages. In this Butterfield and his contemporaries were following the contemporary practice of producing what they thought medieval builders would have done supposing they had 19th-century technology. In choosing bricks, however, Butterfield preferred the texture of hand-moulded ones and the use of burnt headers rather than uniformly glazed bricks although he was fond of the precision in brick sizes that improved kiln technology, provided which allowed him to have bricks laid in English bond with narrow joints. No-one could emulate Butterfield: his style was too individual. Yet he was highly influential, not least for the architects of the Arts and Crafts who admired his understanding of materials and his awareness of their possibilities.

Mechanization and Industrialization

Brick and iron in French architecture 1850–1900

In most of France, and in Paris in particular, brick had been unpopular as a building material for use on the exterior of buildings, although it was frequently used for the core of walls faced with stone. It was only in the middle of the 19th century that it began to return to prominence. One of the most important structures constructed in this period and no doubt responsible for a renewal of interest in its possibilities was the great covered market of Les Halles in the centre of Paris.

Designed by architects Victor Baltard and Félix Callet and built in two different phases in 1854–57 and 1860–66, Les Halles were the most important markets in Paris. The buildings consisted of iron columns supporting brick vaults. Although the emphasis was purely on functionality rather than decoration and the rationale behind the use of brick was of course fire-proofing, the brick outer walls were decorated with garish diaper patterns of red bricks on a yellow background. The combination of brick and iron had proved itself effective and over 40 brick and iron markets were subsequently constructed in the city and beyond. Les Halles itself was demolished in 1971 to make way for a huge underground shopping centre. Some of the smaller markets still survive.

Paris underwent a massive expansion in the middle of the 19th century, its population climbing to one million in 1841. Under Napoleon III and Haussmann, the streets were re-planned and massive boulevards were carved through the centre. Regulations specified that buildings on those boulevards must be faced with stone.

The structures behind and buildings elsewhere could be built in brick. Haussmann's Engineer in Chief of the parks, J. C. Alphand, built a number of park pavilions in the new brick and iron style.

The movement towards increased use of brick was given further momentum by the Expositions held in 1878 and 1889 and by a series of publications in the following decades. The first of these was Eugène Emmanuel Viollet-le-Duc's *Entretiens sur l'architecture* published in two parts in 1863 and 1872, which illustrated a number of outlandish schemes for buildings with iron frames and brick or stone infill. In these he built on his theories of the structural rationalism which he saw as being embodied in Gothic architecture and projected them forward to provide an architecture for the future. His arguments would be deeply influential for the use of iron in architecture. In contrast to Viollet-le-Duc's work, J. Lacroux and C. Detain's *La brique ordinaire* (published in two parts: the first in 1878 and the second in 1886) was devoted entirely to brick. Its text and 108 coloured plates looked mainly at houses but also contained diagrams of bonding patterns and designs

for colleges, factories and apartment blocks. It was followed by Pierre Chabat's *La brique et la terre cuite*, published in 1881 (with a further volume in 1889), which showed grander buildings and had a more comprehensive text including a history of brickwork. These books were gaudily coloured and sought to encourage a new style of architecture which mixed polychromatic brickwork with a range of other materials in a variety of styles.

Opposite and above
The Covered Market (1902),
Albi, France, typical of the brick
and iron architecture used
for railway stations, factories
and utilitarian structures at
the end of the 19th and
beginning of the 20th century.
The structure is iron with
capitals and ornamentation.
The surfaces between are simple
panels of 230 x 110 x 55mm
white and red bricks laid
in lively decorative
bonding patterns.

Left A 19th-century colour
plate of the Menier Factory
(1871–72), Noisel, near Paris,
designed by Jules Saulnies, one
of the most colourful examples
of the 'brick and iron style'.
Illustrations like this in
19th-century books played
an important part in
popularizing the
new style.

This page The Rijksmuseum (1876–85), Amsterdam, designed by Petrus Cuypers (1827–1921), was built to hold the Dutch national art collection and remains one of the most important art museums in the world.

Opposite Amsterdam Central Station (1885–89), also designed by Cuypers, sits in front of the harbour so that ships could unload directly to the trains. In so doing, however, it severed the city's connection with the port which had previously been its focus.

Mechanization and Industrialization

Petrus Cuypers and the Gothic Revival in Holland

The dilemma revealed in Viollet-le-Duc's theories, discussed in the last section, between a wish to revive the past and a desire for structural rationalization, was also evident in the works of Petrus Cuypers, one of the most important Dutch architects of the last quarter of the 19th century.

Petrus Josephus Hubertus Cuypers (1827–1921) was born in Roermund in the Catholic south of the Netherlands. He went to the Academy of Antwerp,

Belgium, graduating in 1849 with the Prix d'Excellence. Many of his ideas were formed during a short stay in Paris where he went to meet Viollet-le-Duc. His ideas

had a significant effect on the young Cuypers, who is said to have often repeated the former's dictum that architectural form should arise exclusively from an expression of structure. Cuypers was, however, less dogmatic in his architecture than this might suggest. He subsequently returned to his native town where in 1850 he set up as an architect and furniture designer. Two years later he founded Cuypers and Stoltenberg, a furniture-making workshop which supplied architectural decoration for churches. It was here that he formed ideas similar to those of William Morris on the relationship of the craftsman to architecture and design and the importance of honesty in the use of materials, in particular brick, while his thoughts on the importance of ornament had a lot in common with John Ruskin.

The introduction of laws in 1853 allowing freedom of worship meant that Catholics could once again build churches. Cuypers found himself engaged on a series of churches as well as the restoration of medieval structures which, following Viollet-le-Duc's example, he restored to what they should have been, rather than what had existed before. It is not, however, for his brick

churches nor for his restorations that Cuypers is chiefly remembered, but for his two great secular works: the Rijksmuseum (1876–1885) and Amsterdam Central Station (1885–1889).

Cuypers had moved his practice to Amsterdam in 1865 as the amount of work he had in the city had become unmanageable from a distance. On starting the Rijksmuseum he was disappointed to realize that there were too few craftsmen of sufficient skill and he immediately set about rectifying this, founding the Rijksmuseum School (later renamed the Quellinus School) where he himself taught applied arts and art history.

Cuypers believed that the brickwork of the exterior of a building should reflect its internal layout and should be structurally in keeping with the principles of Viollet-le-Duc, but he was not slavish in his medievalism and indeed the Rijksmuseum is composed of many styles, as befitted a museum that sought to celebrate the whole of Netherlandish history. Moreover, he believed strongly in the importance of art in building, commissioning craftsmen to design and ornament the various parts. He saw architecture as

evolving from a mixture of sources and thought nothing of combining brickwork, stone, gilding and terracotta in a single façade to create a particular effect. In this Cuypers's work is emblematic of the sort of Gothic Revival architecture that was being carried out all over northern Europe in the late 19th century. His railway station also highlights a problem faced by this revivalism. Like St Pancras in London, the brick façade of Amsterdam Central Station sits unhappily in front of an iron train shed, designed by the railroad engineer L. J. Eijmer. Cuypers did mix iron with Gothic in his Dominicuskerk built near the station between 1882 and 1886, which had an iron roof, but his primary interest always remained in designing in a Gothic manner.

It was a younger man, Hendrik Petrus Berlage (1856–1934) who sought to resolve these issues in his theoretical and built work. Unlike Cuypers, Berlage was fond of writing as well as building. In his *Grundlagen und Entwicklung der Architektur* (Foundations and Development of Architecture) he set out his ideas which had been influenced by Semper, Morris, Muthesius and others, and would find echoes

in Wright and Loos, that beauty could only be found in things which had a utilitarian purpose. He believed that applied ornament should be avoided. He preferred mechanically produced bricks and admired the massive unadorned brick structures of the Romans and praised the material for its low cost. Bricks and mortar, he maintained, symbolized the ethical rectitude of the democratic society, the bricks representing individual worldly endeavours and the mortar the binding agent of intellectual society from which the perfect edifice could be constructed. He put his ideas into practice in a number of buildings, the most famous of which is the Stock Exchange in Amsterdam. The principles and ideas of both Berlage and Cuypers, while different, were not entirely contradictory and had an important influence on the generations of architects in the Netherlands that followed and in particular on the Amsterdam School.

Left and opposite above
Colegio Teresiano (1888–90),
Barcelona, by Antoni Gaudí i
Cornet (1852–1926), a convent
school for Catholic teachers, is
more austere than much of
Gaudí's later work. Its structure
relies on the strength of brick
parabolic arches. These are
used on the façade and
to form internal cloisters.
The building was constructed
on foundations laid by a
previous architect. It was
badly damaged in the Spanish
Civil War but has since
been restored.

Opposite below Casa Vicens
(1883–88), Barcelona, also by
Gaudí. In this early work, Gaudí
uses painted bricks and tiles
to create a rich and playful
language reminiscent of
Mudejar architecture in
Spain but not derivative of it.

Gaudí and the search for the organic

Casa Vicens (1883-1888) stands in an unremarkable back street in Barcelona. Its façades corbel out over the road. A riot of colour, every surface is made of a different texture. Although it is obviously brick, few bricks are visible. The eye is drawn inexorably across it as it is drawn over the details of a Baroque interior, but this is not Italian Baroque. In Barcelona at that time, a movement called *modernista* played with historical references to produce a new type of organic architecture which has parallels with Art Nouveau in France. In some senses Casa Vicens belongs to this style. In its interior one can also see strong references to Spain's Mudejar past. But more than anything else, Casa Vicens is the particular creation of that most innovative of late 19th-century designers, Antoni Gaudí i Cornet (1852–1926).

Gaudí was born in Reus in Catalonia, the son of a coppersmith. The two great influences on his early life were nature (which he observed at length during long walks) and his religious education. He decided not to follow the family tradition of going into metalworking but to study architecture instead. He was influenced by Ruskin's ideas on ornament and Viollet-le-Duc's theories on the role of structure in architecture. Even as a student his schemes were considered outlandish by his teachers and he graduated without distinction.

Gaudí was convinced that architecture was necessarily a reflection of nature which in turn was a reflection of God. The development of his architectural language can be seen as a progression away from the rectilinearity of traditional architecture to an increasingly organic and curvilinear architecture of his later work. Casa Vicens marks the earliest stage

Above Pavilions Guëll (1884–87), the gate pavilions of the Guëll Estate. The joints are galletted with broken pieces of glazed tile (top).

Opposite The Crypt of the Colonia Guëll Church (1898), originally intended as the crypt of a larger church which was never completed.

in this process. Here bricks are used to form ornamentation that is original in its design but still basically rectilinear. The façade is composed of a large number of planes that intersect and cantilever out from the surface.

This is taken one step further in his design for the Colegio Teresiano, a convent school located at 319 – 325 calle de Ganduxer, Barcelona, built between 1888 and 1890. Here Gaudí used the parabolic arch as a generating form both for the internal structure and the façades. This looked back directly to the structural rationalism of Viollet-le-Duc. The parabola is the most efficient shape for an arch. What is more when steep parabolas like those Gaudí uses at the Colegio Teresiano are constructed out of brick there is no need for formwork. Each course is simply projected slightly further over the one beneath. This gave the parabolic arch an immediate advantage over the traditional voussoired semi-circular or Gothic arches typically used by other architects of the period. The result is a building that conforms to no particular style but grows directly out of its structural rationale. Nevertheless this is not an exercise in modernist functionalism. Gaudí believed strongly in the importance of ornament and brick is used to create detailed patterns across the façade.

In the Pavilions Guëll (1884–1887), gate pavilions for entry into the Guëll estate, Gaudí used bricks to produce a wide variety of effects and form a background for brightly coloured mosaic ornament, alluding to Oriental traditions. Mosaic is also inserted in the mortar. The practice of inserting coloured stones in mortar joints was used in the Middle Ages. The English term for this technique is 'galletting'. Medieval galletting was employed partly to protect the mortar, but Gaudí used it entirely for decorative effect.

The main pavilion is roofed using a particular technique of brick vaulting where the bricks are laid flat in layers. This technique, which has a long history in Spain, is called *la tabicada*. The bricks employed are more like large, square and flat tiles. They are laid flat, in the plane of the vault. The upper surface and joints are covered in gypsum mortar and a second layer of tiles at 45 degrees to the first is laid on top. The use of gypsum mortar is the key to the whole technique. Its quick drying properties mean that each tile can be held in place by a simple wooden prop and by hand. The vault can thus be built with the minimum of support from underneath. The art is to place the bricks at the correct angle to create the curve accurately. Vaults are commonly built from two or three layers and called *doblades* and *tresdoblades* accordingly.

This technique has been used in Spain from at least the 16th century when brick began to replace stone as

a cheaper alternative. Recorded early examples include the vaults of the gallery of the courtyard of the Tavera Hospital in Toledo, built by Alonso de Covarrubias in the 1540s, and of the church of the monastery of Santo Domingo el Antiguo de la Cuidad, built by Juan de Herrera in the 1570s. The technique became common in the 17th century. Although the thin shells created were not used to support structures they were perfectly adequate to hold the loads of people walking on them.

Historically such vaults were carefully set to exact curvatures, a practice that Gaudí himself followed in his workshops for the Sagrada Familia. However, it also presented the opportunity to create more complex freeform curves. Gaudí used it for precisely this purpose in one of his most remarkable buildings, the Crypt of the Colonia Guëll (Guëll Colony) (1898).

Gaudí's surviving drawings and models for the Chapel of the Guëll Colony show that he had planned a grandiose structure. In the event only the crypt was completed before his clients lost patience and withdrew their support. The result is nonetheless impressive. The plan of both the crypt and the superstructure that would have stood above it was curvilinear, assymetric and complex. In the crypt Gaudí worked from his principle that the structure should emulate nature and, as nothing in nature was vertical, the columns and walls should incline. He mixed materials freely, using stone and brick, together with overburnt slag from the local iron foundry in the walls and a combination of arches and *la tabicada* for the vaults.

Gaudí's architecture partly arose from his working method, which involved being closely involved in the building operations. He chose the stones himself and stood on site supervising their placement. It was this obsession with controlling every aspect of the construction of a project that gave each of his works its individuality. However, equally his inability to delegate and failure to create a way that his architecture could be communicated in drawings or models to others meant that his work inevitably progressed at a snail's pace. He was less inclined to use brick in his later work as his shapes became increasingly organic. Brick imposed a discipline and order on the construction that was ultimately antithetical to Gaudí's approach. The brick is rectangular and thus not a natural form. He increasingly turned to stone and concrete, which were more suited to the creation of his twisting, writhing, inclined and contorted structures and his search for his very individual interpretation of the organic in architecture.

Richardson and American brickwork

In the 1860s, America was still looking to Europe for inspiration, yet by the 1870s there were signs of a new generation of American architects beginning to emerge whose originality was to extend the vocabulary of American architecture and provide it with a character of very much of its own. Among these was Henry Hobson Richardson (1838–86).

America was as inspired by the writings of Ruskin as Britain, prompting a move away from Neo-classicism and towards Gothic. Ruskinian polychromatic Gothic was used for the first time in the United States in 1860 in the Trinity Church Parish School in New York, designed by Jacob Wrey Mould, a young English designer who emigrated to America. It was the National Academy of Design in New York, however, which brought the style to public attention. This building, designed by Peter B. Wight, was a rather literal re-interpretation of the Doge's Palace in Venice which Ruskin had praised so highly. Thereafter the fashion for polychromatic building, particularly in brick, grew apace. The Museum of Fine Arts in Boston (1870–76) used a mixture of brick and terracotta inspired by the museums in London's South Kensington. The terracotta initially had to be imported from England, but it was not long before American manufacturers were supplying increasing quantities at home. Leopold Eidlitz introduced brightly coloured diaper brick patterns to New York in his Church of the Holy Trinity, completed in 1873. A similar riot of colour was on display in the Memorial Hall, Harvard

University, Cambridge, Mass. designed by Henry Van Brunt and William R. Ware, although Van Brunt accused Ruskin of being a 'dictator on the questions of art' divorced from practicalities of building. He preferred the writings of Viollet-le-Duc.

Henry Hobson Richardson was born on 29 September 1838 in Louisiana, growing up on his father's plantation and in New Orleans. He spent a year at the University of Louisiana before entering Harvard in 1856. After graduation in 1859, he travelled to Paris where he spent the next five years, part of the time at the École des Beaux-Arts. On his return he went into practice with Charles Dexter Gambrill (1834–80) and designed in the styles of the day (mostly Gothic and Second Empire). By the late 1870s, however, he had formed a style very much his own.

Sever Hall (1878–80), Harvard University, is certainly the finest building he ever constructed in brick. Richardson typically built in local materials and most of his larger works were constructed in stone. Sever Hall stands in Harvard Yard, the oldest part of the University. Brick was chosen with regard to the neighbouring 18th-century buildings. Richardson makes no further concessions and that is as far as the similarities go. The Hall uses precise red bricks from the North Cambridge brickyard of M. W. Sands. These measure 300 x 90 x 55mm and are laid in English Garden Wall bond with 10-mm joints. The heads of the windows use flat cut brick arches (jack arches in American terminology) which are set between Longmeadow stone insertions that act like bookends and emphasize the outward thrusts. Similarly large projecting corbels support the base of the arch which forms the main entrance on the yard side. Thus stone plays an important role in the structure but it is not used for decoration. Instead the surfaces are enlivened with inserted panels and moulding made from red terracotta chosen to match the brick and blending closely with it. Other panels are made from decorative brick bonds. The result is a highly original building, which uses brick in sophisticated and original ways.

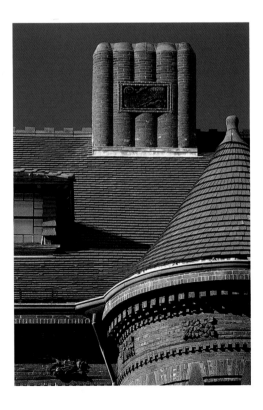

Above Sever Hall (1878–80), Harvard University, Cambridge, Mass., USA, by Henry Hobson Richardson (1838–86), paid for by a bequest from James Warren Sever. The building contains classrooms and has been little altered since its construction. The west front is approached along a brick path.

Left Richardson grouped the chimney shafts into a block and added a terracotta plaque.

Opposite above The façade is enlivened by areas of cut and moulded bricks.

Opposite below Richardson paid great attention to every aspect of the construction.

Mechanization and Industrialization

Prairie Style brick: Frank Lloyd Wright

The figure of Wright deservedly looms large in the history of American architecture. His effect on 20th-century house design was marked. His plans were organized not in rooms but in interconnecting spaces, relying on subtle changes in ceiling height and floor level to introduce divisions. Externally his houses consisted of long low planes, so that through a series of external platforms the house was raised above the landscape, appearing to sail through it like a ship. Brick played an important part in defining what he called the Prairie Style.

Wright had a genius for architectural composition and massing and an unwavering originality and self-belief. Perhaps the greatest inspiration for Wright's early work was his mentor Louis Sullivan. Wright had entered the office of Adler and Sullivan in 1888. At this time it was the most important practice in Chicago and Louis Sullivan was the creative force behind the practice. Most of the work was for large office buildings, the first skyscrapers, which were constructed with iron or steel frames and clad in stone or terracotta. Sullivan created breathtakingly beautiful designs for the ornamentation of these buildings which were transferred into working

drawings by George Grant Elmslie from which the terracotta was fabricated. It was the introduction of the iron frame in Chicago in the late 19th century that was to impress later generations looking back. But for Wright it was probably Elmslie's and Sullivan's decorative schemes that were more directly influential.

Frank Lloyd Wright worked in the office of Adler and Sullivan between 1887 and 1892 during some of the practice's most successful years. Although Wright had attended an engineering course at the University of Wisconsin, he appears to have been a poor student and

left before completing his studies. Instead he learnt architecture the more traditional way, through working in an office, first under Cecil Corwin, head draughtsman for Joseph Lyman Silsbee. When he had gained in confidence he approached Sullivan. It is said that Wright claimed at interview to be conversant with Sullivan's work and to have made a number of designs in his style. Sullivan called his bluff and asked to see them and Wright had to stay up all night producing suitable drawings which he showed him the following day. Whatever the case, Sullivan took the young man on and he worked in the practice until it ran out of work five years later and Wright set up on his own. By that time he had already designed a number of houses on his own account and was rapidly developing what he would later call his Prairie Style of architecture.

The Prairie House Style that Wright created was not dependent on any single material. Prairie houses were built of timber clad in shingles and stone as well as in brick, but brick had certain advantages over the others: it was cheaper than stone and longer-lasting than timber. In addition, brick could be used to emphasize that key element of the Prairie House: the horizontal. This Wright did in a number of ways. The first was to use what are mistakenly called 'Roman bricks'. These were long thin bricks that Wright laid with wide raked horizontal joints and the vertical ones either very thin or, as is the case in the Robie House (1906), with the joints filled flush with mortar of the same colour as the bricks. The effect is to provide long horizontal stripes

across the façade emphasizing the horizontals. The bricks themselves were not Roman: they were simply longer than normal. The bricks at the Robie House are 295 x 100 x 42mm. It was the way in which they were laid (set in 15-mm horizontal joints with 5-mm perpends) that gave them a Roman character. At the Arthur Heurtley Residence (1902), Wright had already gone further, recessing some courses and projecting others to create distinct horizontal bands within the brickwork.

Although Wright experimented with concrete blocks in the Usonian Houses and concrete walls elsewhere, he returned to brick whenever he felt it was suitable for the context and the design at hand. For instance in 1948 he used 'Roman brick' for the arched façade of the Morris Gift Shop in San Francisco and he used regular bricks for the Meyers Medical Clinic in Dayton, Ohio (1956) and the Sterling Kinney Residence in Amarillo, Texas (1957). None of these, however, use brick in such a mannered fashion as his early work.

Above left Nathan G. Moore Residence and Stable (1895), Oak Park, Chicago, designed by Frank Lloyd Wright.

Top and above right Frederick C. Robie Residence (1906), Chicago. Often said to be built out of Roman bricks, the bricks are simply larger versions of standard bricks.

CHAPTER SEVEN

INTO THE 20TH CENTURY 1900 – 2000

More bricks were produced and laid in the 20th century than in any other century in history. It is surprising that although brick continued to be one of the most common building materials, many perceive the 20th century as being a period of decline. Some of the blame can probably be ascribed to architectural historians, who have often given the impression that all buildings in the modern era were wholly constructed in concrete, steel and glass. Even a brief examination of 20th-century architecture shows that this was not the case. Despite the rhetoric to the contrary, brick prospered in the 20th century and some of the greatest modernist architects produced their most sensitive buildings using it.

The Modern Movement in architecture gained enormous momentum after the horrors of the First World War. In its aftermath, it was not unnatural that many sought to reject anything that was rooted in traditional values, which were held responsible for the war itself. Modernist architectural tracts called for mass-production and for buildings to be constructed of new materials, especially steel, glass and concrete. In brick the modernists were faced with an awkward dilemma. On the one hand the material was the epitome of mass-production, a regular repeated unit produced by the million by machine for next to nothing, yet on the other it was embarrassingly old. In fact most of the other materials were similarly not as modern as the modernists would have liked: iron had been used in building construction by the Greeks and iron structures had developed in the 19th century. Concrete and glass were both used by the Romans. Just as the modernists were willing to accept those as truly modern materials by a convenient fudging of historical fact, so brick was also let in through the back door and even the staunchest supporters of steel, glass and concrete rhetoric, such as Mies van de Rohe and Le Corbusier, built buildings in brick. There were also more embarrassing episodes such as the building of the famous Einstein Tower by the Prussian modernist Erich Mendelsohn (1887-1953). This building was built in Expressionist curving shapes to exploit the new potential of concrete; in the event it had to be constructed in brick and painted to look like concrete, which was hardly an exercise in the modernists' principle of truth to materials.

The opening section of this chapter looks at the crucial role played by brick in the development of the skyscraper. This is contrasted with the use of brick in the Arts and Crafts Movement in England, here represented by a building by Edwin Lutyens.

Expressionism in architecture flourished in Germany and can be found in works such as Fritz Höger's Chilehaus (1923) in Hamburg, but perhaps the most dramatic example of this sort of northern Expressionism is the Grundtvigkirke by Peder Jensen Klint in Copenhagen, Denmark, which is the subject of the next section. In Holland, it developed into a style called the Amsterdam School. This is discussed through the work of its leading exponent, Michel de Klerk (1884-1923).

The chapter goes on to look at the development of Art Deco in the 1920s. Today we tend to think of skyscrapers as being clad in glass but many of the most famous Art Deco skyscrapers were clad in brick, the most famous of which is the Chrysler Building in New York. By the 1930s, the clean lines of modernist design were well-established in Holland through the influence of De Stijl, a group of artists and designers identified by the magazine they produced. One of the leading buildings in the style, Hilversum Town Hall, was actually designed by an architect working outside the group, called Willem Marinus Dudok. The construction of this seminal building is discussed in detail as it went on to influence many architects worldwide.

Developments in 20th-century brickmaking are then examined with particular reference to the mechanization of brick factories in Europe and the United States. In Britain a key development was the discovery of so-called Oxford Clay around the village of Fletton near Peterborough in 1881. These deep-bed clays were dry enough to be pressed into bricks and fired immediately and the oil within the clay dramatically reduced fuel costs. *Flettons*, as they were called, were first made in late 19th century and represented a sizeable percentage of all brick production in the UK by the 1920s but as

the process depends entirely on the availability of suitable clays it was not widely used elsewhere.

The chapter then turns to a discussion of mass housing, which became one of the main markets for bricks in the 20th century. The Second World War destroyed much of Europe's housing stock and in the aftermath brick was a vital material in helping to re-build. The Byker Wall in Newcastle, England, is used as an example of how brick played an important role in this process.

The second half of the chapter examines various issues in the use of brick through examples of works by famous architects. Alvar Aalto's work is looked at through his Baker Housing project for MIT in Cambridge, Mass. Lewerentz's puritanical attitude to the use of the brick is examined in the context of St Peter's Church at Klippan. Kahn's ideas about technological rationalism are explored through his library for Philips Exeter, New Hampshire. Renzo Piano's use of terracotta is discussed with reference to his extension to IRCAM in Paris. The environmental advantages of thermal mass are examined in the context of Erik Sørenson's Crystallographic Data Centre in Cambridge, England; the use of structural brick by looking at the opera house at Glyndebourne, England by Patty and Michael Hopkins; the cavity wall through Rick Mather's extension to Keble College, Oxford and the role of brick in creating decorative surfaces in the cathedral by Mario Botta at Evry in France.

The chapter ends with a brief discussion of two important topics: the role of conservation in preserving skills in brickwork and the part played by brick in building in the developing world where the increasing use of mud bricks brings history around full circle.

Opposite The extension to IRCAM (1988–89), Paris, by Renzo Piano uses perforated bricks supported on rods in metal frames which act as rain-screen cladding to the staircase and lift shaft.

Chilehaus, Hamburg, Germany

Grundtvigkirke, Copenhagen, Denmark

Battersea Power Station, London, England

Scheepvaarthuis, Amsterdam, Netherlands

St Peter's Church, Klippan, Sweden

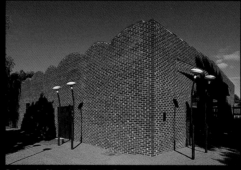

Flatiron Building, New York, USA

Folly Farm, Sulhampstead, England

Philips Exeter Library, New Hampshire, USA

Spaarndammerbuurt Complex, Amsterdam, Netherlands

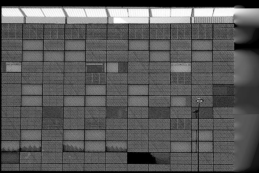

Research Centre, France

Tate Modern, London, England

Evry Cathedral, France

Chrysler Building, New York, USA

Crystallographic Data Centre, Cambridge, England

Spaarndammerbuurt Complex, Amsterdam, Netherlands

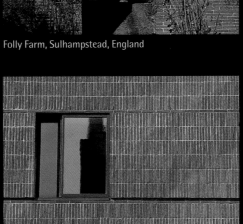

Folly Farm, Sulhampstead, England

Flatiron Building, New York, USA

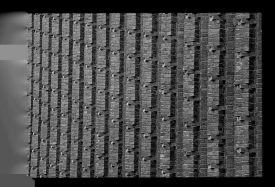

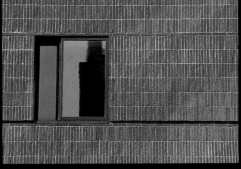

Into the 20th Century

The American dream and the lure of the skyscraper

If one building type can be said to sum up the 20th century more than any other, it is surely
the skyscraper. The race to build ever higher dominated American construction and design.
Yet the contribution of the brick to the skyscraper's design goes virtually unnoticed.

The story of the skyscraper can be traced back before
the 20th century. It starts with the factories and mills
and the developments of iron in building discussed in
the last chapter and with the great fire that swept
through Chicago in 1871. At that time, two-thirds of
the buildings in the city had been constructed in wood
while the larger commercial buildings had brick
façades and iron columns supporting timber floors. The
fire started in a barn on De Koven Street on 8 October
and burned for 48 hours. In that time it destroyed over
a third of the value of the property in the city, reaping
$192,000,000 of damage and making 100,000 people
homeless. Re-building began immediately and with
extraordinary speed but it was not reckless, for the city
had learnt its lesson and building owners demanded
that their architects build fireproof buildings to replace
those lost. The answer was to adopt the methods of
iron construction that had already been developed in
Europe. The invention of the elevator offered new
possibilities: for the first time it was realistic
to build higher. Elisha Otis (1811–61) had developed
his safety lift in 1850. The first steam-driven elevators
were installed in Chicago buildings in 1864 and
the first hydraulic elevator in 1870 in the store
and warehouse of Burley and Company on
West Lake Street.

    The structure of the post-fire buildings was simple.
The exterior walls and lift cores used masonry
construction. They were either completely brick

or brick faced with stone. Internally iron columns
supported beams for the floors. The foundations were
simply walls that stepped out beneath ground level.
Obviously the thickness of the load-bearing outer
walls had to increase with the height. Chicago
architects generally reckoned that 12 inches of wall
were required to support the first storey with an extra
four inches for every additional storey. Such building
methods were typical of the 1870s and 1880s.
The use of masonry walls put a generally accepted
limit on height on the building of ten storeys.
Only one building using this method exceeded this:
the Monadnock Building constructed at
53 West Jackson Boulevard between 1889
and 1891.

Right Monadnock Building,
Chicago (1889–91), by Burnham
and Root, one of the tallest
brick buildings ever built.
At its base the walls are over
six-feet thick.

The Monadnock building is 16 storeys high, six
storeys higher than was thought possible for a building
using masonry construction. Its parapet is 215 feet
above the pavement. Although it is not as tall as the
tower of Siena Town Hall, it is a great deal bigger and
remains one of the tallest brick buildings in the world.
To support the weight of 16 storeys of masonry the
walls on the ground floor are six feet thick. It was
designed by Daniel Burnham and John Wellborn Root.
It is so heavy that they expected it to settle 8 inches
into the ground during construction. In fact it dropped
20 inches in the following decades so that pedestrians
have to step down into the building from the
pavement. While the Monadnock represented the
limit of a particular type of construction, at the time it
was being built it was already outmoded. Other tall
buildings were already being constructed that used not
just internal iron floors, but complete iron skeletons.

The problem of iron-framed buildings was again one
of fireproofing. Although iron does not catch fire, other
parts of the building will burn and when the iron
reaches a relatively low temperature it loses most
of its strength and the building collapses. The early
skyscraper builders solved this problem by cladding the
iron with the best fireproof materials to hand: brick.
The oldest surviving skyscraper in New York, the
Flatiron Building (completed in 1902) is an example
of just this sort of construction. The brick and
terracotta clad skyscraper was born.

Left and opposite below
Views of the house from the
garden with the 1912 extension
in the foreground. Lutyens's
1906 extension to the original
house can be seen in the
background (opposite
below right).

Opposite above The tumbled
brickwork of the arcade under
the 1912 extension.

Below The garden paths, walls
and ponds are all constructed
out of brick.

Into The 20th Century

Edwin Lutyens, the Queen Anne style and
Arts and Crafts: Folly Farm, Sulhampstead, 1906–12

Sir Edwin Lutyens was the most important architect in Britain between 1900 and 1930.
He had trained under two of the greatest architects of the late 19th century:
Richard Norman Shaw and Philip Webb. Shaw was the great exponent of the Queen Anne
revival which consisted of red brick houses with white stone details. For Shaw the plan
was critical but bricks were just colour added to the façade. Philip Webb by contrast was
an architect immersed in the Arts and Crafts school which believed firmly that buildings
should respond to their contexts and should be built out of traditional materials, preferably
taken from the site on which they were built. Materials and craftsmanship were for them
the key to architecture and good design. Lutyens learnt from both schools and Folly Farm
is an excellent example of the result.

Folly Farm is a mature work, many of Lutyens's early
houses were in Surrey where he had used local stone.
It was only when his clients appeared further afield
after 1900 that he began to build in brick. He preferred
not to mix brick and stone where he could avoid it.
He later wrote: 'A building of one material is for
some strange reason much more noble than one
of many. It may be the accent it gives of sincerity,
the persistence of texture and definite unity'. He was
a great admirer of Roman brickwork and experimented
with using Roman bricks but found that making
them in England was too expensive and difficult.
His walls were typically laid in a version of
Flemish Garden Wall bond, with five stretcher
courses to every one of headers, although he chose
to depart from this at Folly Farm to produce
other effects.

Folly Farm was a small cottage when Lutyens was
first employed in 1906 to enlarge it. This he did by
adding a large symmetrical house onto the side of the
original house, which became relegated to the role of
kitchen wing in the new plan. As so often, the change
in orientation and organization of the house was
managed by completely re-ordering the approach to
the house and re-designing the garden. The house itself
is decorated in Queen Anne style but with a Lutyens
twist. The walls are built in grey bricks with red
introduced in the bricks used for the quoins and
window surrounds. To produce a uniform effect the
75mm high grey bricks are laid in Stretcher bond.
The red bricks used for the details are thinner
(approximately 50mm high) and thus course three red
bricks to every two grey ones, providing an interesting
change in rhythm at the openings.

In 1912 a new owner asked Lutyens to expand
the house once again. This time the symmetry created
in the previous addition presented a considerable
problem; one that Lutyens again solved by careful
re-planning of the garden and a judicious change
of style. The new wing is much more vernacular and
relaxed than the previous one with large roofs coming
low to the ground over a quiet cloister surrounding

a large pool. The new extension is constructed from 50-mm bricks throughout, this time laid in Flemish bond interspersed with tiles that are used to express the more difficult junctions. This use of tile and brick was typical of the Arts and Crafts detailing of the previous century.

Lutyens's architecture was typical of the general conservatism that continued in Britain long after Europe and America had embraced modernist theories of design. His was a cosy architecture of village cricket and afternoon teas with children playing croquet on the lawn. Such nostalgia for a past that had never been was difficult to shake off and remained popular in mass-produced suburban housing built in England throughout the 20th century. Brick as a traditional and long-lasting material was an important part of this suburban dream.

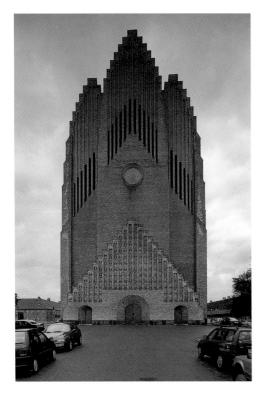

Into The 20th Century

Peder Jensen-Klint, the Grundtvigkirke
and the Danish functionalist tradition (1913–1930)

The ideals of the Arts and Crafts Movement that inspired Frank Lloyd Wright in America and Lutyens in Britain were mirrored in the ideas and buildings of the Danish architect Peder Vilhelm Jensen-Klint whose greatest work, the Grundtvigkirke and its associated housing became an icon of what became known as the Danish functional tradition.

The façade of the Grundtvigkirke is frequently shown in books on the development of modern architecture. A blank wall of brick rises the full height of the building, pierced by a tiny door at the base. This great façade is approached on an axis down a street of housing. It appears like a giant organ case, at once Gothic and strangely modern. Only the size of the bricks gives away its true scale. This is a grand monumental façade that seems wholly 20th-century.

Like much about the church, this frontal view is highly misleading and can be understood only with reference to traditional Danish architecture. Walking around the side of the church, one realizes that the grand façade is in fact the front of a tower which, in traditional Danish fashion, is carried across the whole width of the building. This tower is far taller than the nave behind and only one bay thick, with red pantile roofs behind the façade parapets. Inside the building is even more surprising. Its exterior, its structure, and its interior are entirely constructed in 225 x 102 x 50-mm yellow bricks. Even the

floor, the altar and the pulpit are made from brick. Cut bricks are avoided where possible and details are simple and devised to work in whole numbers of bricks. Despite all this, however, the church is essentially Gothic in design. The key to understanding the link between the medievalism of the form and the carefully crafted use of materials lies in the name of the church.

Nikolai Frederik Severin Grundtvig (1783-1872) was a Danish philosopher, theologian and social reformer. He was a scholar of Danish mythology and a priest who became convinced that the education system in Denmark was élitist and failed to address the basic needs of the working class. To answer this he formed Folk Schools where the emphasis was on the spoken word rather than texts, and readings were to be in Danish rather than Latin. Open debate between pupils and teachers was to be actively encouraged and classes were to be organized accordingly. The first such school was set up in 1851 and between 1866 and 1869 40 further Folk Schools were founded.

The architect of the Grundtvig Church, Peder Jensen-Klint, was a keen follower of Grundtvig's ideas. He had graduated from the Technical University of Denmark in engineering in 1877, but entered the Royal Academy in Copenhagen to become a painter before finally settling on architecture as his chosen medium. He believed passionately that architecture should grow out of an honest expression of materials and the skill of experienced craftsmen. Yet increasingly he saw the place of craftsmen within society threatened by the growth of the academically trained architect whose knowledge was based on books and photographs, rather than experience on site. He declared that he wanted 'to give architecture back to the people' and to create a 'real architecture' comparable to the Gothic of the Middle Ages. He called himself a 'master mason' rather than an architect. The Grundtvigkirke was where he sought to put all his ideas into action. The church was designed, together with the houses that surrounded it, as a focused community dedicated to Grundtvig's ideals. As it turned out, construction progressed slowly through shortage of funds. The project which began in 1913 was still not finished when Jensen-Klint died in 1930. The work was carried on by his son, Kaare Klint, and it was finally completed in 1940.

Michel de Klerk and the Amsterdam School (1912–30)

The term Amsterdam School was coined by the architect and critic Jan Gratama in 1916 in an article he contributed to the *Festschrift* celebrating Berlage's 60th birthday, where it was applied to the work of Michel de Klerk and Piet Kramer. The term was also later extended to cover G. F. la Croix, Margaret Kropholler, Johan van der Meij, J. F. Staal, and Hendrik Wijdeveld. Collectively their work was seen as being directly opposed to that of the De Stijl movement. The most significant difference lay in their choice of materials, the Amsterdam School preferring traditional materials like brick and tile, while the De Stijl movement preferred steel and concrete.

The most important early building accredited to the Amsterdam School is the Scheepvaarthuis (Shipping House), at Prins Hendrikkade and Binnenkant, just east of the railway station in central Amsterdam. It was designed by Johan van de Meij who delegated the detailing to Piet Kramer and Michel de Klerk who were working in his office. Constructed between 1912 and 1916, much of the sculptural detail on the Scheepvaarthuis was assigned to individual artists following the method used on the Rijksmuseum. All these elements are successfully brought together in the façade, in such a way that the wall seems to blend seamlessly with the sculpture and be part of it.

The Scheepvaarthuis has a concrete frame which supports the floors. The walls thus have nothing more to do than to support their own weight. All the windows above the ground floor are placed flush with the outer surface to emphasize the thinness of the walls. Above the lintels, the bricks are laid vertically, imitating the flat arches of the 17th century. The bricks used throughout are brown in colour and were hand-made in the Opijnensche brickworks. They are laid with thick horizontal joints and narrow vertical ones in English bond. The upright windows, hand-made bricks and the sculptural decorations all followed Berlage's call that architecture should evoke each country's particular power and consciousness. The Scheepvaarthuis drew architectural links with the 17th and 18th centuries when Holland had been at the height of its maritime, economic and political power. However, Berlage had called for the ornamentation of the building to reflect the structural system employed. In the Scheepvaarthuis the brick façades show where the concrete columns are behind but no concrete is on display. The use of brick as an expressive and particularly Dutch material is seen as more important.

This understanding of the importance of traditional materials used in a modern way and their role as bearers of meaning and references to history was to become one of the defining features of the Amsterdam School. It marked a critical departure from the teachings of Berlage and, more importantly, from the growing interest in modernism which came to be represented in Holland by the De Stijl movement.

While Michel de Klerk was still working in van der Meij's office he started carrying out private work. It was probably the commission for a residential housing district in the Spaarndammerbuurt that prompted him to set up on his own. Spaarndammerbuurt was a triangular area of land bordered by a main road on one side and the railway tracks on the other. De Klerk was to design three separate blocks here between 1914 and 1921, the last two for a housing association called Eigen Haard (One's Own Hearth). The buildings are for the most part masonry construction with timber floors,

although concrete and iron were used to create the cantilevers and the ground floor of the third block which is the most interesting and elaborate. De Klerk was a keen socialist and his ideas about town planning were rooted in the writings of Camillo Sitte (1843-1903). He introduced changes in height and aspect along the façades to create picturesque vistas and a sense of place. Like other members of the Amsterdam School, he was influenced by the Arts and Crafts Movement in England and the writings of Ruskin and Morris. He rejected the notion that modern architecture need necessarily be bound to modern materials and distrusted the links that groups, such as the Deutsche Werkbund, were making with industrialists and manufacturers, seeing architecture as an art that should remain aloof from industry. Instead the architects of the Amsterdam School favoured the use of traditional materials liberated from the ties of historical styles to be used in new and expressive ways.

The Scheepvaarthuis, Amsterdam (1912–30), by Johan van der Meij, Piet Kramer and Michel de Klerk.

Opposite The entrance tower and staircase.

Above Views of the west façade, which bends to follow the canal.

Below Details of the west façade. The sculpture was carried out by different artists, co-ordinated by the architects into a harmonious composition.

The Dageraad complex, which de Klerk worked on with Piet Kramer, consisted of a central courtyard block and surrounding streets. The surrounding streets are built in sandy brown bricks with red pantile roofs. They exhibit a strongly maritime iconography with windows shaped like the prows of boats and long streamlined curves. The bricks are typically laid in a Flemish bond with two stretchers between every header, the joints pointed flush, although, over entrances and windows and in other areas picked out for decorative treatment, other bonds are used or the bricks are turned on end or set in patterns. At the main corner, where three streets meet the two corner blocks there are rolling curved façades culminating in set back towers. The roof lines and doorways throughout are also elaborated.

De Klerk took this expressive language a step further in his third block for the Spaarndammerbuurt complex, which is triangular and close to the railway line. Here each façade is completely different. Most walls are faced in red brick, but other colours are used. The shortest side is curved inwards to create a small square which is provided with an ornamental spire as a focus. The Oostzaanstraat side is the tallest and has long thin projecting timber windows towards a prow. The side nearest the railway line appears to cantilever out at each floor, and the corner between Hemburgstraat and

By this method they sought to draw on notions of domesticity and cultural rootedness that these materials embodied and to use a wide variety of plans and elevations to produce a sense of individuality. Two schemes by de Klerk illustrate

these ideas particularly well: the housing scheme for the Dageraad (Dawn) housing association in south Amsterdam (1919–21) and the third block of the Spaarndammerbuurt complex (1917–21).

Zaanstraat is marked by an extraordinary cyst-like window that bursts forth from the façade.

De Klerk died of pneumonia on 27 November 1923 on the eve of his 39th birthday. The movement that he had helped to create limped on without him until about 1930 but its greatest exponent was gone. He was mourned by the residents of his blocks who seem to have been genuinely fond of them and admired him. Critics were less kind, describing his work as 'piquant', 'decadent' and at times 'ridiculous'. Howard Robertson writing in the *Architectural Review* in 1922 gave a

more sympathetic account, praising in particular the Director of Housing: 'One cannot help admiring the spirit which permits the designer to provide, in the courtyard of a block of tenements, a structure such as the little group crowned with de Klerk's fantastic tiled flèche. The practical utilization of this delightful touch is almost nil. The reason for its presence merely to afford piquancy and delight to the eyes which peep from behind courtyard casements.'

Opposite The Dageraad complex (1919–21), Amsterdam, by Michel de Klerk: overall view and details.

The third block of the Spaarndammerbuurt complex (c. 1917–20), Amsterdam, by Michel de Klerk.

Top Corner of Zaanstraat and Hemburgstraat.

Above left Detail of the Zaanstraat façade.

Above right Tower at Hembrugplein in the same complex.

The skyscraper and Art Deco

By the 1920s the skyscraper had come of age and architects and developers were vying with each other to produce ever taller and more lavish designs. Brick was the cladding of choice and Art Deco was the style of the moment.

The name Art Deco is given to the decorative style that flourished in Europe and America in the 1920s and 1930s. The term is derived from the 'Exposition des Arts Décoratifs et Industriels Modernes' held in 1925

in Paris. In the same way that Art Nouveau had developed a system of ornament from organic forms, its lines imitating the twisting tendrils of plants, Art Deco sought its inspiration in machines. The aesthetic that evolved was usually applied to furnishing and decorative arts, but it lent itself naturally to skyscraper design. Architects quickly realized that the design of very tall buildings required new solutions. Traditionally buildings had been seen in a context in relation to both human scale and to other buildings around. The skyscraper towered over its neighbours. Although its base was like any other building, its top was only visible from afar, where it had to create a definite and lasting impression.

The result can be seen in Raymond Hood's American Radiator Building built in New York in 1924. Hood creates a generous entrance hall to direct users to the banks of lifts. However, above these storeys the façade is simply divided into vertical strips emphasizing the verticality of the structure. These are left relatively unadorned. By contrast, the top is a mass of elaboration and ornament, a golden crown created from various materials, sitting like one building on top of another. The set backs at roof level are partly to do with the 1916 zoning laws, but this is clearly not the

only motivation. Hood is creating an impact and providing his building with a particular stamp or motif that is instantly recognizable at a distance.

The brickwork in the American Radiator Building is supported off a steel frame at each floor. Structurally the steel frame supports the weight. The brickwork constructed as a series of bands wrapped around the building at each storey acts only to keep the rain off and provide fire protection. Nevertheless the illusion of permanence is provided: the American Radiator Building looks like a masonry building with all the longevity that implies.

The ultimate masterpiece of Art Deco skyscraper design is the Chrysler Building, built in 1928–31 and designed by William Van Alen (1888–1954). Van Alen was born in Brooklyn and went on to study architecture there at the Pratt Institute. In 1908 he won a scholarship to study at the École des Beaux Arts in Paris, setting up in practice on his return. He became one of the foremost New York skyscraper designers of the 1920s, but it is chiefly for the Chrysler Building that he is remembered today. At the time, the building was involved in a race with the Bank of Manhattan building which at 282.55m was to be the tallest in the world. When the latter was completed in

Opposite above and right
The Chrysler Building
(1928–31), New York, designed
by William Van Alen. The whole
skyscraper is clad in glazed
bricks apart from the top
which is timber clad in
metal sheet.

Opposite below   American
Radiator Building (1924),
New York, by Raymond Hood.

1929 it seemed to have won, but Van Alen, who was a
master showman, had secretly built a 56.39-m spire
within the top of the Chrysler Building. It took 90
minutes to hoist into position, raising the height of
the 77-storey building to 319m. The top parts of the
Chrysler Building were clad in timber frames covered
with metal sheet, but the lower sections were covered
in brick. Advertising in the 1930s, the Hydraulic Press
Brick of St Louis was proud to say that it had supplied
the 3,000,000 bricks involved. They were examples of
the Equitable No.128, described as a 'white matt
finished glazed brick'. Today they appear light blue
rather than white and the mortar is black.

The Chrysler Building did not retain its height
record for long. In 1931 the Empire State Building
overtook it, at 381m. It too was clad in bricks
(although they were covered by stone). Over
10,000,000 were used in the construction and
supplying them on time and in the right place became
a critical part of the building's planning. Brick may no
longer be used in the design of skyscrapers, but there
can be no doubt that it played a decisive role in their
development.

Dudok and Hilversum Town Hall

Hilversum Town Hall is one of the most influential buildings of the 20th century.
Built in the late 1920s, it was the masterpiece of Willem Marinus Dudok (1884-1974),
municipal architect of the town. Judging by its design, with its dominating planar surfaces
and abstract composition, it is easy to presume that Dudok was a member of the De Stijl
movement. In fact for much of his career he had been more interested in the
Amsterdam School and Berlage.

The De Stijl movement which opposed the Amsterdam School from 1917 to 1930 took its name from a magazine edited by Theo van Doesburg (1883–1931). The first issue appeared in October 1917. The movement included the artist Piet Mondrian, and architects Jacobus Johannes Pieter Oud (1890–1963) and Gerrit Thomas Rietveld (1888–1964). They stood for a search for universal values in art. This universality was linked to idea of mass-production, which was seen as holding the possibility of breaking down class barriers and making way for a utopian vision of the future. In architecture this translated into an interest in making buildings that had no stylistic or regional references but were instead composed of rectangular planes of simple colours. The main materials used were deliberately modern: concrete, steel and glass. The most obvious example of this type of architecture is the Schröder House in Utrecht. Ironically they chose to ignore brick, despite being the most obviously mass-produced material in use at the times. The reasons for this were simple: the use of brick in traditional architecture was seen as being an undesirable link with a degenerate past.

Hilversum Town Hall, one of most significant buildings in this style, came from outside the movement. It obeys De Stijl principles of composition but Dudok had shown no particular interest in their theoretical debates and felt free to build in any material he chose.

Dudok was born in Amsterdam and studied at the military college in Breda. After graduating he did some work for the army before taking up a temporary appointment as Director of Public Works in Leiden from 1913 to 1915. Here he collaborated with Oud on a small housing complex built in a traditional style reminiscent of the architecture of the Amsterdam School. He left Leiden to take up the post of Director of Public Works in Hilversum, a town with a population of 100,000 about 30km south-west of Amsterdam.

Initial designs for a town hall for Hilversum began soon after Dudok's appointment in 1915. In the following decade various sites were discussed and rejected until eventually the council managed to buy a large area of land on the edge of the town yet close enough to the centre to be practical. The final design was accepted by the town council in November 1924

but work was further delayed by financial constraints so that the foundation was not laid until March 1928. Dudok's vision was for a magnificent town hall set in a beautiful park. The visitor approaching it first sees the building across the lake with the tower in the background.

After such a long gestation, the architect had been given ample time to consider the materials to be used. He had a number of sample walls constructed using standard bricks but rejected each, eventually settling on a purpose-made 233 x 113 x 43-mm yellow brick (thereafter called the Hilversum brick) produced by Alfred Russel in Tegelen. Some 680,000 were ordered.

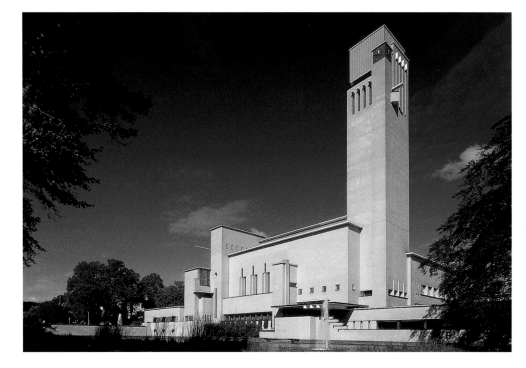

Above Close-up of the top of the tower which sits over the main staircase.

Left The view across the lake.

Opposite The ceremonial entrance. Newly married couples emerge from the Town Hall and descend down this staircase flanked by their guests. Note the large glazed coping blocks which were especially made for the Town Hall.

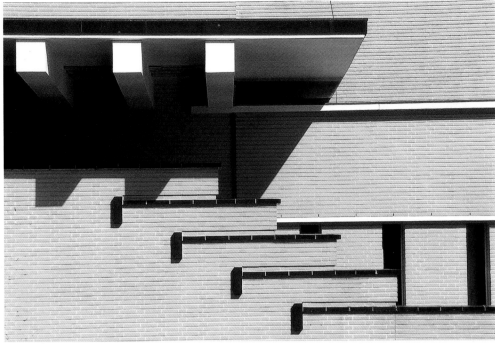

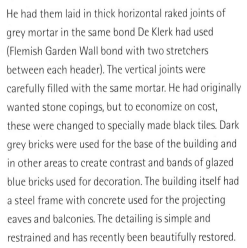

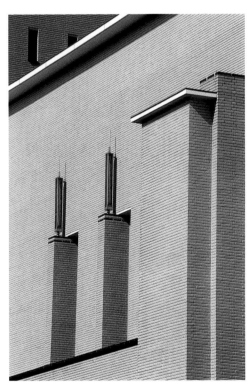

He had them laid in thick horizontal raked joints of grey mortar in the same bond De Klerk had used (Flemish Garden Wall bond with two stretchers between each header). The vertical joints were carefully filled with the same mortar. He had originally wanted stone copings, but to economize on cost, these were changed to specially made black tiles. Dark grey bricks were used for the base of the building and in other areas to create contrast and bands of glazed blue bricks used for decoration. The building itself had a steel frame with concrete used for the projecting eaves and balconies. The detailing is simple and restrained and has recently been beautifully restored.

Opposite View from the main approach to the Town Hall from the city centre.

Top View of the side entrance to the hall.

Above left Each office on this façade has its own balcony overlooking the lake.

Above right Close-up of the windows to the main council chamber. Dudok paid attention to every detail including the lights.

Above Modern UK factory production. Bricks are stacked by robotic arms onto huge carriages that are then moved around the factory on rails. The whole operation is controlled by computer.

Right Workers check the bricks as they go past on conveyor, removing any that have been damaged during production.

New techniques for brick production

The 20th century saw changes in brick manufacturing which were even more remarkable than those of the century before. At the beginning of the 20th century most bricks in Europe and America were still moulded by hand. By its end they were being made in highly sophisticated and heavily automated factories.

Some of the most obvious and important advances were made in the way clay was dug from the ground. In 1900 a few of the larger operators used steam-powered chain grabs but most clay was still dug by hand. The invention of the internal combustion engine in 1876 would lead to the development of tractors and fixed-blade bulldozers although these were not in general use in clay pits until after the First World War. Pneumatic hand shovels also appeared in this period. Clay was typically cut from the pits using cable-operated diggers (hydraulic excavators first appeared after the Second World War but were not widely available until after the 1960s). By the end of the century, a wide variety of diesel grading machines, large dumper trucks and hydraulic excavators were being employed.

Once cut, the clay had to be transported to the factory. On the very largest sites, overhead ropeways were already being used for this purpose in the first decade of the century, as were cable-driven railway systems. Diesel locomotive trains replaced these and by the last few decades of the century these had largely been replaced in turn by belt conveyors. On smaller sites, clay was dug close to where it was used and transported by horse and cart, later replaced by diesel tractors and trailers.

The clay was typically tempered by leaving it in heaps, where it would be turned over and thoroughly mixed. When it was required, it was then transferred to the sorting and grinding machinery by a series of belts and conveyors. The grinding machinery itself changed remarkably little in appearance over the century. The main development was in the change in source of power from steam to internal combustion engine to electricity (either locally generated or taken from national power sources).

The moulding machines too remained similar in operation to their 19th-century equivalents but naturally came to incorporate a wealth of small improvements and features to increase safety of operation. The major improvements were made after the 1970s when electronics allowed increasingly complicated control devices. The introduction of computerized control systems also had a major impact on the stacking and setting of bricks within the factory

in the last decades of the century. Handling was increasingly done by machine, including the stacking and setting of bricks in preparation for firing which became possible with the development of robotic arms specially designed for the purpose. Once moulded, the bricks were set onto cars that passed around the plant on tracks controlled by computers. In dry press plants they passed directly into the kiln, while those using damper clay first passed through drying ovens which used heat reclaimed from the kilns.

Perhaps the largest change made during the century was in the development of better kilns. At the beginning of the 20th century a brick plant typically consisted of a number of buildings each dealing with a particular aspect of the process: sorting and grading, moulding sheds, drying chambers, and then finally kilns. By the end of the 20th century, all these operations were being carried out under one roof in a controlled environment.

The most common type of kiln used for mass-production in Europe by the end of the 20th century was the gas-fired tunnel kiln. In a tunnel kiln the bricks pass very slowly through a single long chamber on cars. Gas jets heat the centre of the furnace to white heat and the hot gases pass along the kiln, warming the cool bricks up. The tunnel kiln was first introduced for use in the porcelain industry in the 18th century, but could not be made to work satisfactorily because of the problems of sealing the bottom of the cars against the heat. For this reason in 1911 Alfred Searle wrote in his *Modern Brickmaking*, 'in spite of their advantages, tunnel kilns are scarcely likely to become popular'. By the second edition of his book, circumstances obliged him to revise his entry. He reported that tunnel kilns were 'wholly satisfactory' and could achieve 'astonishingly large outputs'. Nevertheless the industry was slow to change its practices and Hoffmann kilns and their derivatives predominated in brick manufacture until the 1970s.

The final area of change in the century was in packing. At the beginning of the century, bricks were still being delivered to site by horse and cart, with longer distances being handled by rail transport. By the century's end, bricks were packed on wooden

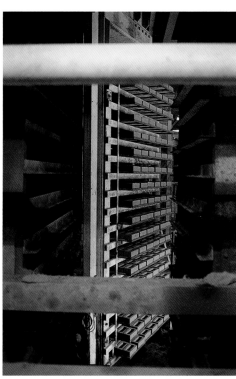

Top Clay is unloaded from lorries and carefully graded, crushed and milled. Sensors above the conveyors detect intrusive objects and make sure it has the correct moisture content.

Above Sorting machines automatically stack and unstack green bricks before and after they have passed through the drying sheds.

pallets of 400–500. Around the yard pallets of bricks were handled by fork lift trucks. The bricks were wrapped in cellophane at the end of the production line before being stacked in the yard for dispatch. Transport was mainly by lorry with a hydraulic handling arm to unload the pallets at the site.

Post-war mass housing

In addition to the devastating loss of life, the Second World War destroyed an unprecedented number of houses, leaving large numbers of people homeless. In the United Kingdom 225,000 homes were destroyed (some 7% of the total) and another 550,000 were severely damaged. During the war there had been 2 million marriages but no more than 200,000 houses were built. However, such figures seemed minor compared to the destruction that the war had wrought on the mainland of Europe. In West Germany one-fifth of all dwellings had been destroyed (some 2,300,000 homes) and an even higher number had beeen badly damaged. In the Netherlands and France some 8% of the housing stock had disappeared. At the end of the war one of the most pressing problems facing the governments throughout Europe was how to house their populations. Mass housing was required like never before.

Pre-war housing in many countries had been in brick but brick manufacturing had virtually stopped during the war. In England most brickyards had been shut because the kilns could not be blacked out during air raids. Getting such plants up and running, recruiting new employees and finding people to run them took time. There was of course an equal shortage of bricklayers. Brick production in England rose from 3,500,000,000 in 1946 to 6,000,000,000 in 1950 and over 7,000,000,000 in 1953.

The more immediate housing needs had to be met by using alternative materials. A great deal of research went into pre-fabricated dwellings, large numbers

being erected after the war which, although designed to last ten years, ended up being used for 40 years or more. Another alternative was concrete, which proved particularly suitable for high-rise housing. In England these proved to be highly unpopular in the long term, although many of the failures can be put down to poor maintenance and design. An alternative were the so-called New Town schemes which created large numbers of units in low-rise developments. One of the most successful social housing projects, the Byker Wall Housing project in Newcastle, unusually combined both high-rise and low-rise development in a highly successful way. Its architect was Ralph Erskine, an Englishman who had spent virtually all his working life in Sweden.

Ralph Erskine (1914-) studied architecture at Regent Street Polytechnic in London, graduating in 1932. In May 1939 he set off with a bicycle, a rucksack and a sleeping bag for Stockholm where he found work in an architect's office, married and settled down. After the war he set up his own practice taking a particular interest in the design of social housing.

Erskine was an early exponent of what would later be called community architecture. He observed that 'in many societies over half those who live a housing district are relatively stationary' either because they are old, children or parents looking after young children. It was essential that housing included all the

basic amenities: churches, schools, shops, health centres, pubs etc. He also believed in producing architecture in consultation with the residents. Most importantly he developed a playful architectural language that sought to engage the inhabitants rather than alienate them and would be easy to maintain. Brick and timber were the two most important materials used in his projects.

The Byker Wall is a large multi-storey block that forms the rear of the site and which Erskine placed there to protect the housing from northerly winds and the noise of main road that passes behind. Most of the 2,317 dwelling units are small houses arranged around pathways, roads, squares and private gardens. These are built in brick in a deliberate reference to

the traditional housing materials used in Newcastle. Special large wire-cut hollow bricks are used measuring 285 x 85 x 90mm. The size and colour of these bricks provides a scale similar to a child's building block. Care has been taken to differentiate individual dwellings and provide the residents with balconies and gardens while cars are restricted to certain areas allowing children to play freely.

The Byker Wall Housing Project (1968–80), Newcastle, England, designed by Ralph Erskine. The site is a mixture of low-rise (**above left and opposite below left**) and high-rise units (**right**), some of which form a long 'wall' to the back of the site overlooking a main road (**above**).

Alvar Aalto, Baker House (1946–49) and Scandinavian modernism

No account of the history of brickwork in the 20th century would be complete without making mention of Alvar Aalto. He was born in 1898 in Kuortane in Finland. He set up the 'The Alvar Aalto Office for Architecture and Monumental Art' in Jyväskylä, Finland, just two years after he completely his diploma in architecture at the Helsinki University of Technology. In 1929 he attended the second Congrès Internationaux d' Architecture Moderne (CIAM) held in Frankfurt and was elected a member of the inner circle of CIAM responsible for preparing the agendas for its meetings. Here he came into contact with the leading members of the Modern Movement including Walter Gropius, Lázló Moholy-Nagy and Le Corbusier. By this time Aalto had turned away from the classical language of his early works and towards modernism. His architecture of this period is characterized by its use of timber and white rendered walls. His first major project to use exposed brick was built in America.

In 1946 Aalto was appointed as a Visiting Professor at the Massachusetts Institute of Technology, in Cambridge on the opposite side of the Charles River from the city of Boston. His sojourn in the United States gave him the opportunity to visit Frank Lloyd Wright, who had been very impressed by Aalto's Finnish Pavilion at the New York World's Fair of 1939. More importantly, it led to his first major exposed-brick building, a new hall of residence for final year students at MIT.

Baker House occupies a magnificent site overlooking the Charles River and separated from it by a wide road. Aalto's provocative and unconventional plan attempted to maximize the views from the student bedrooms by placing them in a single long curving block. The rear elevation was more orthogonal and for the most part devoted to circulation. Large stairs were cantilevered from it . Aalto intended to clad these stair elements in tile. In the event such a move was precluded on cost grounds and much to the detriment of the building they were rendered instead. The main façade, however, was exactly as Aalto intended it and was finished in bare brick.

Aalto later told a story of how his interest in the material had been re-kindled on hearing a speech by Frank Lloyd Wright: 'Brick is an important element in the creation of form. I was once in Milwaukee together with my old friend Frank Lloyd Wright. He gave a lecture that began, "Ladies and gentlemen, do you know what a brick is? It is small, worthless, ordinary thing that costs 11 cents but has a wonderful quality. Give me a brick and it becomes worth its weight in gold." It was the first time I had heard an audience told so bluntly and expressively what architecture is. Architecture is the turning of a worthless stone into a nugget of gold'.

In Baker House smooth factory-made bricks were used on the interiors of the rooms interspersed with plaster walls. For the exterior Aalto wanted a more primitive effect and chose locally produced hand-made bricks. Describing them later he said: 'The bricks were made of clay from topsoil exposed to the sun. They were fired in manually stacked pyramids, using nothing but oak for fuel. When the walls were erected, all bricks were approved without sorting, with the result that the colour shifts from black to canary yellow, though the predominant shade is bright red'. The bricks are 190 x 85 x 55mm with the horizontal 15-mm joints raked out and mortar left in the vertical ones, a trick he may have learnt from Wright. Aalto's innovation was to allow warped bricks to be included in the wall although it is doubtful that this was done as randomly as Aalto suggested.

William W. Wurster, Dean of the School of Architecture and Planning, described its progress in the summer in 1948, 'It is very beautiful. The brickwork is *just* right. It is wonderfully free of any smooth thin feeling. It honestly makes me think of Florence'.

Above Baker House (1946–49), MIT, Cambridge, Mass., designed by Alvar Aalto (1898–1976), one of the great leaders of the Modernist Movement in architecture. The curved façade is designed to provide the rooms with the best views of the river.

Opposite below Details of the brickwork showing the twisted and distorted overburnt bricks used at intervals to add interest to the surface of the walls.

Into the 20th Century

St Peter's Church, Klippan (1963–66):
Sigurd Lewerentz and the brutality of brick

In a century when architects took great pride in their outspokenness and in their wish to tell other people how they should live, Sigurd Lewerentz (1885–1975) stood out. He was reticent, ambiguous and elusive, qualities that were no doubt frustrating to his contemporaries but which have led those who have discovered his work to examine it for what it was, not for what the architect said it was. The silence of the architect has meant that Lewerentz's buildings are open to interpretation, each writer looking at the buildings with their own preoccupations and finding in them new resonances and meanings.

St Peter's Church, Klippan, Sweden was one of Lewerentz's last buildings, completed in 1966 when he was over 80 and is seen by many as the summation of his life's work. Like much of Lewerentz's later buildings, it is a difficult work born out of certainty, stubborness and a lifetime of quiet contemplation. One of the keys to understanding it is his obsession with detail. Lewerentz shared the modernists' interest in materials but preferred masonry to steel and glass. St Peter's is Lewerentz's homage to brick.

What Lewerentz saw in the brick that no-one else had seen fit to express before was the primacy of the module. This he understood made it different from stone which is cut to size. The brick is made in a certain size and cutting it is difficult and to be avoided. It took an architect like Lewerentz to turn this observation into a building, stating that not a single brick should be cut during construction. Moreover, he was determined that the bricks should be laid in such a way that their intactness was obvious: in Stretcher

bond. To make such a system work he had to set the bricks in thick joints which could vary in size. The mortar was spread roughly and loosely over the bricks and scraped off giving a flush joint. Indeed the lime mortar was so thick that Lewerentz mixed it with flint to try to increase its strength.

Lewerentz apparently likened this method to Persian brickwork. Persian bricks are square in plan and thus laid in Common (rather than Stretcher) bond. Moreover, Persian bricklayers treated bricks like stone. They were frequently cut and laid with recessed joints.

Lewerentz had never been to Persia and was probably unaware of all this. His interest was in the nature and poetry of the brick not historical accuracy. The thick, rough joints of his brickwork have an immediacy about them that reminds the viewer that they have been laid by hand rather than by machine. The varying thickness of the perpends implies a casual approach to detail, a deliberate harsh primitivism

which is, of course, directly at odds with the carefully worked out and rigidly adhered to system that is used throughout.

Once Lewerentz had set the rule it was not departed from. There are no cut bricks in St Peter's, Klippan. All the bricks are of a uniform standard size. Bricks with flaws were carefully selected from discard bins in the Helsinborg brickworks and placed in key areas to attract the eye. Paving bricks were individually positioned according to colour under the architect's direction. Windows are made without frames, the glass fixed to the outside of the walls with steel clasps and sealed with mastic.

The church, entered through a narrow door, dimly lit from narrow frameless windows. The left of the entrance is the font, which is a fissure in the floor. The edges are staggered whole bricks, the floor heaves up in a curve and then drops away into a deep hole filled with water. Above this, a steel frame supports a huge shell from which water continually drips into the pool below. Beyond the font, the church slopes to the altar, a great slab of brickwork. Behind large doors open through which the congregation pass at the end of the service, the architecture becoming part of the ceremony.

Opposite The façade of the Meeting Hall. Lewerentz designed a small complex made up of church, meeting hall and offices, all of which form an intimate group, and through which the church is entered.

Above left The rigid orthodoxy of the uncut brick is demonstrated in this detail of the meeting hall.

Top The offices look out onto a garden.

Above The west façades of the church and meeting hall overlook gardens and the pond.

Opposite Everything is brick - the walls, the floor and the ceiling, which is the source of its 'bunker-like' intensity. The one non-brick structural element, the steelwork, symbolizes the cross.

Right The first view of the nave from an adjoining room. The first impression is its extreme darkness. At the end of a service, large doors at the west end are flung open, leading the congregation out into the light.

Below left The altar and seating for the clergy are brick, and lie at the lowest point of the sloping floor. The congregation sit on chairs arranged to match the brick patterns - these chairs are deliberately lightweight, insubstantial and temporary.

Below right and overleaf Piercing the silent intensity of the space is the constant dripping of water from the overflowing shell of the baptismal font into an invisible pool below the gash in the floor.

Louis Kahn, Philips Exeter Library (1969–71) and what the brick wants to be

'*The brick was always talking to me, saying you're missing an opportunity...
The weight of the brick makes it dance like a fairy above and groan below',*

Louis Kahn on the Philips Exeter Library, quoted in the *New York Times*, 23 October 1972

Philips Exeter Library is a solid cube of brick which sits enigmatically in the centre of
a neo-Georgian secondary school in Exeter, New Hampshire. Like so many of the works
of the American architect Louis Kahn (1901–74), its appearance is monumental.
It is a ruin from a lost civilization, a piece of the Palatine Hill dropped down in the middle
of New England, to be re-used as a library. From the outside it betrays nothing of its purpose
and there is no obvious way in. Yet this ambiguity was precisely Kahn's intention.

Philips Exeter Library (1969–71), New Hampshire, by Louis Kahn.

Opposite Views from the lawns surrounding the building.

Top The cloister that runs around the base of the building.

Above Detail of the flat arches above the openings at each level.

Philips Exeter Academy was founded in 1781 by
Dr John Philips, a graduate of Harvard and resident of
the small town of Exeter, New Hampshire. Today it is
one of America's leading private schools with some
1,000 students taught by 200 teachers, an annual
operating budget of about US $50 million and an
endowment of over US $500 million. It specializes in
teaching according to the Harkness method involving
interaction in classes of 12 students gathered
round oval tables. Such an intense environment
breeds success and its students go on to leading
American universities. It is thus anything but
a conventional school.

In November 1965, after considering a number of
architects, the school commissioned Kahn to build a
new library, giving him a central site on the campus
and a budget of US $2 million. Their brief included a
stipulation that the building must 'encourage and
insure the pleasure of reading and study' and that
individual carrels must be provided for half the readers.
Kahn's design solution was a mausoleum to house
books as sacred objects, a church for the words
of the departed.

At first it seems to be a relatively simple building.
Its rectangular façades appear to be regularly
punctured by rectangular windows and it is the same
on all four sides. A 'pseudo-arcade' reminiscent of a
monastery cloister runs around the bottom and the
entrance is off this, on one side. From there the reader
ascends one of two symmetrical curved stairs to the
catalogue room in the centre of the library, a space that
rises through its complete height, allowing the books
to be glimpsed through the massive concrete circles of
the internal structure.

Brick was an obvious choice of material from the
outset, because it blended easily with the surrounding
neo-classical buildings. Kahn had used brick

throughout his career. In early projects such as his Yale
Art Gallery and Richards Laboratories; here he had used
it mostly as an infill for walls in concrete frame
construction, although both buildings do contain load-
bearing brick. The brick in these early buildings is laid in
Stretcher bond and unremarkable in detail or texture.
His discovery of its architectural possibilities began
with his project for the Indian Institute of
Management at Ahmedabad and Sher-e-Bangla Nagar
(Dhaka), the capital of Bangladesh. In both these cases
brick was seen as an appropriate material because it
was cheap and readily available locally. While concrete
was also used (for instance, for the main assembly
building at Sher-e-Bangla), the steel reinforcement it
required was a significant cost. The Indian climate led
Kahn to devise a new architecture where the outer
walls provided shade for inner walls set back with
glazing. This division allowed him to ignore internal
floor levels on the external facades which became huge
and monumental, punctured by gigantic round and
semi-circular openings made using brick arches.
Throughout his career Kahn was prone to poetic
outpourings and at the end of his life he reflected on
his use of brick in the Indian Institute of Management :
'I had to learn to lay brickwork from scratch...Why hide
the beauty of open brickwork? I asked the brick what
it wanted and it said I want to be an arch, so I gave it
an arch'.

Brick arches became a recurring theme of Kahn's
work thereafter. He was particularly fond of putting an
arch above an inverted arch to produce a circular
opening. Inspired by visits to Rome, he used relieving
arches in walls and curved arches in drums and to
produce a shallow arch he invented a system of tying
the feet of the arches together using concrete beams.
His primary concern was always that the brickwork
carried the load and was seen to carry it.

In initial designs on the library for Philips Exeter he
drew a large central hall enclosed by four tiers of
Roman arches, surrounded by book stacks, which in
turn were surrounded by the reading carrels looking
out through arched windows. The arrangement of
central hall, book stacks and carrels remained, but
through a series of revisions forced by costs and client
comments, the present external and internal elevations
evolved. Four years after being commissioned, and with
budget estimates reaching nearly twice the original
sum, work began on site.

The walls of the completed building are built in
English Garden Wall bond with one course of headers
to every seven of stretchers, using 190 x 85 x 55-mm
hand-made bricks. Kahn later related how he found a
local brickmaker who made the bricks that had been

used in building Cambridge, Mass. These are the same
bricks that Aalto used 20 years before in the Baker
Housing and, just like Aalto, Kahn leaves the warped
over-burnt headers projecting from the surface,
which is otherwise finished with 10-mm flush joints.
The resulting variations in colours and textures provide
detail in what could easily be an uninterestingly large
expanse of brickwork.

The arches are flat (jack) arches and these are
restrained by concealed concrete beams that project
down from the concrete floor slabs in the pillars
between. Despite these, the structure is basically load-
bearing brick with concrete only providing restraint to
the ends of the arches. The external brick pillars carry
all the weight and to emphasize this they taper, getting
smaller towards the top. Internally brick circular arches
were replaced with concrete ones at a late stage in the
design, but the principle remains the same.

What then appears at first to be a very simple (even
primitive) building is actually on closer inspection
surprisingly complex one. Kahn's monumentalist
approach to brick is developed in the work of the Swiss
architect Mario Botta, while the inspiration of ancient
Rome can be seen in a more literal, and arguably less
successful form in Rafael Moneo's National Museum
of Roman Art (1986) in Mérida, Spain.

Renzo Piano and the search for lightness

Louis Kahn's architecture was structurally heavy. Renzo Piano by contrast has always been concerned with lightweight structures. At the risk of over-simplification it might be said, that for Piano architecture since 1900 has been about frames supporting skins and design is about choosing the right frame and the right skin for the job. Of course Piano would no doubt be the first to protest that his architecture is about more than this, but it is fair to say that his own writings have continually stressed the importance of these elements in design and that masonry is very rarely used in his buildings.

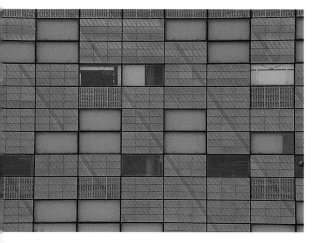

Renzo Piano was born in Genoa in 1937. He studied architecture in Florence and at the Milan Polytechnic, graduating in 1964. When he was not at university he worked for his father, who was a builder, and in the studio of Franco Albini. In 1965 his father helped him set up his first office, Studio Piano, where he began his research into lightweight structures. Later he formed partnerships with Richard Rogers (1971–78) and the engineer Peter Rice (1978–80) before setting up his present office, the Renzo Piano Building Workshop, in 1981.

In 1977 Richard Rogers and Renzo Piano designed and constructed the Institute for Research and Co-ordination of Acoustics and Music (IRCAM) in Paris. This essentially consisted of a number of large box-shaped studios underneath the Place Igor Stravinsky next to the Pompidou Centre. These were designed so that their acoustics could be very accurately controlled and altered so that the studios themselves became instruments in their own right.

A major shortcoming of the design was that it lacked a formal entrance or space for offices, libraries and other areas that were better placed above ground.

Piano was approached and asked to design an
extension which was to contain these elements and
integrate with the existing buildings on the site and
the previous project.

Piano's solution was a lightweight glass and steel
frame structure which would act as a bridge between
the old and the new. The library and meeting rooms
were placed within the older building. The entrance
itself was then in a central portion which was
structurally glazed, while the section of the building
on the corner which contained the fire escapes and
lifts was clad in terracotta to match the brick in colour.
Piano artfully creates a block of masonry which is
actually only a cladding on a steel frame. Initially it
appears to be brickwork, albeit in Stack bond. On closer
inspection the observer can make out the metal frames
that divide the façade into panels. Each 275 x 50 x 50-
mm 'brick' is perforated and three bolts through these
perforations hold it to the metal frame. The bricks are
held apart by washers, creating even joints which are
not filled. The whole system acts as a 'rainscreen',
waterproofing being provided by bitumen painted
concrete behind.

Since IRCAM, terracotta rainscreens have become
increasingly popular and proprietary systems are now
available. The terracotta elements are usually
lightweight and hollow and vary widely in size
according to specification. In general, larger units are
more economical but with increases in size come
associated problems in handling (the units are brittle
and can be easily damaged). Like bricks, the effect is
dependent on the way they are spaced. A research
block at Evry near Paris by the French practice Canale 3
has tried to play on the regularity created by using
large terracotta units by placing window elements of
the same size in an apparently random pattern across a
large façade. The external effect is intriguing, although
internally the indiscriminate placing of windows is
presumably rather frustrating, with some people
having to put up with windows at foot or knee level
rather than getting a view out.

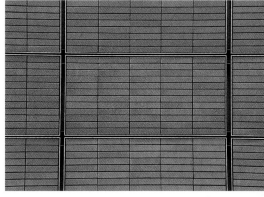

Eric Christian Sørensen
and the environmental advantages of brick

The relationship of frames to façades is a vexed one in late 20th-century architecture. Frames can be erected quickly, providing an advantage in time and cost. They also allow large spans which means long distances between columns. As columns reduce the flexibility of spaces this too is an advantage. Frames have come to predominate as the main way of organizing the structure of larger buildings. As has already been shown, bricks can be incorporated into framed buildings and were used in the early American skyscrapers to great effect, but the early skyscrapers were erected using traditional bricklaying carried out on high scaffolds. The modern building industry is always looking for safer, more efficient, quicker and cheaper options. For some architects this has meant a move away from brick façades altogether, to metal or glass cladding, while others like the Danish architect Eric Christian Sørenson have sought to incorporate the frame within a more traditional approach to materials. His Cambridge Crystallographic Data Centre is one of the most sensitive essays in the use of brick to be constructed in the last decade of the 20th century.

The Cambridge Crystallographic Data Centre is a non-profit organization which holds a database for the identification of organic and inorganic compounds from the results of spectroscopy. The basic requirements for its building were for a quiet working environment in which the researchers could sit at computers, as with any office. Sørenson's response was far from the dull speculative office block that could so easily have resulted from such a brief. He made an entrance with a low timber ceiling, mysteriously lit from above through a water-filled pool. Taking the lift to the first floor the visitor finds

that the main space is a well-lit double-height room. A curved reflector draws light down a large wall at the back of the space in the centre of the building. Researchers sit at desks looking into this space or out of windows to the outside world.

The internal walls are brick and the large spaces and hard surfaces could easily have created a difficult and noisy acoustic environment. In fact, in the finished building the reverse is true. Sound is absorbed by carpeted floors and specially formed timber acoustic ceilings, while the bricks used are 103 x 168 x 228-mm acoustic bricks laid in Flemish bond. These provide an interesting pattern and are also absorbent. Each surface is thus provided with a distinctive texture derived from the choice of materials and helps to reduce any sound that might disturb the workers. In addition the use of bricks on the inside walls provides a feeling of a working environment rather than a domestic one.

The outside of the building is formed by a thick outer wall, varying between 550 and 628mm. The building is situated to the rear of the main University of Cambridge Chemistry Laboratories, facing a large brick car park in a narrow back street. This is a dull environment of bland unmodulated 1970s Stretcher bond brick façades. The Data Centre responds to this by also employing brick, but instead of using a conventional half-a-brick thick outer skin which would have to be laid in Stretcher bond, Sørenson's thick wall allows games to be played within the depth of the façade. The windows are sunk in groups into shallow recesses. Stone dressings are used to break up the mass and the corner is enlivened

by a quartz relief. The main surfaces are laid in a complex repeating variant on Flemish bond. At the corners, the whole depth of the wall is exposed by slit windows on the sides. These are placed to emphasize that the wall is just a skin and not load-bearing, although its thickness implies the reverse.

In fact, the wall consists of four layers:
• An outer skin of specially imported thin Danish bricks measuring 230 x 103 x 40mm, Their thinness makes them prone to warp in firing, giving a pleasing uneven mortar joint which is approximately 10mm thick. This outer skin is up to 400mm thick and laid in a weak 1:1:12 cement mortar to avoid the necessity for expansion joints.
• Insulation in the form of rigid aluminium-backed sheet.
• A large void which accommodates the members of the steel frame.
• An inner layer of acoustic bricks with headers to produce a Flemish pattern.

Such a thick wall system certainly allows certain design options on the façade, but might easily be viewed as uneconomic for normal building purposes. Professor Olga Kennard, the chair of the committee in charge of the building, was an enthusiastic fan of the architect and there is no doubt that he was given a freer rein than most.
Yet it would be wrong to dismiss Sørenson's design out of hand as an act of over-indulgence. The thick wall design offers much more than just the ability

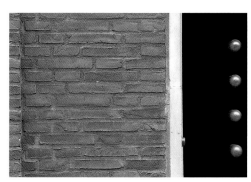

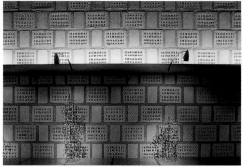

to experiment with the façade. The advantages of speed and long spans are still incorporated into the design by retaining a frame system which can be erected first. It has the added advantage that the wall when completed protects the frame embedded within it from fire and from the weather and avoids the problems of condensation and cold-bridging which plague infill-panel solutions. More importantly, the great thickness and weight of the wall provides enormous advantages in heating and cooling the building by creating what is called 'thermal mass'.

Cambridge Crystallographic Data Centre (1990–92), Cambridge, England, designed by Eric Christian Sørensen.

Opposite Looking up at the underside of the gallery in the main office space, showing the acoustic timber soffit.

Left, top Detail of glass entrance door and adjacent brickwork.

Left, middle Detail of acoustic brickwork in main office space.

Left, bottom View from the top floor gallery into the main space.

Above A slot window on the corner reveals the depth of the main façade. The entrance is flanked by a quartz relief making reference to the purpose of the centre. The thick front wall allows the façade to be peeled back in layers for decorative effect.

Typical lightweight steel frame and curtain wall clad buildings can be made to be well-insulated, but they heat up and cool down fast: that is they have a low thermal mass. Large masonry walls by contrast heat up and cool down slowly, a property known as high thermal mass. In the English climate which is generally mild, but can experience great fluctuations in temperature over a single day, this is an advantage, preventing the building from over-heating in the midday sun, whilst reducing heat loss at night. During the day the occupants and their computers provide heat which is absorbed by the walls, and rises through the large open space. Opening windows provide ventilation and prevent over-heating. At night the heat is retained by the thick walls, reducing the need to heat the space in the winter. In summer, the windows can be left open, cooling the fabric down overnight.

The use of thick brick walls in the Crystallographic Data Centre thus represents an environmentally sensitive approach to building design, producing a building that uses less energy to run which offsets slightly higher construction costs. In addition, the sensitive choice of materials and their disposition following an understanding of traditional methods provides a text-book example of how lessons can be learnt from the past and used to provide a building that is still uncompromisingly modern and of its time.

Opposite The main space of the Crystallographic Data Centre, which is on the first floor. The space is lit by large roof lights above and by smaller openable windows at desk height. The relatively low light levels allow monitors to be seen. Most of the work in the centre is carried out on computer.

Above The main space is clad internally in acoustic bricks to reduce noise. Likewise the ceiling is constructed using timber inserts. The result is a very calm quiet space which changes as the light moves around throughout the day.

Michael and Patty Hopkins:
Glyndebourne (1991–93) and structural brickwork

The principle of 'truth to materials' is often seen as being central to modernism. The structure of a building being meant to be easily legible to the observer is not a new idea. French architects in the 18th century, for instance, were as concerned with structural rationalism as the architects of 20th century. Nevertheless, producing a structure that conforms to modern standards of waterproofing and insulation is a considerable challenge. An attempt to face these issues can be found in the new theatre constructed at Glyndebourne, East Sussex, England.

Here the architects were particularly concerned that the construction of the building should be instantly legible. Brick was chosen for the walls for contextual reasons: the country house which is next to the opera house is built out of it. To maintain the texture of the existing brickwork, they specified a brick that matched those used on the house measuring 220 x 106 x 60mm. This was slightly thinner than the standard metric brick (215 x 105 x 65mm) and was moulded by hand by Selbourne Brick Limited. The order represented the small company's entire production output for 1992.

The building is oval in shape and to follow the architect's call for structural rationalism, all external brickwork was load-bearing. The structure was very similar in appearance to that used by Louis Kahn at the Philips Exeter Library (but avoided the concrete framing he employed to restrain the arches). The opera house façade was divided into equal bays divided by piers which tapered as they rose up the building to reflect the smaller loads being applied at the top. The tapering also provided the haunches to support flat (jack) arches which formed the lintels over the openings at each level. The piers were 2 bricks thick (448mm) while the walls between them (and the arches) where 1½ bricks thick (334mm). The piers at the base are 1,018mm wide, reducing to 780mm at the lowest arch, 562mm at the next and 220mm (a single brick) at the top. The internal floors are supported on pre-cast 264 x 220-mm concrete

beams which pass through the wall, emerging as visible squares on the external surface. Internally the walls are left unplastered throughout.

The laying of the bricks had to be carried out with considerable precision. The whole building was set out to brick dimensions assuming 8-mm joints for the walls and 6-mm joints for the arches, the bricks laid in English bond. Forty bricklayers were employed, carefully selected by the foreman who watched each of them for three hours to see whether they were up to the job.

The arches required particular skill. They were made up from bricks especially cut to shape and numbered at the brickworks before firing and required more skilful laying. Initially only two of the bricklayers on site were capable of laying them and it took five days to construct each one. They had to be built with great accuracy, achieving a 25-mm camber over a 2,768-mm span, to ensure that the loads were evenly transferred to the piers.

Thermal expansion and contraction were a major concern on a building of such size, particularly as the architects wanted to avoid expansion joints. The solution was to use a lime mortar which was tested by Ove Arup Engineers for strength and found

to be perfectly acceptable. Tests were also carried out to confirm that there would be no problems with damp penetration.

Glyndebourne is thus deceptively simple in construction and amply demonstrates the knowledge and effort required on the part of both architect and craftsman to produce a beautifully crafted finished product.

Opposite top left View across the garden of the main house and the new opera house.

Opposite below A typical arch. Note the square of the concrete beam which supports the floors behind projecting from the brickwork.

Opposite top right View from the front of the family home showing how the bricks were chosen to match those of the older house.

Above Juxtaposition of old technology with new. The brick wall of the new opera house and the teflon-coated entrance canopy.

Below The first-floor terrace preserves the idea of being in a marquee in a garden.

Rick Mather: Keble College extension, Oxford (1991–95) and the cavity wall

Most British 20th-century brickwork is laid in monotonous Stretcher bond. In continental Europe, hollow clay patent bricks are commonly used to provide a degree of thermal insulation and these are then faced with normal facing bricks or other facing blocks. In Britain these blocks have never been popular. Instead, since the 19th century most walls have been built with a central cavity.

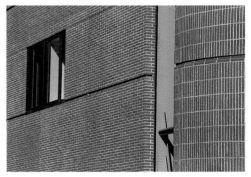

The first printed references to cavity walls appear in the 19th century. William Atkinson's *Views of Picturesque Cottages with Plans* (1805) suggested that 'in constructing walls for cottages or other edifices in brick a great saving might be made in materials without sacrificing much in regard to strength by leaving the walls hollow'. He pointed out that the 'hollow wall will be much warmer also than any other kind in consequence of the air confined in the cavity which is one of the best non-conductors of heat and cold'. Various ways of constructing cavities were tried in the 19th century. Rat-trap bond was the most common. A variant using special closers was called Dearne's bond after Thomas Dearne, who recommended it in his *Improved Method of Building* (1821). Other writers noted the advantages of cavity walls in guarding against damp penetration. S. H. Brooks even advocated using the cavities to circulate hot air around a building to produce a form of central heating in his *Designs for Cottage and Villa Architecture* (c. 1839). The introduction of cavity wall construction to the United States is credited to Ithiel

Town, who in the 1850s used this type of construction widely in New Haven, Connecticut. All these examples used bricks to tie the walls on either side of the cavity together at regular intervals. The use of wrought-iron cramps for this purpose is first mentioned in Gwilt's *Encyclopaedia of Architecture* in the 1860s, where it is stated that they were used in Southampton, England. It was the latter method with metal and plastic ties that was to become widely adopted in England in the 1920s and 1930s. By 1945 virtually all brick walls in England were built using cavity wall construction. Because of the shortage of bricks after the war it also became increasingly common to build the inside leaf of the wall in concrete blocks. By the 1970s this practice was virtually universal and the cavity itself was increasingly being filled partially or wholly with insulation.

One of the problems with cavity wall construction is that the outer leaf is invariably half a brick thick resulting in the use of uninspiring Stretcher bond. Some designers specified half-bricks (called snapped headers) to create a fake bonding pattern. A more elegant solution was provided by Rick Mather in his

new hall of residence for Keble College.

Completed in 1995, the new block provided 93 residential student rooms on four floors with a basement floor containing seminar rooms opening out into a sunken part of the garden. The building has concrete floors supported on the inner block walls. Thus the outer brick walls bear only their own weight. To express this Mather had the corner towers laid in stretcher bond but the main façades constructed in stack bond with the 248 x 102 x 41-mm hand-made Welsh bricks laid upright as soldier courses. Bricks laid in this way clearly cannot be bonded back into the wall behind except by steel ties, and the stack bond emphasizes the precarious nature of the outer wall, so the construction method is made explicit. Yet Mather's façade is not quite as straightforward as it seems. At the sides of windows (the jambs) the stretcher bond pattern appears to continue uninterrupted around the corner. Special bricks which are square on plan are used to create this effect and close off the cavity at these points. The window sills are also made from special bricks with deep recesses to form drips. These are carried around the whole façade.

Right, opposite top and opposite below Details of the garden façade showing the use of stack bond to express the non-load-bearing nature of the brickwork.

Opposite middle The junction between the stack bond and the more conventional bonding on the other façade.

Into the 20th Century

Mario Botta and Evry Cathedral

Of all the architects of the late 20th century, few have used brick more forcefully than Mario Botta. His buildings draw inspiration from Le Corbusier, Carlo Scarpa and Louis Kahn. He does not build exclusively in brick, but it is a material he has used frequently throughout his career. His most powerful brick building to date is the cathedral at Evry, just south of Paris near Orly airport, which was designed between 1988 and 1992 and built 1992–95.

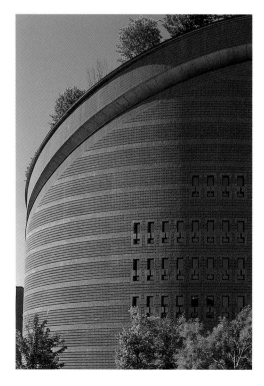

Evry is an industrial town with a modern town centre. The cathedral sits next to the town hall and near a main road. The challenge for a new building in such a situation was to create an impact within a locality that already contains a number of very large modern buildings vying for attention.

In common with Kahn, Botta has always had a strong interest in the use of symmetry and geometry to produce monumentality in building. It is always difficult to fit routes and rooms for purposes which are usually asymmetrical into buildings that are strongly symmetrical on plan. This was one of the reasons why the functionalists among the early modernists had rejected symmetry. Nevertheless there is no doubt that buildings that have a strong symmetry and a simple shape create a lasting impression on even the most unsympathetic viewer. Kahn had understood and exploited this and this is exactly what Botta does at Evry. The main body of the church is cylinder cut off at an angle. The roof appears to be a public space with trees on terraces circling the top, although in practice these terraces can only be reached from within the cathedral and are not open to the public. Internally such a building could easily have been banal, but Botta avoids this by creating a porch at an angle to the main axis that serves to direct the congregation down a single ramp into the main space. A dimly lit private prayer chapel sits beneath the entrance lit by a single shaft of light from the pavement above. The focus on the interior is on a huge projecting section of the ceiling that billows out into the space. This asymmetrical entrance,

the asymmetrical arrangement of the various elements (font, lectern, altar, organ) all serve to introduce a movement into the space which by its shape creates a feeling of repose. The result is a surprisingly complex and powerful space, the entire decoration of which relies solely on the use of brick, inside and out.

Botta's achievement at Evry is to use standard 210 x 100 x 45-mm bricks and lay them in bonding patterns to divide the façade into zones sub-divided into stripes made up of repeating numbers of courses. Thus a Dog-tooth course is separated by three courses of Stretcher bond. This pattern repeats six times,

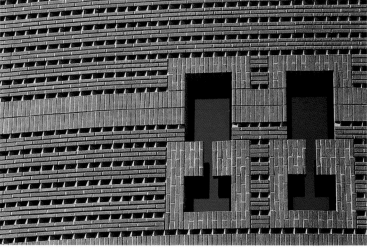

Opposite above Side view from the courtyard showing the slot in which the stairs climb to the roof and the trees above.

Opposite below The view of the cathedral from the town square in front of the town hall. The punched windows let light into rooms at various levels behind. The main space is lit from above.

Above The entrance façade with its dramatic roof-top garden. The block in the foreground contains offices and flats.

Left Detail of the brickwork on the main façade. The patterns are created by alternating three courses of Stretcher bond with Dog-tooth brickwork. Note also the use of Soldier course round the windows.

forming a horizontal band separated from the next by two soldier courses laid in Stack bond. To further emphasize the horizontal bands, all horizontal mortar joints are raked while the vertical ones are set flush, a light sand-coloured mortar being used throughout. Great care was taken in the setting out of this brickwork to ensure that the exact numbers of bricks were used. The brickwork in the cathedral is purely decorative, covering in situ concrete walls which are structural inside and out. The concrete allows Botta to create large openings in the façade and the dramatic overhang on the interior. By using this method of construction Botta is rejecting

the idea that materials have to be used 'truthfully'. Instead the presumption is that the viewer is sufficiently sophisticated to realize that modern buildings consist of lightweight cladding over structural skeletons. The brickwork is used like a fabric wrapped around the structure, a versatile cladding whose bonding mimics the weave of a material, an idea that Gottfried Semper had put forward in the late 19th century.

Opposite above left The courtyard created by the cathedral and its associated housing. One side is yet to be completed.

Opposite above right The main altar of the cathedral. The brick wall bulges dramatically out into space. Above and behind this structure is a large meeting room.

Opposite below The entrance façade with its dramatic cantilevering brickwork.

Above The interior, like the exterior, is entirely faced with brick. Lighting is provided from above through an elaborate steel roof structure. The space is entered down the ramp to the right. The altar is to the left.

Appropriate technology and the developing world

The processes and techniques described so far relate to industrialized brick production in the Western world, but bricks form a vital part of the building industries of many developing countries. In the 1980s India had some 115,000 brickmaking yards annually producing over 50,000 million bricks and employing 1.5 million people. Bricks made locally reduce transport costs. They represent a vital alternative to imported materials like steel, aluminium and plaster and avoid wasting precious timber supplies.

Most bricks in India are burnt in Bull's trench kilns. This type of kiln derives its name from its inventor, William Bull of Pembroke Hall, Redhill, Surrey, England. In his patent (dated 25 October 1893) it was noted that he was an engineer and had recently left England for India. It was presumably Bull himself who brought his new kiln to the country where it has been used ever since.

The Bull's trench kiln is similar in principle to the Hoffmann kiln. Instead of constructing a building above ground, the kiln is made by digging a large trench and lining the walls with bricks. Just like a Hoffmann kiln, the Bull's trench kiln is continuous and relies on the heat of bricks being fired at one point to heat up the next batch. Gases are distributed by the arrangement of the bricks to be fired and usually extracted using moveable chimneys (variants exist which have permanent chimneys). The capacity of such kilns varies between 200,000 and 300,000 bricks and they typically produce about 30,000 bricks a day. They can burn a wide variety of fuels from car tyres to wood and palm roots, but are most commonly fired using coal. Their two greatest disadvantages are that firstly, like Hoffmann kilns, once started they need to be kept stocked with bricks (thus they do not respond well to fluctuations in the market) and secondly they are highly polluting and relatively wasteful of fuel. Nevertheless, they still represent an important advance over reinforced concrete and steel construction which are both expensive and wasteful of resources. As a result, brick is encouraged by architects such as Laurie Baker.

Laurie Baker has worked as an architect in India since 1945 and has been a leading advocate of local building techniques to supply India's housing needs. Brought up as a Quaker in England, Baker trained as an architect at Birmingham School of Architecture, graduating in 1937. He enrolled in the Friends Ambulance Service in the war and tended the sick and wounded in China and Burma. He was suspicious of the idea of Westerners working in India but on a ship back to England from Bombay he had a chance encounter with Mahatma Gandhi who persuaded him to change his mind and in 1945 he returned to India

Opposite Wire cut perforated bricks stacked to dry before firing, Isfahan, Iran.

Below 'Jali' walls, from Laurie Baker's *Cost Reduction Manual.*

Below centre Setting out the bricks to dry, Pagan, Burma.

Right Moulding bricks, Pagan, Burma.

Bottom The firing of a scove kiln in Pagan, Burma.

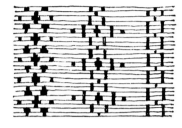

to build leprosy hospitals. Marrying an Indian doctor, he devoted the rest of his life to building for the poor.

Housing is an immense problem in India. Baker objected to the huge bureaucracy surrounding the government's attempts at alleviating the situation. He advocated from the beginning that all building work should be carried out and supervised locally. Vast government architects' departments, he claimed, just used up necessary funds and typically produced costly designs for concrete and glass buildings that were unsuited to local conditions. The result was fewer, more expensive units. His solution was to use materials made locally. In Kerala in southern India this meant bricks. Windows were to be avoided. Instead he suggested the use perforated walls (*jali*). In his *Cost Reduction Manual* he set out in easy to understand diagrams how brick buildings could be reduced to very simple construction that could be built by anyone, using the least materials possible. Over his career he has constructed literally thousands of houses using these methods and is recognized as one of the leading exponents of what is now called 'appropriate technology'.

Conservation of brick and the heritage industry

Although building conservation movements can be traced back to at least the 17th century and made great leaps forwards in the 19th century with the founding of organizations such as the Society for the Protection of Ancient Buildings (SPAB) in England, it was only in the second half of the 20th century that building conservation came to be taken seriously internationally. The Foundation for the Conservation of Museum Objects was founded in 1950. This was followed by the founding of the International Centre for the Study of the Preservation and the Restoration of Cultural Property under the auspices of UNESCO in 1959. In 1964 the Venice Charter was published after the Second International Congress of Architects and Technicians of Historic Monuments and a year later the International Council of Monuments and Sites (ICOMOS) was founded. All these organizations aim to identify endangered monuments around the world and the best methods for their preservation. In many developed countries legislation has been enacted that seeks to protect buildings of particular interest. Elsewhere legal protection tends to be less common and certain political régimes have even actively sought to destroy their cultural heritage.

As this book has shown, bricks are in general resilient materials which can, if well-made and kept clean and properly maintained, last for thousands of years. Nevertheless neglect, frost, persistent exposure to water and loss of mortar can all lead to damaged brickwork. In urban areas acidic pollution can damage both brick and terracotta, especially where soft brickwork was used for decorative effect. Sadly, even greater damage is often caused by the use of the wrong cleaning methods employed by unscrupulous contractors. Shot-blasting and acid cleaning can destroy or damage brick and terracotta irreparably. Cleaning and conserving buildings is specialist work and requires professionals and craftsmen to be correctly trained and experienced.

One of the problems faced by countries such as Britain and Italy, with a large number of protected buildings, is the lack of skilled craftsmen in the construction industry. This is most evident in bricklaying, which is difficult and strenuous work requiring a long period of training and thus seen as undesirable by young people looking for a trade. As a result highly skilled bricklayers are in short supply and can command high rates of pay. Certain types of brickwork, especially cut and rubbed work, can only be carried out by a small number of specialist contractors and the skills are in danger of dying out altogether.

In contrast to this, the amount of conservation work around as a result of the legislation has created an increase in the demand for old bricks. Some of this is met by recycling. A large number of specialist building merchants keep stocks of bricks and tiles re-claimed from demolished buildings. The remaining demand is met by a small number of very active specialist brickyards where bricks are moulded by hand to suit individual orders and fired using traditional methods. Such bricks cost about four or five times the price of normal bricks but are more desirable than reclaimed bricks and may be the only alternative where matching bricks of a particular type or size cannot be obtained by other means. Increasingly such bricks have also found a place in new building works where their particular textures and characteristics have been chosen in preference to those obtainable using machine-moulding techniques. Terracotta is similarly still being made by a very few manufacturers almost entirely for the conservation industry.

In the developing world there are obviously other priorities and the response to heritage varies. The creation of World Heritage Sites has encouraged some countries to spend valuable resources in protecting monuments in the hope of increasing tourism with its associated benefits. This has often involved re-building monuments (anastylosis), a highly controversial process which creates a false impression of history. Elsewhere many countries have lacked the resources adequately to protect sites uncovered by archaeological excavation and great brick complexes like those at Mohenjo Daro in Pakistan are in danger of disappearing altogether.

Opposite and above
Bricks are produced to traditional patterns in wooden box moulds.

Opposite bottom left
Plain tiles and ridge tiles are made to order.

Opposite bottom right
Wooden moulds for making bricks are kept for future use.

Photographs taken at the Bulmer Brickworks, Suffolk, England.

WHAT FUTURE FOR BRICK?

This book has provided an overview of the whole history of brick. It has discussed the problems involved in brickmaking and how it developed from a craft in the Neolithic period to a modern manufacturing industry. It has looked at the craft of the bricklayers and traced the myriad of forms that they have produced transforming simple fired blocks of clay into patterns of astonishing complexity and beauty. It has examined the ways in which designers (architects, master craftsmen, patrons, engineers) have used bricks since the beginning of civilization to shape the built environment and how the qualities of the brick have been exploited to produce an extraordinary range of structures from humble drains to great ziggurats, from the cottages of peasants to the palaces of kings. Finally it has traced the development of the brick itself and how it has changed from a simple clod of earth kneaded into a loaf-like mass by hand to the metric-sized precision moulded factory-produced object made today. One question remains: what if anything can this tell us about the future?

Brickmaking has obviously come a long way since mud was rudely shaped into lumps in Neolithic Jericho. But of all the aspects of brickmaking moulding has changed least. The ancient Mesopotamians first used open-bottomed wooden moulds to shape bricks and the same method is used across the globe today. When bricks began to be fired they were still moulded in much the same way and Byzantine brick moulders were using tools that would have been familiar to the ancient Egyptians. The first great leap forward was the moulding bench which seems to have appeared in the Middle Ages in Europe. Then there was the introduction of the stock over which the mould fitted and the wooden pallets that allowed the brick to be transported without losing its shape. Finally there was the barrow onto which it was loaded to be taken to the drying ground. However, these were refinements in a basic technique that varied little in thousands of years.

It was only in the 19th century that machines began to be used in any numbers for moulding bricks. As late as 1850 Edward Dobson could still confidently maintain in his *A Rudimentary Treatise on the Manufacture of Bricks and Tiles* that 'the actual cost of moulding bears so small a proportion to the total cost of brickmaking, that in small brickworks the employment of machinery would effect no ultimate saving, and therefore, it is not to be expected that machinery will ever be generally introduced for brickmaking'. What of course Dobson had not realised was that in the developed world the economics of mass-production would mean that brick-moulding machinery would force the smaller manufacturers out

of business. In the Western world bricks are now only made by hand for special purposes and cost four to five times their machine-made counterparts. In other parts of the world, where labour is cheap, they still remain the norm.

Most of the techniques for machine-moulding bricks were devised in the 19th century; the 20th and 21st centuries have merely automated the control systems. Where the traditional processes required weeks, the new ones take hours. In the past brickmakers and bricklayers craved the very uniformity that machines seemingly effortlessly create. Today, by contrast, money and time is expended in producing bricks by machine that look like they were moulded by hand. Yet one limitation still remains: flexibility. It takes time to reset machines to produce different shapes of bricks making 'specials' (as they are called) expensive to produce. Most factory-produced bricks are a 'standard' size. Although it is already theoretically possible, the days when designers will be able to ask a factory to produce hundreds of slightly different bricks from computer drawings to their own specifications still appear to be a long way off. In this regard at least hand-moulding remains more sophisticated than modern manufacturing.

The development of kilns has been similarly varied. As we have seen in Chapter Two, the simple updraught kilns where bricks were stacked in a separate chamber above the one where the fuel was burned were used in Roman times and had probably already been in use for several thousand years before then. The cheaper alternative, the temporary clamp, was certainly used in the Middle Ages. The West only caught up with

Opposite and above
Housing (1991–2000), Java Island, Amsterdam. The blocks are all different but carefully coordinated by architect Sjoerd Soeters of Soeters Van Eldonk Ponec. Brick is used alongside other materials to create the illusion of a city that has grown up over time. Each block is given its own identity. Brick has once again become fashionable in Dutch architecture.

China's downdraught kiln technology in the 19th century. Progress was very limited before the middle of the 19th century. Since then, however, with the development of continuous kilns, there have been considerable advances in efficiency. Pollution and fuel use still remain problems and no doubt improvements will continue to be made in this regard.

Some inventors have of course tried to do without the kiln altogether. Calcium silicate bricks are made by compressing a mixture of damp sand and lime and then curing the result with saturated steam in an autoclave. The process was invented in Germany in 1880s but has never been particularly popular. It was soon superseded by the concrete block, which used Portland Cement to bind an aggregate together. The colour and density of the aggregate determined the colour, weight and performance of the blocks. As they could be made lighter than fired clay bricks by using low-density aggregates, they were soon

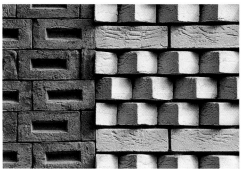

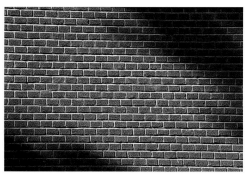

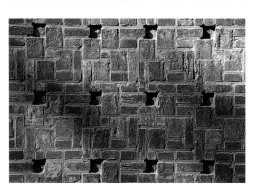

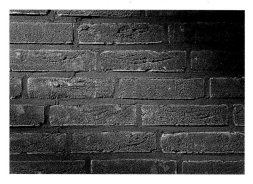

Top The Openluchtmuseum, Arnhem, Netherlands. Founded in 1912, it displays rescued historic buildings. The entrance wing was designed by Francine Houben, founding partner of Mecanoo Architects. It consists of a dramatic 143m long wall forming one boundary of the site, built out of a patchwork quilt of bricks.

Above Details from the wall: 40 different types of brick are laid in 28 different bonding patterns, forming a dramatic permanent exhibition of the versatility of brick.

made in larger units that allowed walls to be built more quickly. Today the concrete block presents the greatest threat to the brick manufacturing industry in many developed countries. Yet in the developing world, where Portland Cement is expensive, bricks still predominate. The increasing interest in sustainable building materials may yet create a move away from Portland Cement and back towards fired bricks and lime mortar elsewhere.

Trends are also discernible in bricklaying. The division between brickmaker and bricklayer has, if anything, widened in the last century, but as we have seen it already had a long history. In adobe construction it is not uncommon for the householders to make the bricks and lay them, but the use of fired bricks generally implies a division of labour. Sometimes, on large projects built over many years, brickmakers and bricklayers have worked closely together and many moulded brick details were produced as a result. In other cases, the brickmaker supplied the raw material and decorative work was carved by the bricklayer.

Most of the techniques of bricklaying today have, as we have seen, a very long history. The use of distinct bonding patterns, for instance, can be traced back to ancient Mesopotamia. The Romans developed pointing. Yet the ingenuity of man is such that advances continue to be made. Brunel had experimented with reinforcing brickwork with iron in the 19th century and many variations on this technique were tried with steel in the 20th century, allowing brick buildings to be built higher and with thinner walls. Le Corbusier carried out detailed research into Catalan vaults which he used in some of his houses. Engineers have developed the diaphragm wall (an extra thick cavity wall that could use thin leaves of brick to carry large loads). Advances in epoxy adhesives make it possible to build previously unachievable structures.

While brickmaking has become highly automated, bricklaying is largely untouched by modern technology. Most bricklaying tools now have a long history. For instance, the Romans used trowels, set-squares and plumb rules. Moxon's 17th-century illustration (page 173) shows many of the tools that are still used today. The brickaxe, a sort of double-ended chisel, was developed in the Middle Ages and replaced in the 19th century by the bolster (the large bricklayers' chisel) that is used today. The plumb rule and square were only replaced on site by the spirit level in the 20th century. Yet there are no automatic bricklaying machines and no robotic bricklayers.

But while the tools have remained the same, in many parts of the world methods of training bricklayers have changed dramatically. Apprenticeships and guild memberships have disappeared. The skilled bricklayer in the Middle Ages would have trained for at least seven years. Today the craft is often learnt at colleges in only two or three years, sometimes part-time. Employers are rarely involved in the process. This makes it much more difficult for the bricklayers to acquire the same level of skill as their forebears and puts more of the burden on the individuals to teach themselves. Certain skills which are not in regular demand are in danger of dying out altogether.

One of the most important developments in the building industry over the past five hundred years has been the changes in the role of the designer. Architects and engineers, as distinct from master craftsmen, rarely have experience of handling building materials or the opportunity to experiment with them on site as the building is being constructed. Modern contracting methods increasingly require all decisions to be made at an early stage so that the works can be accurately priced. This method of drawing up contracts was not common before the 18th century in Europe. During the Renaissance the architect could often change his mind as the building progressed, the workers usually being paid by the day. In the Middle Ages, of course, the master craftsmen would have already been intimately familiar with the materials that they were using, although they only would have tended to put them together in tried and tested ways. The later architect had more freedom to experiment but needed a knowledge of materials acquired from education or books with all the limitations that implied. To make things more difficult, in the 20th century the range of materials that could be acceptably used in building increased.

Modern technology has freed up the possibilities of building for architects. The designer has more power than ever before. No longer do buildings have to look a certain way or conform to a certain style. However, with this freedom of choice has come an extraordinary burden of responsibility. Today the architect is expected to be conversant with the possibilities of a bewildering array of different materials. Where in the past the architect could look to craftsmen for advice, there are frequently no craftsmen to ask at the design stage and a contractual arrangement that puts the burden firmly on the designer's shoulders.

A book like this runs the risk of giving the history of brick a misleading unity and sense of continuity, but as I have tried to show this has not been the case. The history of brick is full of instances when political and social events have disrupted a particular path of development. Invasions and disasters have changed or destroyed economic and political structures that underpinned one method of construction or substituted others in their place. Skills, on which a person's or company's livelihood depends, are closely guarded secrets. Rarely published or even publishable, they tend to disappear without trace when the demand for them ceases. No-one wants to train under those who have a skill that is no longer needed, so techniques can easily be lost within a generation. For example, the glazed brick technologies of the Babylonians were never used by the Greeks and were effectively lost when they conquered Persia, only to be later partially rediscovered in the Middle Ages, and again in the 19th century. As this work has shown, histories of manufacturing technologies do not conform to simple evolutionary theories or general notions of progress. It is more complex than that. If analyzed in isolation they appear to move in jumps or starts, followed by regressions, but they do so because they are affected by changes in society as a whole. In this sense technology is not a driving force in society so much as a reflection of it and its preconceptions and inclinations.

History is concerned with the past, with attempting to establish what happened and venturing to ask why events turned out they way they did. An understanding of history is essentially an understanding of how we arrived at where we are today. History can show us that the brick has a large number of advantages and possibilities and how countless generations have sought to exploit these. Where, in balance, does all this leave the future of the brick? Ultimately, athough history can provide an invaluable source of information and inspiration for future designers, it cannot be used to predict the future. Nevertheless, having seen how successful brick has been over so many thousand years, it does not seem unreasonable to suggest that brick will be with us for some time to come.

GLOSSARY

American bond another name for English Garden Wall bond.

Anda the spire on the top of a Buddhist stupa.

Apron a projecting panel below a window sill, sometimes richly ornamented. Found in some 17th- and early 18th-century Western European architecture.

Arris the straight edge formed where any two faces of a block meet. The sharpness of the arrises will determine how closely bricks can be laid together.

Backsteingotik German term for the brick built Gothic architecture that prevailed in northern Europe during the Middle Ages.

Bat a *brick bat* is a brick that has been cut to fit across its width (or especially moulded to shape) to make up the dimensions of a wall. Where the brick is cut in half it is called a *half-bat* and where the piece used is three-quarters the length of the original a *three-quarter bat* (see Fig.1). Where a brick is cut along its length it is called a **Closer** rather than a bat.

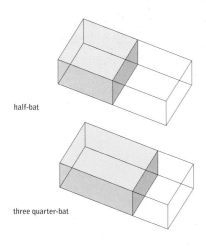

half-bat

three quarter-bat

Fig.1 **Bat**

Bed joint the horizontal joint between one brick and the one beneath it. The vertical joints are called Perpends.

Beehive kiln specific term for a circular enclosed downdraught kiln with a domed roof where the gases are directed from stoking holes around the base up through the bricks to the top of the dome and then drawn down to be exhausted through a duct in the floor leading to a tall chimney to one side (see illustration on pages 210–11).

Belgian kiln a continuous kiln invented by Dubois-Enghiens in 1891, which was similar to a **Hoffmann kiln** but was stoked and controlled from ground level (fuel in Hoffmann kilns is loaded from above) and was usually rectangular. Commonly used in Britain and elsewhere for making Facing bricks.

Bessalis smallest Roman brick (derived from *bes* meaning two-thirds of a unit) is two-thirds of a Roman foot (200mm) square and usually about 45mm thick.

Bipedalis the largest Roman brick, measuring two or more Roman feet square. Those found vary between 590 and 750mm square and are usually 65mm thick.

Black mortar obtained by mixing soot with the sand. Commonly used in the 19th century for re-pointing existing work and for building new walls using machine-made bricks.

Blind Window a false window, with head, jambs and sill, but a wall instead of glass and frame, usually included in a regular façade, where a window is not required on the interior, to preserve symmetry. In rarer cases the result of bricking-in to avoid taxes levied on the number of windows.

Bonding the arrangement of the face of brickwork in a pattern for strength and to create decorative effect. Different arrangements have been given names to distinguish them, most of which were only coined by writers in the 19th century, although the patterns they describe all have a longer history. Fig.3 shows some of the different types of bonds.

See also : American bond, Chinese bond, Dearne's bond, Dutch bond, English bond, English Cross bond, English Garden Wall bond, Flemish bond, Flemish Garden Wall bond, Flemish Stretcher bond, Flying bond, Header bond, Mixed Garden bond, Monk bond, Quarter bonding, Quetta bond, Raked Stretcher bond, Rat-trap bond, Silesian bond, Stack, Stretcher, Sussex, Yorkshire.

Bonding courses through-courses of brickwork inserted at regular intervals in a rubble or stone wall to bond the structure together (also called Lacing courses).

Bond timber, or **Bonding timber** a timber inserted into the thickness of a masonry wall to add

strength. Common in many types of construction. Examples are found in ancient Mesopotamia. Used in Byzantine times as temporary support during construction, but in the late Middle Ages and after in northern Europe more commonly intended as an important part of the permanent structure, which can lead to structural problems if timber decays.

Box mould a wooden mould consisting of a box with sides and a bottom (but no top) into which the clay is pressed. Often used for making tiles and complex shapes.

Breeze cinders or ashes from domestic fires, consisting of incompletely combusted material, often used in firing clamps or kilns and in the 18th century in making **London stock** bricks as an additive (then called **spanish**) to the brickearth.

Brickearth generally the material from which bricks are made.

Brick-end plugs plugs of decorated mortar or plaster inserted into extra wide perpends between the bricks (see pages 115–21).

Bricknogging brickwork when employed as infill panels in timber frame construction.

Brick on edge bricks laid with the headers on their sides exposed on the front surface of the wall (Fig.2). Compare with **Brick on end** and **Soldier course**, **Stretcher** and **Header course**.

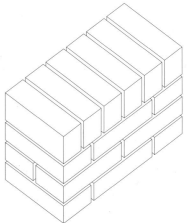

Fig.2 **Brick on edge**

Brick on end brick laid upright, displaying the stretcher face. If laid in a course this is called a **Soldier course**.

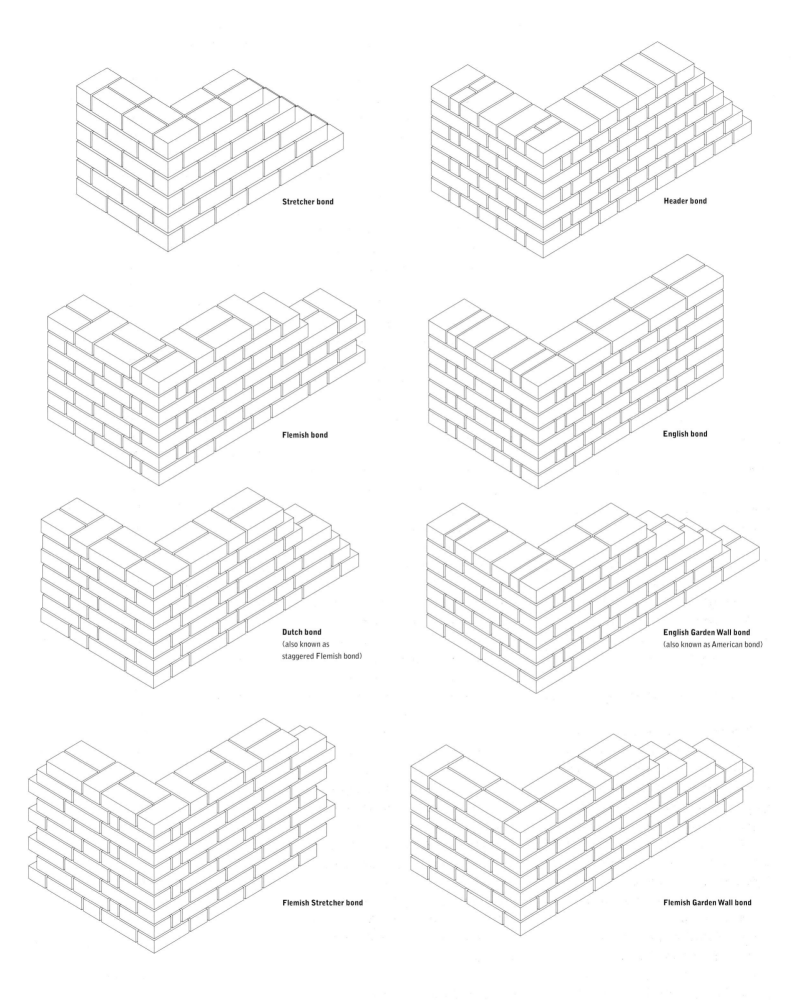

Stretcher bond

Header bond

Flemish bond

English bond

Dutch bond
(also known as
staggered Flemish bond)

English Garden Wall bond
(also known as American bond)

Flemish Stretcher bond

Flemish Garden Wall bond

Fig.3 **Bonding**

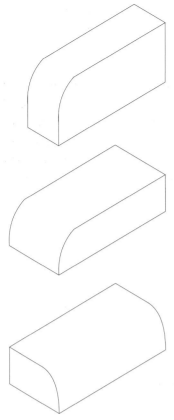

Fig.4 **Bullnose Bricks**

Brick slips thin vertical slices of bricks, either cross-ways or length-ways, usually used to cover beams or lintels to make them match surrounding brickwork.

Brick tiles another name for **Mathematical tiles.**

Bullnose bricks brick which has been especially moulded to have a semi-circular edge rather than a sharp edge. Use in situations where a sharp arris might be damaged or for decorative effect (see Fig.4).

Bulls-eye a small round or oval window.

Bull's trench kiln a continuous kiln patented by an English engineer, William Bull, in October 1893 which was based on the **Hoffmann kiln** principle but using a large trench in place of a building, the fires being lit from one side under the bricks and the gases extracted using a mobile chimney. It has the advantage that it makes a large number of bricks quickly, cheaply and continuously. Widely used in modern China, India and the developing world. Creates great problems with air pollution and is relatively fuel inefficient. The **Vertical shaft kiln** has been proposed as a more efficient alternative.

Burrs discarded bricks which have been fused together by excessive heat in a kiln.

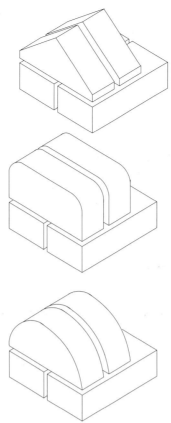

Fig.5 **Capping Bricks**

Calcium silicate bricks bricks which are not fired but made instead from sand or crushed flint which is mixed with a hydrated lime cement, moulded under pressure and allowed to dry. Also called **Sand-lime** bricks or **Flint-lime** bricks.

Cant brick an especially moulded brick with one or more corners cut off diagonally (see Fig.6).

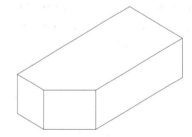

Fig.6 **Cant Brick**

Capping brick a moulded brick shaped to be laid on edge to form the top of a wall but not projecting beyond it to form a drip (which would be a **Coping brick**). The standard forms are bullnose, half-round and saddle-back (see Fig.5).

Carved brickwork decorative brickwork formed from bricks which are carved after firing, as distinct from **moulded** or **sculpted** bricks which are shaped before firing.

Casings bricks used on the outside of a clamp as a cladding to keep off the rain and as insulation.

Cavity wall a wall constructed in two leaves with an air gap in between to provide thermal separation. Various methods are used to fix the leaves together structurally. Bricks can be used and a number of bonding patterns have been invented to enable this to be done, most notably: **Chinese bond** also known as **Rat-trap bond, Rowlock bond** or **Silverlock's bond;** and **Dearne's bond.** Today the leaves are more commonly tied together using metal or plastic wall ties specifically designed for the purpose.

Cement mortar mortar made from sand, water, and Portland Cement, instead of, or in addition to lime. The term is used to distinguish it from **Lime mortar.**

Centering temporary timber structures used to support the stones of an arch or vault during construction. Also called formwork.

Chequered brickwork either: brickwork in **Flemish bond** with headers which are vitrified so that they become grey or black and contrast with the stretchers; or brickwork where the bricks are laid in squares contrasting with panels of other materials such as flint.

Chinese bond a type of bonding used to make a cavity wall, constructed by laying the bricks on edge in Flemish bond, also called **Rat-trap bond, Rowlock bond** or **Silverlock's bond.** The term 'Chinese bond' refers to the fact that the Chinese used similar patterns (see Chapter One), although Chinese brickwork was far more various and the bond in question was made with large flat bricks in the Far East.

Chuffs discarded bricks that are soft and full of cracks when drawn from the kiln or clamp, perhaps because of inadequate drying.

Clamp a temporary kiln made from the un-fired bricks, as opposed to a **Kiln**, which is a permanent structure for firing bricks. When the outside of a clamp is covered in mud or plaster it is called a **Scove kiln** in the United States.

Clinker term used in 17th-century England for a small hard type of Dutch brick, commonly used for paving.

Closer a brick that has been cut to fit along its length (or especially moulded to shape) to make up the dimensions of a wall. See also **King closer** and **Queen closer**. Where a brick is cut along its width it is called a **bat** rather than a closer.

Common bond a type of bonding, sometimes used to mean **Stretcher bond** but more correctly applied to the simplest method of laying square bricks. Although the wall appears to be composed of identical bricks laid in Stretcher bond, to bind it back to the wall behind, the outer surface will be composed of alternating patterns of full and half bricks. These will not be distinguishable on the surface.

Common brick a poor quality brick, often with surface blemishes which is thus unsuitable for facing, but still adequate for the interior of a wall. The converse is a **Facing brick.**

Compass bricks (also called **Radial** or **Radiating** bricks) a tapered brick moulded or cut for use in making semi-circular arches or **Bulls-eye** windows.

Continuous kiln any type of kiln designed so that one part of the kiln is being fired while other parts are being cooled down or emptied. Examples are **Bull's trench kilns**, **Hoffmann kilns**, **Belgian kilns**, and **Tunnel kilns**. The opposite is an **Intermittent kiln.**

Coping brick a brick moulded especially for use in the capping of walls, where the edges project beyond the faces of the wall and are formed with drips to throw off the rain (see Fig.7). By contrast see **Capping bricks.**

Corbel table a row of small projecting arches used as cornice in medieval architecture, usually beneath the eaves of a roof.

Corbelling successive courses of projecting bricks used to provide projecting elements in a building façade such as bay windows (see Fig.8).

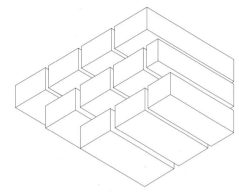

Fig.8 **Corbelling**

Course a single layer of bricks laid horizontally in a wall.

Cow-nose brick a special brick made with a semi-circular end (see Fig.9).

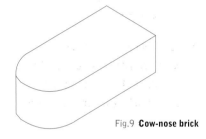

Fig.9 **Cow-nose brick**

Crinkle-crankle wall termed in America a **Serpentine wall**, a wall usually only half-a-brick in thickness, which derives its stability from its curving shape on plan (see Fig.10).

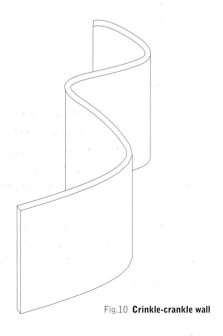

Fig.10 **Crinkle-crankle wall**

Cutter: also called a **rubber**, a type of brick of a particularly uniform texture which makes it ideal for carving.

Dearne's bond a type of bonding devised to save bricks, where the bricks are in **English bond**, but with the stretchers laid on edge, creating a cavity (see Fig.11). Named after Thomas Dearne (1777–1853), architect and writer, who suggested its use in *Hints on an Improved Method of Building*, 1821.

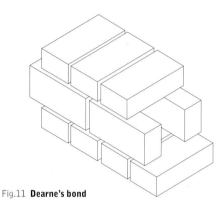

Fig.11 **Dearne's bond**

Dentilation (Dentilated brickwork) the projection of alternate headers in a course to mimic the projecting blocks or dentils in a Greek entablature, usually found at eaves level.

Diaper diagonal patterns of bricks created by using vitrified headers.

Didoron type of brick invented by the Romans, described by the Roman author Pliny the Elder as being the same size as the **Lydion**.

Dog-leg bricks special bricks made to fit obtuse angles in walls (see Fig.12).

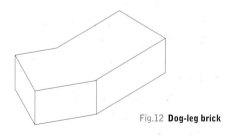

Fig.12 **Dog-leg brick**

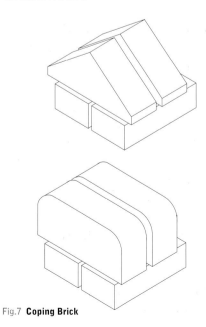

Fig.7 **Coping Brick**

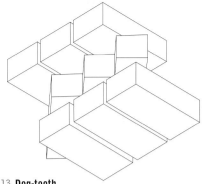

Fig.13 **Dog-tooth**

Dog-tooth (Hound's tooth, Mouse tooth)
the laying of bricks diagonally so that a triangular
shape projects from the face of the wall, designed
to create a decorative effect.

Downdraught kiln a type of kiln where the exhaust
gases pass up to the roof and are then drawn back
down to grates in the floor by using a tall chimney.
The opposite is an **Updraught kiln**, where the fires are
lit at the bottom and the gases simply escape upwards.

Dressings parts of a wall (typically the corners and
window and door surrounds) that are made in finer
rubbed and gauged brickwork contrasting with the
normal brickwork of the main wall surfaces.

Drying hack the stack made from green bricks
which have just been moulded and are set out to dry,
prior to firing.

Dry press term used by brickmakers for a
mechanized process of brick moulding where the clay
is so dry that when it is pressed into shape no further
drying is required before it goes into the kiln.

Dutch bond another name for **English Cross bond**
confusingly sometimes also used for **Flemish
Cross bond.**

Dutch gable a confusing term used in England
to describe shaped gables of the 17th century
which are surmounted by pediments. Not especially
Dutch in origin.

Engineering brick dense uniform hard machine-
made bricks which lack porosity and tend to be
employed in engineering works.

English bond type of bonding where courses of
headers alternate with courses of stretchers.

English Cross bond a type of bond based on English
bond where the courses alternate between headers and

stretchers, but each row of stretchers is shifted half a
length so that only alternate stretcher courses line up.
Also known as St Andrew's and Dutch bond and called
Flemish bond in Germany.

English Garden Wall bond a variant of English
bond where two or more courses of stretchers occur
between every course of headers. Also called
American bond.

Face the side of a brick placed on the outside
of the wall and thus visible.

Facing brick a uniformly coloured brick without
blemishes suitable for use on the visible face of a wall,
as opposed to a **Common brick.**

Faïence strictly a particular type of glazed terracotta
where the terracotta is fired at high temperature,
then a glaze is applied and it is re-fired at a lower
temperature, but more usually the term given
to all glazed terracotta.

Firebrick bricks made from **Fireclay** which are
suitable for resisting high temperature and are thus
used in chimney lining, kilns, etc.

Fireclay type of clay found in coal measures
with a high silica content which when fired
produces **Firebricks.**

Fireholes chambers in the side of kilns where
the fuel is burned.

Flat arch (also called a **Straight arch, Jack arch,** or
French arch), a lintel made from tapering bricks, held
in place by the shape of the bricks and friction.

Flemish bond one of the basic bonds, where each
course is made of headers alternating with stretchers,
where each header lies above the middle of the
stretcher beneath. The bond has been given many
names in different parts of the world. It is also known
as **Gothic bond** and in Germany as **Polish bond.**
Confusingly 'Flemish bond' is the term used in
Germany for what is known in England as
English Cross bond.

Flemish Cross bond a variant on **Flemish bond**
where in alternate courses the stretchers are all
replaced with headers.

Flemish Garden Wall bond a variant on **Flemish
bond** where in each course there are three stretchers

between each pair of headers. Traditionally the
headers line up vertically. Also called **Sussex bond**
or **Silesian bond.**

Flemish Stretcher bond a variant on **Flemish
bond** where two or more courses consisting only of
stretchers are inserted between every course of
headers and stretchers. If the headers do not line up
then it is called **Mixed Garden bond.** Also called
American Flemish bond.

Fletton strictly a brick made in the Peterborough
area of England from deep Oxford Clays but generally
applied to all bricks made from such clays which have
a high carbon content allowing the bricks to fire
using less fuel. At the beginning of the 20th century
Fletton bricks were produced in enormous numbers
using the dry-press process, primarily as
Common bricks.

Flint-lime another name for **Calcium silicate bricks.**

Flying bond also known as Yorkshire bond or Monk
bond, a variant on **Flemish bond** with two stretchers
between every header.

Formwork temporary timers structures used to
support the stones of an arch or vault during
construction. Also called centring.

French arch another term for **Flat arch.**

Frog the name given to an indentation made in the
top of a brick during moulding, thought to take its
name from the cleft of a horse's hoof, the soft part
of which was called a 'frog' (see Fig.14).

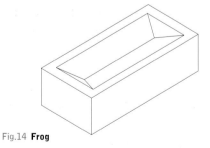

Fig.14 **Frog**

Galletting the insertion of pebbles or other stones
into the joints when wet for decorative effect and to
protect the face of the mortar.

Gauged literally means measured. Used to
mean brickwork with particularly fine joints
where every brick is individually measured and
cut to shape.

Gault bricks strictly bricks made from the chalk-rich Gault clay of eastern England which typically burns to a characteristic yellow, but loosely applied to all pale yellow bricks.

Glazed bricks bricks with one end and one face glazed, made by coating the surfaces with a salt before firing; early examples are found in Babylon in Mesopotamia. Became very popular in the late 19th century because of its easy-cleaning and light reflecting qualities.

Gothic bond another name for **Flemish bond** reflecting its use in northern Europe throughout the Middle Ages.

Great bricks a term applied to medieval bricks of particularly large size.

Green bricks bricks before they are fired.

Gypsum mortar a quick drying mortar made from water and anhydrous gypsum. Soft and white or grey, hydrous gypsum (calcium sulphate) is found occurring naturally among clays and limestones. Anhydrous gypsum is made by burning hydrous gypsum to drive off water.

Hack see **Drying hack.**

Header a brick laid so that the short side is visible.

Header bond a bond consisting entirely of headers.

Header course a course of bricks all of which are headers.

Herringbone bond bond in which the visible parts of the wall are laid in **Stretcher bond** but the inside of the wall is laid in herringbone patterns.

Herringbone brickwork bricks laid diagonally rather than horizontally, sloping in alternate directions.

Hitch bricks patent interlocking hollow bricks invented by Caleb Hitch in 1828 and manufactured in his factory in Ware, England.

Hoffmann kiln the first type of continuous kiln, patented by Frederick Hoffmann in Germany in 1858 (see pages 212–13).

Hollow bricks bricks consisting with 25% or more of hollow spaces.

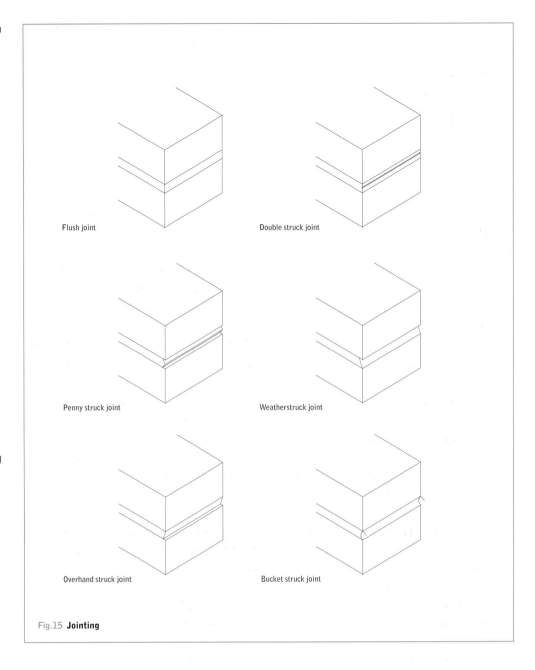

Flush joint

Double struck joint

Penny struck joint

Weatherstruck joint

Overhand struck joint

Bucket struck joint

Fig.15 **Jointing**

Honeycomb brickwork brickwork where the bricks are laid in **Flemish bond** but without the headers so that there are gaps through which the air can pass.

Hoop-iron bond an early type of reinforced brickwork using wrought iron bars, dipped in tar and laid in every sixth horizontal mortar joint.

Hydraulic lime mortar a mortar formed using slaked lime, sand, and another additive with pozzolanic qualities (such as volcanic ash or brick dust), which makes the mortar set underwater.

Hydrogen reduction the firing of brick in an atmosphere with reduced oxygen, so that the brick fires without the materials oxidizing. Used in the early Chinese manufacture, producing characteristic grey bricks.

Imbrex curved Roman roofing tile that fitted over the upstands of two **tegulae.**

Intermittent kiln a traditional type of kiln where the bricks are loaded into the kiln, it is fired, and then allowed to cool before unloading. As opposed to a **Continuous kiln.**

Jack arch the American term for a **Flat arch.**

Jamb the side of a window or doorway.

Jointing ways of finishing the joints between bricks (see also **Pointing**). The most common types are shown in Fig.15, above.

Kiln a permanent structure for firing bricks (as opposed to a **Clamp** which is a temporary structure). Kilns are typically made of fired bricks.

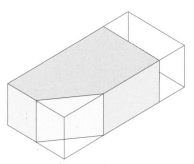

Fig.16 **King closer**

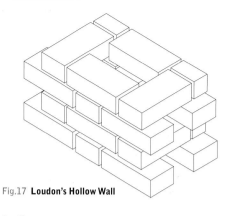

Fig.17 **Loudon's Hollow Wall**

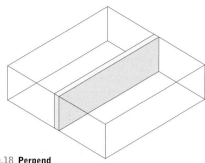

Fig.18 **Perpend**

King closer a three-quarter bat with half header further cut on the diagonal to reveal a face equivalent to a closer, the diagonal being hidden within the wall (see Fig.16).

Kokoshniki in Russian architecture, decorative arches commonly found in tiers on the roof of Russian churches.

Lacing courses through-courses of brickwork inserted at regular intervals in a rubble or stone wall to bond the structure together (also called Bonding courses).

Lime mortar mortar made from slaked lime. Lime itself is naturally occurring as limestone and chalk. It is burnt in a kiln to produce quicklime which is then mixed with water to produce slaked lime. This, when mixed with sand, produces a mortar which dries slowly on contact with air.

Lime putty another name for slaked lime.

Lintel the structural element which spans across an opening, typically timber in traditional building but stone was also employed. Today lintels are often concrete or steel.

London stock brick a brick that is made with clay to which ash (called **spanish**) has been added. The ash burns when the brick is fired so that less fuel is required. The technique is said to have been discovered after the Great Fire of London in 1666. Not to be confused with **Stock bricks**.

Loudon's Hollow wall a system of bonding devised for cavity walling. The bricks are laid in **Flemish bond** but with a 50mm cavity between the leaves (see Fig.17). The headers are used to bind the leaves together and a 50mm bat is used at one end of each to provide a flush face. The bond was invented by John Claudius Loudon (1783-1843), a Scottish writer and landscape gardener.

Lydion type of mud brick said to have been used by the Romans by the Roman author Vitruvius who says they were rectangular and measuring one foot by one and a half.

Mathematical tiles tiles specially made and designed to be hung on the outside of a building to imitate bricks.

Mixed Garden bond a version of **Flemish Stretcher** bond where the headers do not align vertically.

Monk bond also known as Yorkshire bond or Flying bond, a variant on **Flemish bond** with two stretchers between every header.

Mortar any paste spread between the bricks to both bind them together and to keep them apart.

Mould the box or container into which clay or brick earth is pushed to produce a regular shape.

Moulded bricks bricks made in a mould, particularly used in the context of especially shaped bricks to distinguish them from bricks that are cut to shape after firing.

Muqarnas in Islamic architecture the graduated subdivision of a squinch (an arch across the corner of a square space on which a dome rests) into miniature arches and squinches producing a rich decorative pattern.

Newcastle kiln a rectangular horizontal-draught intermittent kiln, with stoke holes at one end of a chamber and a chimney at the other. Used particularly in the north-east of England in the 19th century. The kilns were often placed back-to-back sharing a central chimney.

Non-hydrated lime mortar lime mortar made by burning lime to produce quicklime and then mixing it with water to produce slaked lime. The slaked lime is then mixed with sand to make a slow-setting mortar. Hair was sometimes used as a binder and other ingredients were added with the aim of improving the setting time. Such ingredients which varied according to local custom and were often of dubious efficacy, have included beer, urine, eggs, camel's milk, rice gruel, and animal fat.

Open mould type of mould most commonly used for hand-moulding bricks, consisting of a box with four sides but no top or bottom.

Pallet boards thin boards used for carrying bricks from the moulding bench to the place where they are set out to dry (see the illustrations on pages 174–75).

Patent bricks the various types of bricks proposed and patented by inventors in the 19th and 20th centuries, usually attempting to solve a particular building problem. Typically known by the owner of the original patent (eg. Hitch Bricks: interlocking hollow bricks which were invented by Caleb Hitch in 1828).

Paviour bricks bricks specifically made for use in paving and floors which are typically of low-porosity and particularly hard-wearing.

Pedalis type of Roman brick, one Roman foot (295mm) square and usually about 45-50mm thick.

Pentadoron type of mud brick said to have been used by the Greeks by the Roman author Vitruvius who says they were square and five palms long in either direction.

Perforated bricks bricks with vertical holes passing through the thickness of the brick, usually made using the wire-cut process by using special dies.

Perpends the vertical strips of mortar between bricks (see Fig.18).

Place bricks terms used in the 17th century to mean a brick made using a moulding process that pre-dated the use of pallets (stock-moulding) where the bricks were turned straight from the mould onto the ground where they were dried. As these bricks were generally inferior to those made by the stock moulding process the term came to be used in the 18th century for any inferior brick including those that were poorly burnt.

Plinth brick a brick with a chamfer cut in the face to provide for a reduction in thickness of the wall between a plinth running around the base of a building and the normal wall above.

Pointing the careful application of a layer of superior quality mortar to a raked out joint to produce a joint with a particular profile or finish. Can be used to produce normal **Jointing** profiles or special effects such as Concave pointing, Convex pointing, Tuck pointing and Bastard Tuck (see Fig.19).

Pozzolan substance added to lime mortar that makes it set under water. Takes its name from the area where the Roman extracted volcanic ash which they used to make **hydraulic lime mortar**.

Pressed brick a brick produced by a machine which operates by pressing the clay into a mould. Usually characterised by having particularly sharp arrises.

Pug mill a horse-drawn device for mixing clay (see illustration on page 206). Not thought to have been commonly used in brick manufacture in Europe until the end of the 18th century.

Quarter bonding another name for Raking Stretcher bond. A wall faced in **Stretcher bond** but where the perpends are set at a quarter brick intervals rather than half brick intervals.

Queen closer a brick cut in half along its length (see Fig.20).

Quetta bond a variant of **Flemish bond** for one and one-half brick thick walls where Flemish bond is visible on both interior and exterior faces, leaving hollow vertical shafts in the centre of the wall which are filled with concrete and steel reinforcement to strengthen the wall.

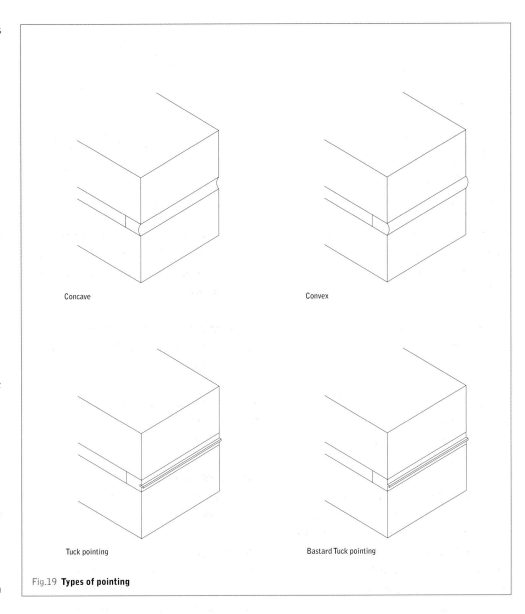

Concave

Convex

Tuck pointing

Bastard Tuck pointing

Fig.19 **Types of pointing**

Quoins projecting bricks at the corners of a building shaped to look like projecting stone features also called quoins.

Raked Stretcher bond also known as Quarter bonding. A wall faced in **Stretcher bond** but where the perpends are set at a quarter brick intervals rather than half brick intervals.

Raking bond another name for Raked Stretcher bond.

Rat-trap bond a type of bonding where all the bricks are laid on their edges in Flemish bond creating a cavity wall structure (see Fig.21). Originally devised in then 19th century when it was advocated for use in the construction of single-storey worker's cottages.

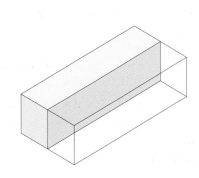

Fig.20 **Queen closer**

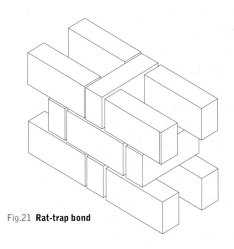

Fig.21 **Rat-trap bond**

Rectangular brick a brick that is rectangular in plan. Usually the length of the brick is twice the breadth plus a mortar joint to simplify bonding.

Relieving arch an arch constructed in the face of a wall rather than over an opening. Relieving arches are typically used to transfer loads to piers within the wall.

Re-pressed brick a brick that has been moulded roughly to shape by hand or machine and is then passed through a brick press to produce a more compact brick with sharper arrises.

Roman kiln the type of brick kiln employed by the Romans consisting of two parts: a lower area where the fuel is burned and an upper area with a perforated floor on which the green bricks are placed to be fired.

Rowlock North American term for laying bricks on edge. Rowlock bond is another name for Rat-trap bond.

Rubber: another name for a cutter .

Rustication a term used in stonework for a method of emphasizing the outline of each stone by carving deep recesses at its edges and making the surface rough and primitive. In brickwork it means that the bricks are cut to imitate stones laid in this way.

St Andrew's bond another name for English Cross Bond.

Samel bricks medieval term for bricks that are found not to have been sufficiently fired when they are taken from the kiln. Such bricks were normally discarded as they would quickly fall apart if used.

Sand-lime bricks another name for Calcium silicate bricks.

Scotch kiln an intermittent updraught kiln that came into use with the adoption of coal-firing in the in Europe (see Fig.22). Essentially little more than a clamp with permanent outer walls of fired bricks in which firing holes are made to allow the coal to be fired under the green bricks.

Sculpted bricks special decorative bricks made by shaping the clay individually by hand prior to firing.

Serpentine wall North American term for what is known in England as a **Crinkle-crankle**. The most famous Serpentine walls were constructed by Thomas Jefferson in the University of Virginia. Contrary to popular myth he did not invent them as they were commonly used in England for garden walls in the 18th century.

Sesquipedalis type of Roman brick which measured one and a half Roman feet (443mm) square and was typically 50mm thick.

Shatyor in Russian architecture, a tent roof or spire.

Silesian bond the European name for **Sussex bond**: a variant on **Flemish Bond** with three stretchers between each header.

Silverlock's bond another name for **Rat-trap bond**.

Skintling the method of stacking green moulded bricks in a hack to dry. If the bricks are too soft then small impressions are left in the surface where the bricks above bear on the bricks below called 'skintling marks'.

Soldier course another name for a brick on end course.

Soft-mud term used by brickmakers to describe mechanical brick moulding processes that mimic hand moulding and thus use relatively soft mud which is pressed or thrown into moulds.

Spanish ash added to brickearth to make London stock bricks.

Square bricks a brick which is square on plan as opposed to merely rectangular.

Squinch one of the four arches placed at each corner of a square room to turn it into an octagon and support the edges of a dome above (see Fig.23).

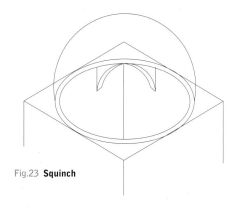

Fig.23 **Squinch**

Stack the shaft of a chimney that projects above the roof line and may contain one or more flues.

Stack bond type of bonding where the bricks are simply stacked on top of each other vertically without overlapping. The orientation of the bricks is not important: a stack bonded façade could be all headers, stretchers, bricks on edge or bricks on end.

Staffordshire kiln a variant on the **Hoffmann kiln** patented in 1904 where the vaults over the chambers were placed transversely. It was used for burning Staffordshire blue bricks, Engineering bricks produced

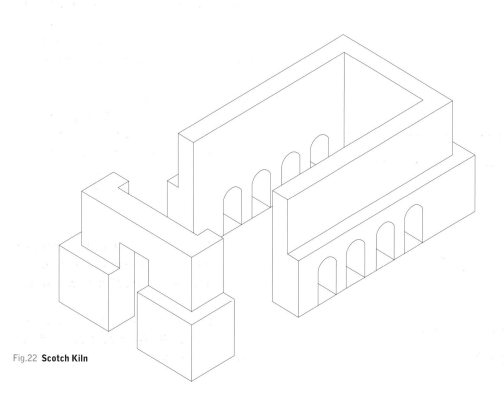

Fig.22 **Scotch Kiln**

in Staffordshire, England, which burned to a grey, blue or purple colour.

Stiff mud term used by brickmakers to describe the wire-cut method of moulding bricks where clay is extruded through a die.

Stock a block of wood attached to the moulding bench over which the mould neatly fits.

Stock brick a brick made using a mould fitting over a stock and wooden pallets. If ash is added to the clay before moulding it is called a **London stock brick**.

Straight arch an arch made of cut bricks which has no perceptible rise in the centre. In North America called a **Jack arch**.

Stretcher a brick laid so that the longer side is visible.

Stretcher bond a brick bond consisting entirely of stretchers.

Strike a straight piece of wood used in the hand moulding of bricks to remove any excess clay from the top of the mould.

Suffolk kiln the term used in England for a **Roman kiln**: the type typically employed there throughout the Middle Ages.

Sussex bond another name for what is known in Europe as **Silesian bond**: a variant on **Flemish bond** with three stretchers between each header.

Tegula Roman roofing tile, rectangular in shape with upstands along the longer sides to receive the **imbrex**. The Latin word *tegula* is commonly used in European building accounts in the Middle Ages to mean a brick.

Terracotta a loose term applied to refined earthenware. In the context of bricks it is generally applied to any moulded object which is substantially larger in format than the rest of the bricks in the wall.

Tetradoron type of mud brick said to have been used by the Greeks by the Roman author Vitruvius who says they were square and three palms long in either direction.

Tunnel kiln a type of continuous kiln first used in the porcelain industry in the 18th century where the wares to be fired are passed slowly through a long tunnel-shaped furnace on fireproof carriages. The maximum temperature is reached at the centre of the tunnel, the bricks gradually heating up and cooling down at the ends. There were a number of problems adapting the process for the manufacture of bricks which were not satisfactorily solved until the 20th century. Gas-fired tunnel kilns are now the most commonly used type of kiln in highly mechanized European and American factories.

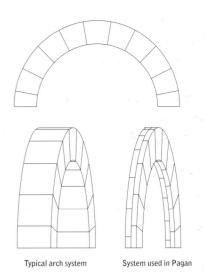

Typical arch system   System used in Pagan

Fig.25 **Voussoir arch**

Updraught kiln any type of kiln where the heat is applied at the bottom of the kiln and the gases extracted at the top.

Vertical shaft kiln recently developed in China, a type of continuous kiln designed to replace the Bull's trench kiln for making bricks in developing countries. The Vertical shaft kiln uses a six to eight metres tall shaft. The bricks are loaded in batches at the top with brick dust spread in layers between them. At the bottom batches are removed one at a time, jacks being used to lower the whole column of bricks down the shaft as each batch is removed. One kiln can fire 4000 bricks a day. Vertical shaft kilns use less fuel and create less pollution (see Fig.24).

Vitrified Headers bricks with glass-like ends caused by applying a glaze to the end of the brick prior to firing or by placing it too close to the source of heat. Used for making **Diaper patterns** and **chequered brickwork**.

Voussoir arch an arch built with wedge-shaped stones. Usually the stones are deeper than they are wide on the face. In Pagan the reverse is true, the stones are used flat, a process which may have reduced the amount of formwork required (see Fig.25).

Wire-cut process for making bricks by machine (also known as the stiff-mud process) by which clay is extruded through a die and cut into bricks using wires.

Yorkshire bond also known as Monk bond or Flying bond, a variant on **Flemish bond** with two stretchers between every header.

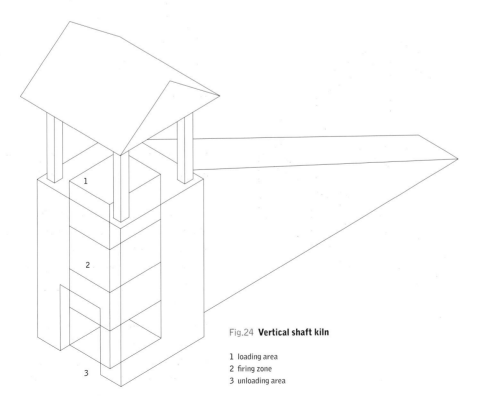

Fig.24 **Vertical shaft kiln**

1 loading area
2 firing zone
3 unloading area

BIBLIOGRAPHICAL ESSAY

It would be impossible to provide a full bibliography of everything ever written relating to the history of brickwork. Therefore the aim of this essay is to provide a general guide, chapter by chapter, to further reading on the topics included in this book. Each of the works listed here contains its own bibliography and list of sources to which the reader can refer for more information. Items are cited in full on their first appearance and assigned a number [in brackets]. Where they are mentioned again later in the essay, only the author's name and that number are used to avoid repetition. Inclusion of an item here does not imply that it is in print. In fact, as will be apparent from the dates of publication, very few of the books mentioned are, but in virtually every case the work cited should be available through major libraries or inter-library loan. Where this might be difficult I have noted it in the text and tried to provide details of where they may be obtained.

Introduction

The history of building construction is one of those subjects that is often described as being interdisciplinary. This is a polite way of saying that it falls outside the subject areas normally taught in universities. Architectural historians, who are often specialist art historians, have tended to view construction history as being too technical and have dismissed it accordingly as being of minor importance. As a result it is rarely touched on in general works on architectural history. Archaeologists who do write on building construction tend to be less interested the more modern the period in question. Material scientists and building technologists are generally more interested in the here and now than the past. Thus it is only with the rise in interest of building conservation over the last 150 years that books have begun to appear on the development of construction from the Middle Ages to the present day and there is still very little in the way of general literature on the subject.

A broad introduction to construction history can be found in [1] Norman Davey, *History of Building Materials* (London: Phoenix House, 1961), [2] Robert Mark (ed.), *Architectural Technology up to the Scientific Revolution* (London/Cambridge, Mass.: MIT Press, 1993) and [3] Rowland Mainstone, *The Development of Structural Form* (Oxford: Architectural Press, 1998) while more recent developments can be followed in *Construction History*, the journal of the Construction History Society, which also provides useful reviews of relevant books and articles in other journals as they appear.

Of the books concentrating wholly on brick, a number of general works provide a useful introduction. One of the

most accessible is [4] John Woodforde's *Bricks to Build a House* (London: Routledge and Kegan Paul, 1976) which was written specifically for the layman. However some of its contentions have now been proved wrong and it contains few references. More international in its approach is [5] Andrew Plumridge and Wim Meulenkamp, *Brickwork: Architecture and Design* (London: Studio Vista, 1993) which in 224 pages ambitiously tries to cover both the history of brickwork and its technical aspects. Its coverage of both is rather brief as a result. A better account of the problems inherent in modern masonry construction today (including stone and block as well as brick) can be found in [6] Günter Pfeifer, Rolf Ramcke, Joachim Achtziger & Konrad Zilch, *Mauerwerk Atlas*, published in English as the *Masonry Construction Manual* (Berlin/Basel/Boston: Birkhäuser, 2001), which has a short introductory historical essay. However, perhaps the best introduction to the history of brickwork all over the world is the excellent collection of short essays included in the [7] *Grove Dictionary of Art*, edited by Jane Turner, 33 vols. (London: Grove/Macmillan, 1996), vol. 4, pp. 767–97.

On brickmaking, [8] Martin Hammond, *Bricks and Brickmaking* (Princes Risborough, England: Shire, 1998) provides an authoritative short (32 pages) illustrated history, including a useful introduction to modern methods and manufacturing terminology. A longer historical account (focusing mainly on developments in the United States) is included in [9] Karl Gurcke *Bricks and Brickmaking: A Handbook for Historical Archaeology* (Moscow, Idaho: University of Idaho Press, 1987). The various editions of [10] Alfred B. Searle, *Modern Brickmaking* (London: Ernest Benn, 1911–1956) also contain very clear descriptions of the principles and processes of brickmaking and are now useful historical sources in their own right.

There is a vast literature on the techniques of bricklaying, much of it aimed at students enrolled in bricklaying courses. A selection of these can be found in any large bookshop. [11] Gerard Lynch, *Brickwork: History, Technology and Practice*, 2 vols. (London: Donhead, 1994) provides a more useful study for those interested in understanding the development of the art, including the history, techniques, tools and terminology of bricklaying and detailed drawings showing bricklayers at work.

Architects and those seeking advice on the repair of brickwork will find [12] John Warren, *Conservation of Brick* (Oxford: Butterworth Heineman, 1999) an invaluable resource. [13] John & Nicola Ashurst, *Practical Building Conservation, Volume 2: Brick Terracotta and Earth* (London: Gower Technical, 1998); [14] A. M. Snowden (ed.),

The Maintenance of Brick and Stone Masonry Structures (London: E & FN Spon, 1990) and [15] John W. De Courcey (ed.), *Brick and Masonry*, 3 vols. (London: Elsevier Applied Science, 1988) are also useful in this regard. A list of references for articles on the deterioration of brickwork can be found in A. Elena Charola, 'Conservation' in Grove [7], vol. 4, p. 797.

An important forum for new discoveries on the history of brick is *Information*, the journal of the British Brick Society (hereafter referred to as *BBS Information*) which appears between two and four times a year. The Society was originally founded in 1972 as a specialist sub-group of the British Archaeological Association with the aim of promoting the study of English brickwork in a wider context. It welcomes members from all countries and occupations and more information can be found on its website.

Chapter One

The origins of brickmaking are understandably difficult to trace. An introduction to the subject can be found in [16] O. Aurenche, 'L'Origine de la brique dans le Proche-Orient Ancien' in M. Frangipane, *Between the River and Over the Mountains* (Rome: University of Rome, 1993), pp. 71–85. The mud bricks in Jericho are discussed in [17] Katherine Kenyon, *Digging Up Jericho* (London: E. Benn Ltd, 1957) and [18] *Archaeology of the Holy Land* (London: Thames and Hudson, 1965). A more detailed report with drawings is given in [19] T. A. Holland (ed.), *Excavations at Jericho, vol. III: The Architecture and Stratigraphy of the Tell*, (London: British School of Archaeology in Jerusalem, 1981). Later use of mud-brick in Mesopotamia is discussed in [20] David Oates, 'Innovations in mud-brick: decorative and structural techniques in ancient Mesopotamia', *World Archaeology*, Vol. 21, no. 3, pp. 388–406.

Egyptian brickwork is fully explored in [21] A. J. Spencer, *Brick Architecture in Ancient Egypt* (Warminster, England: Aris and Phillips, 1979) which contains analyses and measurements of bricks from all the major sites, as well as information on Egyptian brick stamps and bonding patterns. The brick mould is illustrated in [22] W. M. F. Petrie, *Tools and Weapons* (London: Egyptian Research Account Publications, 1916), pl. XLVII, p. 55. The photograph of the mural from the tomb of Rehk-me-Re was kindly supplied by Dr Alberto Siliotti. More details of the tomb itself can be found in [23] Norman de Garis Davies, *The Tomb of Rekmire at Thebes* (New York: Plantin, 1943).

Mesopotamian brickwork has been subjected to similarly exhaustive treatment in [23] Martin Sauvage,

La Brique et sa Mise en Oeuvre en Mésopotamie: Des Origines à l'Époque Achéménide (Paris: Ministère des Affaires Étrangères, 1998) which provides detailed lists of bricks found in all the major excavations, bonding diagrams for the major projects, maps, in-depth analysis of the early development of brickwork and a substantial bibliography, including Babylon and Susa. Accounts of the rituals involved in building are taken from [24] D. O. Edzardo, 'Deep-Rooted Skyscrapers and Bricks: Ancient Mesopotamian Architecture and its Imagery' in M. Mindling, M. J. Gellar & J. E. Wainsborough (eds.), *Figurative Language in the Ancient Near East* (London: SOAS, University of London, 1987), pp.13–24. Koldewey's investigations in Babylon are summarised in his [25] *Excavations at Babylon* (London, Macmillan, 1914) and in more detail in volumes 15, 32 and 55 of the [26] *Wissenschaftliche Veröffentlichung der Deutschen Orient-Gesellschaft* (Berlin-Leipzig). Discoveries at Susa are discussed in [27] P. O. Harper, *The Royal City of Susa. Ancient Near Eastern Treasures in the Louvre* (New York: Metropolitan Museum of Modern Art, 1992).

Chapter Two

There is an enormous literature on the classical world, mostly in specialist journals on archaeology. By far the best book on Greek building techniques is [28] A. K. Orlandos, *Les Matériaux de construction et la technique architecturale des anciens grecs*, 2 vols. (Paris, E. de Bocard, 1966 & 1968) which deserves to be reprinted in a revised edition. Brick is included in volume one. More recent literature is listed in [29] A. W. Lawrence, *Greek Architecture*, fifth edition revised by R. A. Tomlinson (New Haven and London: Yale University Press, 1996).

The best introduction to Roman building technology is [30] Jean-Pierre Adam, *La Construction Romaine: matériaux et techniques* (Paris: Éditions A. et J. Picard, 1989), available in English (translated by Anthony Matthews) as *Roman Building: Materials and Techniques* (London: Batsford, 1994). It covers all aspects of Roman construction and contains a useful bibliography. [31] François Auguste Choisy's, *L'art de bâtir chez Romains* (Paris: Ducher, 1873) is now out of date, but is still worth looking at for the quality of its illustrations.

For writing on bricks and brickwork by Roman authors, all of whom are listed in the text, I have used the relevant parallel translations of the books in the Loeb Classical Library editions produced by Harvard University Press, together with the latest English translation of Vitruvius: [32] Ingrid D. Rowland, *Vitruvius: Ten Books on Architecture* (Cambridge, England: Cambridge University Press, 1999) which contains a particularly useful introduction and commentary.

Detailed studies of Roman kilns and brickmaking can be found in the collected papers in [33] Alan McWhirr (ed.),

'Roman Brick and Tile: studies in Manufacture, Distribution and Use in the Western Empire', *British Archaeological Reports International Series*, Vol. 68 (1979). Information on the naming of the various types of Roman brick can be found in [34] Gerard Brodribb, *Roman Brick and Tile* (Gloucester, England: Sutton, 1987), which despite its title, actually concentrates on Roman bricks and tiles in England. Brick stamps are the subject of extensive literature which is continually growing. A good introduction can be found in [35] Tapio Helen, *The Organization of Roman Brick Production in the First and Second Centuries* AD (Helsinki: Suomalainem tiedenkatemia, 1975).

Bricklaying and construction techniques for different sites are discussed in C. Roccatelli, 'Brickwork in Ancient Times' in [36] G. C. Mars (ed.), *Brickwork in Italy* (Chicago: American Face Brick Association, 1925), pp. 1–47, and in more detail in [37] M. E. Blake, *Ancient Roman Construction in Italy from the Pre-historic Period to Augustus* (Washington D.C.: Carnegie Institution, 1947), [38] M. E. Blake, *Roman Construction in Italy from Tiberius through the Flavians*. (Washington D.C.: Carnegie Institution, 1959), and [39] Marion Elizabeth Blake (edited and completed by Doris Taylor Bishop), *Roman Construction in Italy from Nerva through the Antonines* (Washington D.C.: Carnegie Institution, 1973). The construction of the Pantheon and Trajan's Markets is discussed in [40] William L. Macdonald, *The Architecture of the Roman Empire I* (New Haven and London: Yale University Press, 1982). Pointing in Roman brickwork is explored in [41] C. Tedeschi and G. Cardani 'Historical Investigations on the use of masonry pointing in Italy', *Proceedings of the First International Congress on Construction History*, edited by Santiago Huerta, 3 vols. (Madrid: Instituto Juan de Herrera, 2003), vol. III, pp.1963–1977. The part played by *collegia* in Roman construction is explored in [42] Janet DeLaine, 'The Builders of Roman Ostia: organisation status and society', *Proceedings of the First International Congress on Construction History*, edited by Santiago Huerta, 3 vols. (Madrid: Instituto Juan de Herrera, 2003), vol. I, pp. 723–32 and the cost of brick versus other forms of construction in [43] Janet DeLaine, 'Bricks and Mortar: exploring the economics of building techniques at Rome and Ostia' in D. Mattingly and J. Salmon, *Economies Beyond Agriculture in the Classical World* (London: Routledge, 2001), pp. 230–68.

A good introduction to Byzantine brickwork can be found in [44] Cyril Mango, *Byzantine Architecture* (New York: Harry N. Abrams, 1976). A more up to date summary of scholarship is included in [45] Robert Ousterhout, *Master Builders of Byzantium* (Princeton, New Jersey: Princeton University Press, 1999). [46] Rowland Mainstone, *Hagia Sophia: Architecture,*

Structure and Liturgy of Justinian's Great Church (London: Thames and Hudson, 1988) covers every aspect of the construction of that great church. For Ravenna, a detailed account of the construction of the baptistry of Neon is found in [47] Spiro Kostof, *The Orthodox Baptistry of Ravenna* (New Haven and London: Yale University Press, 1965) while a more general account can be found in E. Verdozzi, 'Brick in the Middle Ages', in [36] G. C. Mars , pp. 47–177. The construction of San Vitale is discussed in [3] Robert Mark, pp. 97–98 and 152–53.

A comprehensive account of the development of Chinese building technology is included in [48] Zhong Yuanzhao and Chen Yangzheng (eds.), *History and Development of Ancient Chinese Architecture* (Beijing: Science Press, 1986) replacing the volumes on building technology in the history of Chinese technology by Joseph Needham.

Introductions to early Islamic architecture can be found in [49] R. Ettinghausen and O. Grabar, *The art and architecture of Islam 650–1250* (London/New Haven: Yale, 1994) and [50] Markus Hattstein and Peter Delius (eds.), *Islam; Art and Architecture* (Cologne: Könemann, 2000). The most readable history of Bukhara that I have found is [51] Richard N. Frye, *Bukhara: the Medieval Achievement* (Norman, Oklahoma: University of Oklahoma Press, 1965). Much of this is based on a Persian abridgement of an Arabic text of the same name by Narshaki translated by Professor Fyre when he was at Harvard as [52] *The History of Bukhara* (Cambridge, Mass.: Medieval Academy of America, 1954). My account of the tomb of the Saminids is based heavily on these and [53] G. A. Pugachenkova, 'The Role of Bukhara in the creation of the architectural typology of the former mausoleums of Mavarannahr' in Attilio Petruccioli, *Bukhara: The Myth and the Architecture*, the published proceedings of an international symposium held at MIT in November 1996. The latter cites a full bibliography of the tomb in [54] M. S. Bulatov, *Mavsovei Samanidov-hudojectvennaia djemchuzchine architecturi srednei aziz* (Tashkent: n.p., 1976) which I have not seen.

Chapter Three

The Middle Ages in Europe represents an age of variable scholarship on brick. A great deal has been on done, for instance, on English brickwork, but very little has been written on the brickwork of the South-east Asia. Everywhere there is a problem with the paucity of documentary sources. Much of the research remains in isolated papers in archaeological journals.

The best introduction to the treasures of Pagan is [55] Paul Strachan, *Pagan: Art and Architecture of Old Burma* (Edinburgh: Kiscadale, 1989) which contains descriptions of many of the structures and a good bibliography. A summary of recent literature on the architecture of Thailand can be found in [56] Clarence Aasen, entertainingly retold in [126] Stephen Halliday, *The Great Stink of London* (Stroud, England: Sutton, 1999).

An account of Soane's use of terracotta pots can be found in Ayres [104]. The development of fire-proof floors is discussed in [127] Lawrance Hurst, 'Concrete and the structural use of cements in England before 1890' in James Sutherland, Dawn Humm and Mike Chrimes (eds.), *Historic Concrete: background to appraisal* (London: Thomas Telford, 2001). Historic accounts of the development of fireproof construction in the United States (including floors) are provided in [128] H. Newlon (ed.), *A Selection of Historic American Papers on Concrete 1876-1926* (Detroit: American Concrete Institute, 1976).

A full introduction to 19th-century terracotta can be found in [129] Michael Stratton, *The Terracotta Revival* (London: Victor Gollancz, 1993). Schinkel's use of brick and terracotta is also discussed in [130] Barry Bergdoll, *Karl Friedrich Schinkel,* (New York: Rizzoli, 1994).

A discussion of polychromy in English brickwork in the 19th century and Keble College can be found in [131] Paul Thompson, *William Butterfield* (London: Routledge and Kegan Paul, 1971). [132] Ruskin's *Seven Lamps of Architecture* (London: Smith Elder & Co., 1849) and [133] *Stones of Venice* (London: 1851-53) have both been reprinted many times. [134] Pierre Chabat, *La brique et la terre cuite* (Paris: Yve Morel, 1881) and [135] J. Lacroux & C. Detain, *La Brique Ordinaire* (Pairs, Ducher, 1878) have also been reprinted, but in highly abridged editions. An account of brick and iron architecture in Paris can be found in Marrey and Dumont [92]

Extensive bibliographies of Dutch architecture and architects for both the 19th and 20th centuries including Cuypers and Berlage can be found in [136] Joseph Buch, *A Century of Architecture in the Netherlands 1880/1990* (Rotterdam: Netherlands Architecture Institute, 1993).

An introduction to Gaudí can be found in [137] Rainer Zerbst, *Antoni Gaudí* (Cologne: Taschen, 1988) and [138] Juan José Laheurta, *Antoni Gaudí* (Milan: Electa, 1992). A history of 'Catalan vaults' is provided in [139] Fernando Marias, 'Piedra y ladrillo en la arquitectura, española siglo XVI' in Jean Guillaume (ed.), *Les Chantiers de la Renaissance* (Paris: Picard, 1991), pp. 71-83.

Richardson's Sever Hall is featured in the sumptuously illustrated [140] Margaret Henderson Floyd, *Henry Hobson Richardson* (New York: Monacelli Press, 1997). There is an extensive literature on both Wright and Sullivan, but good introductions to the architects and their use of materials can be found in [141] Robert Twombly and Narciso G. Menocal, *Louis Sullivan: the poetry of Architecture* (New York: W.W.Norton, 2000), [142] B. B. Pfeiffer, *Frank Lloyd Wright: Master Builder* (London: Thames and Hudson, 1997) and [143] Henry-Russell Hitchcock, *In the Nature of Materials* (London: Elek, 1958).

Chapter Seven

The rise of the skyscraper in Chicago is discussed in [144] Frank A. Randall, *The History of the Development of Building Construction in Chicago* (Chicago: University of Illinois, 1999) and [145] Carl W. Condit, *The Chicago School of Architecture* (London: University of Chicago, 1964). The building of the Flatiron Building is detailed in [146] Sarah Bradford Landau and Carl W. Condit, *The Rise of the New York Skyscraper 1865-1913* (London: Yale University Press, 1996).

Lutyens's work at Folly Farm, Sulhampstead, is the subject of [147] Peter Inskip, 'Wrenaissance' in 'Masters of Brickwork', a special supplement to *the Architects' Journal,* December 1984, pp. 1621, but very little has been written on Jensen-Klint except in Danish. I have not yet been able to find a copy of [148] J. Marstraad's, *Grundtvig Minderkirk paa Bispebjerg* (Copenhagen: 1932) which is said to be the standard work on this great church.

The Amsterdam School and Michel de Klerk are examined in [149] Wim de Wit (ed.), *The Amsterdam School* (Cambridge, Mass.: MIT Press, 1983); and [150] Suzanne S. Frank, *Michel de Klerk 1884-1923* (Ann Arbor, Michigan: UMI Research Press, 1984). [151] David Stravitz, *The Chrysler Building* (New York: Princeton Architectural Press, 2002) provides a fascinating photographic record of the building's construction and the role of terracotta in the architecture of the period is the subject of [152] Sarah Tunick, *Terra Cotta Skyline* (New York: Princeton Architectural Press, 1997).

[153] Herman van Bergeijk and Paul Meurs, *Town Hall, Hilversum, W. M. Dudok* (Naarden, Netherlands: Inmerc, 1995) provides a useful study of the construction and renovation of Dudok's best known work. [154] Herman van Bergeijk, *Willen Marinus Dudok* (Naarden: V+K, 1995) and [155] Poala Jappelli & Giovanni Menna, *Willem Marinus Dudok: architettura e città* (Naples: Clean, 1997) provide biographies of the man.

More information on the Byker Wall can be found in [156] Peter Collymore, *The Architecture of Ralph Erskine* (London: Academy Edition, 1994); [157] Peter Buchanan, 'Byker: the Spaces Between', *Architectural Review,* vol. 170 no. 1018 (Dec. 1981), pp. 334-43; and [158] David Dunster, 'Walled Town', Progressive Architecture, vol. 60, no. 8 (Aug. 1979), pp. 68-73. All the architect's files from the project are deposited with the Royal Institute of British Architects in London.

An introduction to Aalto's work can be found in [159] Peter Reed (ed.), *Alvar Aalto: Between Architecture and Humanism* (New York: Museum of Modern Art, 1998). A short piece on Aalto's use of brick can be found in [160] Esa Laaksonen, 'Alvar Aalto the Brick', *A+U,* No. 373, May 2000 special issue (Brick Architecture), pp. 52-55.

The construction of St Peter's Church, Klippan, is discussed in [161] Colin St John Wilson, *Sigurd Lewerentz*

1885-1975 and the Dilemma of Classicism (London: Architectural Association, 1989) and [162] Janne Ahlin, *Sigurd Lewerentz, arkitekt* (Stockholm: Byggförlaget, 1985),* translated into English by Kerstin Westerlund as *Sigurd Lewerentz, architect* (Stockholm: Byggförlaget, 1987).

A printed bibliography of material on the Philips Exeter Library is available from the College. Kahn's musings on the nature of life and architecture (including bricks) are collected in [163] Alessandra Latour, *Louis I. Kahn's writings, lectures, interviews* (New York: Rizzoli, 1991) and [164] Richard Saul Wurman (ed.), *What will be has always been: the words of Louis I. Kahn* (New York: Rizzoli, 1986).

IRCAM and Piano's other works are discussed at length in [165] Peter Buchanan, *Renzo Piano Building Workshop: Complete Works,* 4 vols. (London: Phaidon, 1993-2000). Sørenson's Chrystallographic Data Centre is examined in articles by Nick Ray, Dean Hawkes and Zibrandsten Architects in [167] *the Architects' Journal,* vol. 196, no. 2 (8 July 1992), pp. 24-37, 39-41, 71-73. The construction of Glyndebourne is described in [168] Kenneth Powell 'A Day in the Life of Glyndebourne', *the Architects' Journal,* vol. 200, no. 14 (13 Oct. 1994), pp. 31-36, 38-39 and a similarly detailed study of Rick Mather's extension for Keble College, Oxford can be found in [169] John Welsh 'Brick Layers', *RIBA Journal,* vol. 102, no.9 (Sept. 1995), pp. 42-49. The complete story of the construction of Evry Cathedral is told by the architect and others in [170] Mario Botta, *La cathédrale d'Evry* (Milan: Skira, 1999). An introduction to the ideas of one the greatest exponents of appropriate technology can be found in [171] Guatam Bhatia, *Laurie Baker: Life, Works and Writings* (London: Penguin, 1994).

Finally, although it is obvious that readers who wish to follow more recent advances in bricklaying can refer to the wide variety of architectural journals available on the market today, its is perhaps worth noting that there are less well known journals such as *Ziegelindustrie International* and *Clay Technology* which provide similar information on current trends in brick manufacturing.

INDEX

Aalto, Alvar
   Baker House, MIT, Cambridge, Mass.
   270, 271
Albi, France 80,98,99
   Cathedral 108-113
   Covered Market 232, 233
Albigensians 108
Al-Untesh-Napirisha, Iran 24-25, 30, 32
Amsterdam, Netherlands 163, 163,
   164, 165
   Rijksmuseum 204, 235
   Central Station 205, 234
   Scheepvaarthuis 246, 256, 257
   Spaarndammerbuurt Complex
   247, 258, 259
   Dageraad Complex 258
   Java Island housing 300, 301
aqueducts 54, 55
arches and vaulting 56
Arnheim, Netherlands
   Openluchtmuseum 302
Aspdin, Joseph 216

Babylon 34-35
Bacon, Nathaniel 185
Backsteingotik 103
Bage, Charles 219
Baker, Laurie 296
Baltard, Victor 232
Barcelona, Spain
   Guëll Pavilions 204, 205, 238
   Colegio Teresiano 204, 205, 236, 237
   Guëll Colony Church 205, 238, 239
   Casa Vicens 237
Berlage, Henrik Petrus 235, 256
Bernard de Castanet 108
Bigot, Paul
   Institut d'Art et d'Archéologie, Paris
   3, 12, 23
Bologna, Santo Spirito 18, 124, 135, 136
   S. Francesco 94
   S. Stefano 94, 95
   Corpus Domini 123, 137
   San Giacomo Maggiore 124, 134, 137
bonding 19
Boston, USA
   'Old South' 161, 163
   State House 163, 185
Botta, Mario
   Evry Cathedral, France 4, 247, 292-95

bricks 14, 15, 32, 50, 174, 176
   mud 14, 33
   fired 14
   dimensions 15
   bricklaying 17
   rubbing and cutting 190, 191
   moulding 206-209
   new techniques of brick making
   266, 267
   conservation of 298, 299
   brick-making machines 206-209
Bristol, England
   Granary Building 204
   Warehouses 219
Brunel, Marc
   cantilevered arch 216
   Thames Tunnel 216
Brunelleschi, Filippo
   Florence Cathedral 124, 126-127
Bukhara
   Tomb of the Samanids 15, 74-77
   Magok-i Attari Mosque 72-73
   The Ark 6-7
   Kalan Mosque 16, 114, 115, 148
   Taq Sarafan 81
   Ali Minaret 115
   Chashmeh Ayub Shrine 117
   Mir-i Arab Madrasa 149
Bull's Trench Kiln 296
Bulmer Brickworks, England 163, 174,
   175, 211, 298, 299
Bulmer and Sharp's wire cutting
   machine 209
Burnham and Root
   Monadnock Building, Chicago 250
Butterfield, William
   Keble College, Oxford 228-31
   All Saints, London 229
Byzantine brickwork 60-69

Callet, Felix 232
Cambridge, England
   Queens' College 81, 138
   St John's College 124, 125
   Jesus College 138, 139
   Crystallography Data Centre 247, 284-87
canals 215
Charlottesville, University of
   Virginia, USA 20, 162, 163, 200, 201
Chiang Mai, Thailand 16, 89

Chicago, USA
   Arthur M. Heurthley House
   20, 204, 242
   Monadnock Building 248,250, 251
   Nathan G. Moore House 204, 205, 243
   Rookery Building 205, 223
   Stock Exchange 242
   Robie House 243
China 70-71, 90-93
   Bersi Ta Pagoda 80, 93
   Great Wall 125, 158, 159
Chinese brickwork 70, 71, 90, 91,
   158, 159
Choga Zambil 24-25, 31, 32
clay 14
Clayton's stiff-mud brickmaking
   machine 207
Coade Stone 192, 193
Coke, Thomas 194
Colchester, England 99
Cole, Henry 222
Constantinople/Istanbul, Turkey
   St Eirene 60, 61
   Kalenderhane Camii 61
   Christ Pantepoptes 62-63
   Hagia Sophia 64-65
Copenhagen, Denmark,
   Grundtvig Church 2, 22, 246,
   254, 255
Cuypers, Petrus
   Central Station, Amsterdam 205, 234
   Rijksmuseum, Amsterdam 204, 235

Della Robbia family 136
Dieulafoy, Marcel 36
Digswell Viaduct, Welwyn, England 204
domes 59, 64, 118, 119, 126, 127
Doré, Gustave 220
Du Cerceau, Jacques Androuet 170
Dudok, Willem Marinus
   Hilversum Town Hall 21, 262-65
Duhammel de Monceau, Henri-Louis
   186, 187

Egypt 28-29
Erskine, Ralph
   Byker Wall, Newcastle 268, 269
Evry, France
   Cathedral 4, 247, 292-95
   Research Centre 246, 282, 283

Exeter, USA
   Philips Exeter Library 278-81

faience 226
Ferrara, Italy
   Castello Estense 105
   S. Carlo 132, 133
   Palazzo Roverella 133
   S. Stefano 137
fireproofing 218, 219
Florence, Italy
   Cathedral 124, 126-29
   Orsanmichele 134
Floris, Cornelius 164
Folly Farm, England 20, 246, 247, 250-53
Frederiksborg Slot, Denmark 168-69

galletting 19
Gaudi, Antoni 236-39
   Guëll Pavilions 204, 205, 238
   Colegio Teresiano 204, 205, 236, 237
   Guëll Colony Church 205, 238, 239
   Casa Vicens 237
Gdansk, Poland 103
Glyndebourne, England, Theatre
   288, 289
Gomme, Bernard de
   Tilbury Fort 162, 180, 181
Grant, John 217
Greek architecture 42
Groombridge Place, England 20, 162,
   176, 177

Haarlem, Netherlands, Vleeshal 166
Hamburg, Germany, Chilehaus
   246, 247
Hampton Court, England 139, 142, 143,
   178, 179
Hangzhou, China 91, 92
Harvard, Cambridge, Mass. USA 205, 240,
   241
Herstmonceaux Castle, England
   18, 104
Hilversum, Netherlands, Town Hall
   21, 262-65
Hoffman Kiln 213
Holkham Hall, England 163, 194-97
Hopkins, Michael and Patty
   Glyndebourne Theatre 288, 289

iron in French architecture 232

Isfahan, Iran 18, 19, 134, 135, 150-57

Islamic brickwork 72-77, 114, 115, 148-57

Istanbul, see Constantinople

Italian Baroque brickwork 133

Italian Renaissance brickwork 128-31

Jefferson, Thomas
  Monticello 201
  University of Virginia 20, 162, 163, 200, 201

Jericho 26

Jones, Inigo 167, 177

Kahn, Louis
  Philips Exeter Library 278–81

Kew Palace, England 163, 172, 173

Khoroshevo, Russia 144

Kiev, Ukraine, Cathedral of St Sophia 144

kilns 15, 48, 49, 186, 187, 210-113, 296

Klerk, Michel de
  Spaarndammerbuurt Complex, Amsterdam 247, 258, 259

Klint, Peder Jensen
  Grundtvig Church, Copenhagen 2, 22, 246, 254, 255

Klippan, Sweden, St. Peter's Church 21, 246, 272-77

Koldeway, Robert 35

Kolomenskoe, Russia 125, 144, 145, 146

Kramer, Piet
  Dageraad Complex, Amsterdam 258

Layer Marney, England 125, 140, 141

Lewerentz, Sigurd
  St Peter's Church, Klippan 21, 246, 272–77

Lottus, William 36

London, England
  Battersea Power Station 20, 246
  Bedford Square 162, 188
  Cumberland Terrace 162
  St Benet, Paul's Wharf 179
  Church Row, Hampstead 188, 189
  Park Square 198
  Carlton House Terrace 199
  Prudential Assurance Building 205, 223
  Midland Grand Hotel 215
  Bank of England 218
  Albert Hall 222

Victorial and Albert Museum 223
  Natural History Museum 224–27
  Howard de Walden Nurses' Home 227
  Tate Modern 247
  All Saints, Magaret Street 229

Lübeck, Germany 80, 102, 103

Lutyens, Edwin
  Folly Farm 20, 246, 247, 250–53

Malbork (Marienburg), Poland 17, 81, 106-7

Mather, Rick
  Keble College extension 247, 290, 291

Monticello, USA 201

Moscow, Russia
  St. Basil's 147
  History Museum 204

moulding 20

Moxon, Joseph 172, 173

Nash, John 199
  Cumberland Terrace 162
  Park Square 198
  Carlton House Terrace 199

Newcastle, England, Byker Wall 268, 269

New York, USA
  Flatiron Building 246, 247, 249
  Chrysler Buidling 247, 260, 261
  So-Ho 247
  skyscrapers 248, 249, 260, 261
  American Radiator Building 260

Noisel, France 233

Oljeitu 78

Ostankino, Russia 124, 147

Ostia, Italy 47, 52, 55, 59

Oxford, England
  Keble College 21, 204, 205, 228-31
  Keble College extension 247, 290, 291

Padua, Italy, S. Antonio 18

Pagan, Burma 17, 80, 81, 82-87

Paris, France
  Institut d'Art et d'Archéologie 3, 12, 23
  Place des Vosges 163, 170,171
  Rue des Archives 171
  IRCAM 245, 283
  Les Halles 232

Piano, Renzo
  IRCAM, Paris 244, 245, 282, 283

Pirenesi, Giovanni Battista 45

pointing 19

Portland Cement 215, 216, 217

Rauwolff, Leonhart 34

Ravenna, Italy
  Arian Baptistery 66
  Mausoleum of Galla Placida 67
  S. Vitale 68
  Baptistery of Neon 69
  S. Maria in Porto 130

Renaissance brickmaking 128-129

Rick, Claudius James 32

Richardson, H.H.
  Sever Hall, Harvard 205, 240, 241

Ringsted, Denmark 80, 97

Roman architecture 43, 46, 47

Rome, Italy
  Colosseum 14, 46, 56, 57
  'Temple of Rediculus' 14, 46, 52
  Basilica of Maxentius 39
  Trajan's Markets 40-41, 48, 50, 51
  Pantheon 58, 59
  Aqua Claudia 54, 55
  S. Maria di Loreto 130, 131

Roskilde Cathedral, Denmark 80, 96-97

Ruabon works 225

Ruskin, John 229

Russian brickwork 144-47

Saminids 75

Saulinies, Jules
  Menier Factory, Noisel 233

Scott, G.G.
  Midland Grand Hotel, London 215

sewers 215, 216, 217

Shanghai, China 81, 90, 204, 221

Siena, Italy
  Palazzo Conmunale 19, 79, 81, 101
  Campo 80, 100

Smythson, Robert 167

Soane, John 218

Soeters, Sjoerd
  Java Island, Amsterdam 301

Sørenson, Eric Christian
  Cambridge Crystallography Data Centre 247, 285-87

Street, George Edmund 229

stucco 199

Sullivan, Louis 242

Sultaniya, Iran 5, 80, 81, 116, 117, 118-121

Susa, Iran 23, 30, 36-37

Suzhou, China,
  Twin Pagodas 16, 90

terracotta 134-37, 140, 141, 222-27

Thebes, Egypt, Tomb of Rekh-mi-Re 28-29

Theodoric 68

Thompson, Arthur E 227

Tilbury Fort, England 162, 180, 181

Toulouse, Saint Sernin 108

Uruk 35

Van Alen, William
  American Radiator Building, New York 260, 261

Van der Meij, Johan
  Scheepvaarthuis 246, 256, 257

Viollet-le-Duc, Eugène 232

Virginia, USA
  Bacon's Castle 162
  St. Luke's Church 162, 184
  Adam Thoroughgood's House 182, 183

Vitruvius 44

Vredeman de Vries, Jan 167

Waterhouse, Alfred
  Natural History Museum, London 224–27
  Prudential Assurance, London 205, 223

Watts, Mary 225

Wharncliffe Viaduct, England 203

Whitehead's wire-cutting machine 209

Willamsburg, USA 163

Wren, Christopher
  Hampton Court Palace 178, 179
  St Benet, London 179

Wright, Frank Lloyd
  Arthur M. Heurthley House, Chicago 20, 204, 242
  Nathan G. Moore House 204, 205, 243
  Robie House, Chicago 243